Disclaimer

The information included in this book is designed to provide helpful information on the subjects discussed. This book is not meant to be used to diagnose or treat any medical condition. For diagnosis or treatment of any medical problem, consult your own doctor. The author and publisher are not responsible for any specific health or allergy needs that may require medical supervision and are not liable for any damages or negative consequences from any application, action, treatment, or preparation, to anyone reading or following the information in this book. Links may change and any references included are provided for informational purposes only.

Instant Pot Cookbook

200 Easy-To-Make Recipes For Fast, Delicious and Healthy Meals

By Susan Hollister
Copyright © 2018

Table of Contents

INTRODUCTION 10
- BENEFITS OF COOKING WITH AN INSTANT POT 11
- SIZES 13
- PRICE 13
- FUNCTIONS 14
- A GENTLE WARNING 15
- A NOT-SO-GENTLE WARNING 15
- ACCESSORIES AND OTHER NECESSITIES 16
- IMPORTANT BASICS YOU NEED TO KNOW 17

CHAPTER 1: START THE MORNING RIGHT – DELICIOUS INSTANT POT BREAKFAST RECIPES 19
- BANANA NUT OATS 19
- BLUEBERRY/LEMON BREAKFAST CAKES 21
- BREAKFAST BURRITO WITH SAUSAGE 22
- BREAKFAST FRUIT COBBLER 25
- BUILD-YOUR-OWN MINI FRITTATAS 26
- CHOCOLATE OATMEAL 28
- COUNTRY HAM AND EGG CASSEROLE 29
- CRUSTLESS VEGETABLE QUICHE 31
- FRENCH TOAST CASSEROLE 32
- FRUIT AND YOGURT 34
- PEACHES AND CREAM OATMEAL 36
- SAUSAGE GRAVY 38

CHAPTER 2: FROM SOUP TO SANDWICH, INCREDIBLE LUNCH RECIPES 40
- BARBECUE BEEF SANDWICH 40
- CHICKEN & CORN SOUP WITH SPINACH 43
- CREAMY BROCCOLI AND CHEDDAR SOUP 44
- FRENCH DIP SANDWICHES 46
- HAMBURGER AND CABBAGE SOUP 48
- ITALIAN CHICKEN SANDWICH 49
- ITALIAN FARM-TO-TABLE VEGETABLE SOUP 51
- NEW FASHIONED CHICKEN NOODLE SOUP 53
- PHILLY CHEESESTEAK SANDWICH 55

 Potato and Leek Soup with Kale 56
 Ramen Noodle Soup 58
 Spicy Pulled Pork Sandwich 60

CHAPTER 3: WORLD CLASS POULTRY RECIPES 63

 Chicken and Brown Rice 64
 Easy Chicken Adobo 65
 Fancy Chicken Cacciatore 66
 Green Chili Turkey Chili 68
 Herbed Turkey Meatballs 69
 Holiday Turkey Recipe 71
 Latin-inspired Chicken Enchiladas 73
 Lemon Chicken Dish 75
 Savory Chicken and Dumplings 77
 Simple and Delicious Chicken Breasts 78
 Spicy Butter Chicken 79
 Sweet Honey Bourbon Chicken 81
 Taco Bowl with Chicken 83
 Tender Turkey Breast and Gravy 84
 Traditional Chicken and Stuffing 86

CHAPTER 4: MOUTHWATERING BEEF RECIPES 89

 Asian Beef and Broccoli 89
 Beefy Burritos 92
 Braised Beef Short Ribs 94
 Country Style Cube Steak and Gravy 96
 Easy Beef Stroganoff 97
 Elegant Beef Burgundy 100
 Fast Meatloaf and Red Potato Mash 101
 Flank Steak Fajitas 103
 Italian Beef and Peppers 105
 Italian Meatballs for Pasta 106
 Melt-In-Your-Mouth Beef Stew 108
 Quick Salisbury Steak 110
 Simple Beef Pot Roast 112
 Sirloin Tips in Gravy 114
 Taste-of-the-East Mongolian Beef 115

CHAPTER 5: SWEET AND TENDER PORK RECIPES 118

Autumn Apple Pork Tenderloin 118
Balsamic Pork Tenderloin 119
Barbecue Pulled Pork 122
Brown Sugar Ham 124
Chili Verde with Pork 125
Chops with Apple Butter 126
Chops and Rice with Vegetables 128
Cranberry Pork Roast 129
Cuban-Style Pulled Pork 130
Finger-Lickin'-Good Pork Ribs 132
Ginger Pork, Japanese Style 133
Green Beans, Potatoes, and Ham 135
Ham and Beans 136
Honey Chops 138
Honeyed Ham 139
Old Fashioned Ham and Potatoes with Asparagus 141
Smothered Pork Chops 142
Sunday Pork Roast with Vegetables and Gravy 144

CHAPTER 6: TASTY LAMB RECIPES FROM AROUND THE WORLD 147

Cabbage and Chops 147
Easy Irish Lamb Stew 148
Elegant Lamb Shanks in Wine Sauce 150
Flavorful Lamb Curry 151
Harvest Lamb Stew 153
Lamb and Sweet Potato Stew 154
Lamb Pot Roast with Potatoes 156
Lamb Stew with Dates and Cinnamon 158
Middle Eastern Lamb Stew 160
Roman Lamb 161
Savory Leg of Lamb 163
Tasty Lamb Ragout 166
Tender Lamb Chops 167

CHAPTER 7: INCREDIBLE SEAFOOD RECIPES 170

Buttery Mussels 170
Clams Steamed in White Wine with Garlic Butter 171
Coconut Curry Tilapia 172

CRAB LEGS IN AN INSTANT POT 174
EASY LOBSTER TAILS 175
FISH IN PARCHMENT 177
FLAVORFUL FISH TACOS 179
GARLIC BUTTER SALMON 180
LIME SHRIMP AND RICE 182
MEDITERRANEAN COD 183
NEW ENGLAND CLAM CHOWDER 184
NEW TUNA NOODLE CASSEROLE 187
NON-TRADITIONAL SEAFOOD BOIL 189
OYSTER STEW 190
QUICK HONEY BALSAMIC SALMON 192
SHRIMP AND BOW TIES 194
SHRIMP AND SAUSAGE JAMBALAYA 196
SHRIMP RISOTTO 198
SPICY HONEY-FLAVORED MAHI-MAHI 199
TASTY INSTANT POT SEA SCALLOPS 200

CHAPTER 8: THE BEST PASTA RECIPES 202

BROCCOLI, SAUSAGE, AND PASTA 202
CHICKEN ALFREDO PASTA WITH SPINACH 203
CHICKEN PARMESAN PASTA 205
CREAMY TORTELLINI ALFREDO 207
EASY CARBONARA 209
EASY SPAGHETTI AND MEATBALLS 210
FAJITA PASTA WITH CHICKEN 212
INSTANT POT BOLOGNESE 213
LASAGNA IN AN INSTANT POT 215
MAC N CHEESE 218
BETTER-THAN-KIDS' MAC AND CHEESE 219
PAD THAI IN AN INSTANT POT 220
PASTA FAGGIOLI SOUP 223
PASTA IN CREAM SAUCE WITH SAUSAGE 225
PENNE IN VODKA SAUCE 227
SATISFYING CHEESEBURGER PASTA 228
SMOOTH AND CHEESY TACO PASTA 230
VEGAN PASTA PUTTANESCA 230

CHAPTER 9: HEALTHY AND TASTY VEGETARIAN RECIPES 233

- BAKED BEANS WITH MUSHROOMS 233
- CURRIED SWEET POTATOES, CHICKPEAS, AND SPINACH 236
- GARLIC FLAVORED QUINOA WITH MUSHROOMS AND CHERRY TOMATOES 237
- LENTIL TACOS 239
- MEXICAN-INSPIRED QUINOA DISH WITH LIME SAUCE 241
- MOROCCAN SWEET POTATO & LENTIL STEW 242
- QUICK PEA RISOTTO 244
- RATATOUILLE IN AN INSTANT POT 246
- SAVORY VEGETARIAN STEW 248
- SPICY VEGAN CHILI 249
- VEGAN POSOLE 251
- VEGGIE CHOW MEIN 252

CHAPTER 10: AMAZING GRAIN AND BREADS RECIPES 254

- BAKED BEANS AND HAM 254
- BANANA BREAD IN AN INSTANT POT 255
- BEAN AND BEEF STEW 257
- CORNBREAD IN AN INSTANT POT 260
- CRUSTY BREAD IN AN INSTANT POT 262
- HEALTHY AND DELICIOUS QUINOA CHICKEN DISH 263
- IRISH SODA BREAD 265
- MONKEY BREAD 268
- PINTO BEANS WITH CHORIZO 269
- PORK CHOPS AND RICE 271
- SAVORY CHICKEN AND RICE 272
- SOUTHERN BLACK-EYED PEAS AND HAM 273
- SPICY CAJUN CHICKEN AND RICE 275
- TASTY GARLIC BEEF AND RICE BOWL 276
- ZINGY SOUTHWESTERN CHICKEN AND RICE 279
- ZUCCHINI BREAD 280

CHAPTER 11: FUN AND DELICIOUS SIDE DISHES 283

- APPLESAUCE IN AN INSTANT POT 283
- BACON AND BRUSSELS SPROUTS 285

BAKED POTATOES – AND TWICE BAKED – IN AN INSTANT POT............ 286
BASMATI RICE 287
CREAMY MAC AND CHEESE 288
CREAMY MASHED POTATOES 290
DEVILED EGGS A LA INSTANT POT 292
GARNISHED REFRIED BEANS 293
POTATO SALAD IN AN INSTANT POT 295
QUICK CORN ON THE COB 297
ROASTED RED POTATOES 298
SOUTHERN GREEN BEANS 299
SUPERFAST SPANISH RICE 300
SWEET AND SPICY GLAZED CARROTS 301
TASTY SCALLOPED POTATOES 303
TWO MINUTE BROCCOLI 304

CHAPTER 12: DELECTABLE DESSERT RECIPES 307

APPLE COBBLER WITH ROLLED OATS 307
BANANA CHOCOLATE CHIP BUNDT CAKE 309
CHOCOLATE LAVA CAKE 310
CREAMY RICE PUDDING 312
DOUBLE CHOCOLATE CHEESECAKE 314
ELEGANT CRÈME BRULE 317
GOURMET BREAD PUDDING 319
LOW-CARB CHOCOLATE MOUSSE 321
MAPLE FLAVORED FLAN 323
NEW YORK CHEESECAKE IN AN INSTANT POT 325
PERFECT STRAWBERRY FRUIT PIE 327
PRESSURE-COOKED PINEAPPLE UPSIDE DOWN CAKE 329
QUICK TAPIOCA PUDDING 331
SIMPLE AND SWEET PEACH CRISP 332
SWEET CRESCENT ROLL APPLE DUMPLINGS 334

CHAPTER 13: FAVORITE BONUS RECIPES 337

BONE BROTH 337
CARAMELIZED ONIONS 339
LIP BALM 341
CHICKEN STOCK 342
COUGH SYRUP 343
DOG FOOD 344

- Eggs 346
  - Hard, Medium, or Soft-Boiled Eggs 346
  - Scrambled Eggs 347
  - Poached Eggs 348
- Herbal Balms/Salves 349
- Herbal Infusions – Water-Based 351
- Herbal Soap 353
- Instant Pot Ice Tea 355
- Hot Sauce 357
- Jam in an Instant Pot 358
- Ketchup 360
- Kettle Corn 362
- Lotion Bars 363
- Dipping Chocolate 364
- Ricotta Cheese 366
- Roasted Garlic 367
- Salsa 369
- Vanilla Extract 371

CONCLUSION 374
MY OTHER BOOKS 375

Introduction

When I was a child, my mother frequently used a pressure cooker to speed up her meal preparation. That ended, however, the day the pressure cooker malfunctioned, shot the lid through the ceiling into the bedroom overhead, spit food all over the kitchen, and caught the curtains on fire! We never did quite get the tomato stain out of that kitchen ceiling! As a result, I've never since used a pressure cooker because, quite frankly, I was afraid of it.

Recently, I decided to buy an Instant Pot, after hearing a friend rave on and on about how easy it was to sauté directly in the pot and to use it as both a rice steamer and a slow cooker. My trusty Crock-Pot had bit the dust, because I used it constantly, so I thought an Instant Pot might serve as a handy replacement.

It was only *after* making my purchase that I discovered one of the Instant Pot's main functions is pressure cooking! Fortunately, today's Instant Pots are much safer than my mother's pressure cooker, so I screwed up my courage and gave it a try. I was amazed at how easy the pot was to use; it cooked meals swiftly and made meat melt-in-the-mouth tender. Thanks to the Instant Pot, I am now pressure cooking with ease and saving a lot of time in the process.

Another friend used to cook all her dinners for the week on Saturday. She would line up everything like a commercial kitchen; then, starting around nine in the morning, she began preparing food. She wouldn't finish until late afternoon. Then, she faced a mountain of dirty dishes. By the time everything was cleaned up, the day had ended and she was completely exhausted.

All that ended the day she brought home an Instant Pot. This marvelous Wonder Pot liberated her from the kitchen on weekends. Now, she gets home after work, throws everything in that pot (including stuff that is still frozen) and dinner's on the table in less than an hour, no matter what.

Not only is your Instant Pot a time saver, it simplifies the cleanup. You can use the same pot to sauté as you do to pressure cook the meat. Almost everything is prepared in one pan, and it is pretty easy to clean.

Typical Instant Pot with Assessories

Benefits of Cooking With An Instant Pot
Here are some of the many advantages you'll enjoy when you use your Instant Pot:

- **Foods are prepared much faster** than with normal methods and you are not bombarding your food with destructive energy from your microwave oven. Some of the recipes can be completed in 70% less time than they would in an oven or on the stove.

- **You use less energy.** Since cooking time is reduced, the appliance is active for less time than if you were using an oven or stovetop. It also takes less energy to run than your microwave, but don't try reheating food in your Instant Pot; it's not designed for that purpose.

- **Food retains more nutrients.** When pressure cooking, heat is distributed more evenly, and less water is used in the processing, so nutrients are not leached away. Not only does food retain its nutrients, it also retains its color. Green beans stay green instead of turning gray. And the texture is much more appealing; no more soggy, mushy vegetables!

- **Grains and legumes are more digestible.** Food is cooked above the boiling point in pressure cooking. Since many forms of rice, wheat, corn, and beans contain aflatoxins (carcinogens introduced by mold), stovetop cooking could introduce these toxins into your body. Not so when you pressure cook. All those nasty things are gone after the food is cooked.

- Cooking in an Instant Pot reduces the pile of dishes in the sink. You wash the inner pot and maybe the steamer basket or trivet and any glass bowl you put inside. That's it. There are no saucepans, frying pans, cook pots and fewer utensils to deal with.

- When pressure cooking, smells do not permeate the kitchen and the rest of the house. I hate cooking fish because of the fishy odor that lingers in my house for days. With my Instant Pot however, I might smell something when the pressure releases, but it is short lived and doesn't stay around for more than a few minutes.

This book is designed to help you get acquainted you with your Instant Pot by using delicious recipes that are sure to satisfy everyone! In this book you'll find incredible breakfast and lunch recipes, along with mouthwatering main dish recipes using meats, seafood, and vegetables. There are plenty of tasty side dishes and desserts as well, even a chapter on weird things you can do with your Instant Pot like making dogfood, soap, or vanilla extract.

Instant Pot

Sizes

Instant Pots come in a range of sizes. The smallest version holds three quarts; then there are the six- and eight-quart varieties. The three-quart pot is a little limited because you can't fit a cake pan or bowl inside it. The six quart appliance is adequate for a few people, but you would be hard pressed to get a large ham or turkey in it. The eight-quart version is more appropriate for cooking large items and will be quite adequate for most settings, but it is also more expensive. I'm currently using a six-quart Instant Pot and find it quite adequate for my needs.

Price

A good six-quart Instant Pot will set you back around $120 to $150 US dollars and an eight quart pot typically runs around $180. This might seem a little expensive, but it is well worth the cost because you can use it in so many ways without ever needing to turn on the stove.

It's also highly energy efficient. I use my Instant Pot all the time and it doesn't raise my electric bill enough to notice. I *know* it has reduced my gas bill.

Functions
Here are the basic functions included in an Instant Pot:

- Slow cooker
- Electric pressure cooker
- Rice cooker
- Steamer
- Yogurt maker
- Sauté or browning pan
- Warming tray

Most Instant Pots allow for a delayed, programmable start time. The pots are easy to clean and you can cook more than one item at the same time, in most cases.

My Instant Pot has helped me streamline my kitchen. Because of its multifunctionality, I no longer need a separate rice cooker, bamboo steamer, slow cooker, yogurt machine, or warming tray.

I fully appreciate that the pressure cooker function is *much* safer than the stand-alone version. Your Instant Pot includes an automatic pressure release valve. You tell it how long to pressure cook the contents and it monitors the pressure for you, releasing it gradually before the end of the cooking time. No more holding a valve open or risking a blow-up.

The pressure cooker functions at 15 pounds per square inch (psi). This is lower than most stovetop pressure cookers, so you may discover that your Instant Pot needs a little longer to cook than a recipe calls for. I have added 10 extra minutes in a few cases, but everything came out fine.

I love the sauté and browning features included in my Instant Pot. They are so effective that I may never again use a frying pan! Rice cooks much faster in an Instant Pot than in a regular rice cooker and it comes out great every time. I have also come to rely on the pot's warming feature. When I have a hard time getting people to the table, my Instant Pot keeps food warm until we're ready to eat.

If you forget to defrost your meat, that's no problem. I would not advise this with the slow cooker function, but the pressure cooker handles frozen meat nicely; just add forty to fifty percent to the cooking time and everything will come out fine.

A Gentle Warning

If you take the time to read the manual that comes along with your Instant Pot it will show you additional ways to make the most of this amazing new cooking appliance. You'll be able to use most of your slow cooker recipes with your Instant Pot and recipes formulated for pressure cookers will also transfer easily, with a slight time adjustment.

You'll want to pay attention to the safety instructions for using your Instant Pot as a pressure cooker. Even though there are built-in safeguards, please remember that there are always dangers when you pressurize a sealed pot. You'll want to be doubly certain that the pressure has returned to normal before you open the lid. Even if the recipe doesn't call for it, I recommend opening the quick release valve before removing the lid.

To avoid steam burns, train yourself to raise first the side of the lid that is farthest away from you. You'll also want to keep your face and hands away from the opening for a few seconds. Steam can rise quickly and easily burn exposed skin.

A Not-So-Gentle Warning

While your Instant Pot can do a lot of things, there are a few things it just was not designed to do. Be careful about overfilling the pot; things tend to expand under pressure, well, at least with pressure cooking. If you're cooking beans, rice, or other grains, don't fill it higher than halfway. Anything you're pressure cooking should not start out filling more than two thirds of the pot.

Don't try to use it as a deep fat fryer and *never, ever* attempt to turn it into a pressure fryer! Why? Because the Instant Pot's pressure is much higher than a commercial fryer's. Besides, you're just askin' for an explosion if you drop a chicken into a pot full of hot grease.

Accessories and Other Necessities

Here are a few items that can help simplify your use of the Instant Pot:

- The pot most likely comes with a trivet you can set in the bottom to raise things above any liquid in the bottom of the pot. When you pressure cook or steam food in your Instant Pot, you will place water in the bottom. Since you don't want the water in your food, you will set a trivet on the bottom and place your food in another container on top of the trivet,
- Your Instant Pot should already come with a small measuring cup to measure out liquids, but you may find a set of heat-resistant measuring cups useful.
- A steam basket is essential; it can double as a trivet, if set upside down.
- Wooden, bamboo, or silicone stirring utensils can come in handy.
- The Instant Pot also sells accessory bundles that include containers designed to fit inside the pot liner. These packages vary but they may include such useful items as heavy-weight steam baskets, silicone egg cups, and slings designed to slip beneath pots and simplify the removal process. Because you will probably be using your Instant Pot all the time, you'll find these accessories well worth the investment.
- I would recommend buying a glass lid if your model has one available. This is essential for preparing popcorn and is helpful in other situations as well.
- You may also have – or be able to easily find – containers that will fit inside your Instant Pot. I rely on a glass bowl, a

springform pan, and a steamer basket that doubles as a colander.

- If you plan to make soaps or other non-food items, I recommend purchasing an extra stainless steel inner pot. Otherwise, you run the risk of your food absorbing some pretty strange tastes!

- I also suggest keeping on hand a couple replacement sealing rings for the lid; they tend to wear out quickly with such constant use. If you have extra sealing rings on hand, it will prevent you from having to live without your Instant Pot while you go after a replacement.

Important Basics You Need To Know

Here are some interesting tips to get you started. **Do Not Skip Reading This Section Or You Might Be Disappointed!**

- Do not expect to put a bunch of frozen ingredients in the pot and have them thoroughly pressure cooked in 10 minutes. Depending on what you put in the pot, it is going to take a while to actually heat up and start producing pressure. It is a Miracle Pot, but not a magical pot!

- If you turn on the sauté function before starting the pressure cooker, it will take less time for the pressure to start to build up, because the pot is already hot. If you are starting out with a cold pot, it will take longer. The pot will indicate when it is warming up. Once the digital clock starts ticking down, the pot is cooking.

- The sauté function also takes a little time to heat up. Always let the pot warm to where it says "hot" on the digital display before starting to sauté food.

- Your Instant Pot has functions that allow the pressure to decrease, either gradually or immediately. Some recipes call for the natural release; the food continues to cook while the pressure goes down. This process can take 15 to 30 minutes to complete.

  Other foods don't need to cook after the time is up. This calls for the rapid release function. You'll want to review your manual to learn how the rapid release works for your particular model. Most pots have a release valve on the lid that you raise to let the steam out. The rapid release process will take three to five minutes and then you'll be able to get to the food inside.

- Just because a recipe says it takes 10 minutes of cooking, you can't assume the cook time will be absolute. Altitude, weather, the size of your meat, and other factors can contribute to alter processing times.

  I always check meat with an instant meat thermometer before I pull it out of the pot. If the internal temperature isn't high enough, I just close the lid, seal the pot again, and let it go on cooking for another few minutes.

As with any new appliance, you can expect a period of trial and error while you explore ways to take advantage of your Instant Pot's capabilities. Don't let that scare you. Cooking with an Instant Pot is the way of the future. It's healthier, it's a huge time saver, and it's good for the environment. Before long you'll wonder how you ever lived without it.

Chapter 1: Start The Morning Right – Delicious Instant Pot Breakfast Recipes

Start the day right with some easy and delicious recipes prepared in your Instant Pot. These recipes use a variety of Instant Pot functions, including the pressure cooker, yogurt maker, steamer, the sauté setting, and the slow cooker option. These recipes work well for a family breakfast or to host a brunch party.

Banana Nut Oats

Banana nut oats provide a hearty, warm breakfast.

Oatmeal is always a great choice for breakfast; this recipe will remind you of a moist and flavorful banana nut bread. Its crunch comes from toasted nuts and chia seeds, both powerful sources of protein. In addition to the nuts and seeds sprinkled on top of hearty steel cut oats, you'll enjoy a touch of sweetness provided by maple syrup.

The pressure cooker setting prepares your oatmeal in about 20 minutes. I've found that if I turn it on as soon as I get up, by the time I've showered and prepared for the day, breakfast is ready to be served.

Yield: 4 servings

Ingredients:

2 cups water

1 cup unsweetened almond milk

1 cup steel cut oats, dry

¼ cup chopped walnuts

2 tablespoons chia seeds

1 large ripe banana, mashed

1½ teaspoon ground cinnamon, divided

1 teaspoon vanilla extract

2 tablespoons maple syrup

1 pinch salt

2 tablespoons toasted walnuts

1 banana, sliced

Directions:

1. Place the water, almond milk, oats, chopped walnuts, chia seeds, mashed banana, one teaspoon of the ground cinnamon, the vanilla, maple syrup, and salt in your Instant Pot.
2. Stir well and place the lid on the pot with the release valve in the sealed position.
3. Set the time to 10 minutes.

4. After the cook time is completed, flip the release valve to "vent".

5. Give the pot 5 to 10 minutes to decompress and finish cooking, and then you can serve up the contents into four bowls, laying banana slices on top and sprinkling over everything the rest of the walnuts and cinnamon.

Blueberry/Lemon Breakfast Cakes

This recipe makes two small muffin-like cakes with a citrusy blueberry punch. They take 30 minutes each to bake. I often bake mine the night before, warming them in the microwave next morning. If you lack buttermilk, you can make your own by stirring a tablespoon of lemon juice into a half cup of milk.

This recipe uses the pressure cooker setting. Each cake will serve about two people.

Yield: 4-6 servings

Ingredients:

 2 cups unbleached all-purpose flour

 ½ teaspoon salt

 2 teaspoons baking powder

 ½ cup unsalted butter, softened

 ¼ cup sugar

 Zest of 1 lemon

 1 egg, room temperature

 1 teaspoon vanilla extract

 ½ cup buttermilk

 2 cups blueberries, fresh or frozen

 ½ cup powdered sugar

 Juice of ½ lemon

Directions:

1. You will need a dish that fits inside your Instant Pot. Grease and flour this dish, then set it aside.
2. In a small bowl, mix the flour, salt, and baking soda. Extract two tablespoons and place in a lidded container.
3. In another small bowl, cream together the butter, sugar, and lemon zest.
4. Add the egg and vanilla, mixing well.
5. Add half of the flour mixture to a mixing bowl, followed by half of the buttermilk. Mix well before adding alternating portions of flour and liquid until everything is thoroughly combined.
6. Place the blueberries in the lidded container and toss with the extracted flour mixture. This will prevent the berries from clumping together. Add to the batter and fold in carefully.
7. Pour two-thirds of a cup of water into an Instant Pot with a rack in the bottom.
8. Spoon half of the batter into the greased baking pan and place inside your Instant Pot on the rack.
9. Select the high pressure cooker function and set a cook time of 30 minutes.
10. At the end of 30 minutes, give the pressure a quick release. When it is safe to do so, remove the pan and empty the cake onto a serving dish.
11. Carefully prepare the cake pan again, pouring in the rest of the batter, and then pressure cook it for another 30 minutes
12. In a small bowl, whisk together the powdered sugar and lemon juice. Drizzle over the cakes before serving.

Breakfast Burrito with Sausage

These breakfast burritos are perfect for morning meals. You actually use ground pork for this recipe; the added spices provide the sausage flavor. This recipe utilizes your Instant Pot's pressure cooker setting.

For southwestern flair, include chopped cilantro, and a lime wedge on the side.

Yield: 6 burritos

Ingredients:

    8 ounces ground pork

    1 teaspoon sea salt

    ⅛ teaspoon ground pepper

    1 teaspoon crushed fennel seed

    1 teaspoon sage

    1 teaspoon thyme

    ⅛ teaspoon nutmeg

    ½ teaspoon red pepper flakes, crushed

    1 teaspoon light brown sugar

    1 tablespoon water

    6 flour tortillas

8 eggs

¼ cup milk

½ teaspoon sea salt

1 pinch ground black pepper

Cheddar cheese, shredded

Salsa

Directions:

1. Mix the ground pork in a large bowl with the salt, pepper, fennel seed, sage, thyme, nutmeg, red pepper flakes, brown sugar, and water. Cover and refrigerate while preparing the rest of the recipe.
2. Take two pieces of aluminum foil and brush with them olive oil where the tortilla shells will rest against it. Lay the tortilla shells in the middle of one sheet, top with the other sheet, and seal the foil edges.
3. Break the eggs into an ovenproof seven-inch-diameter bowl and whisk together.
4. Add the milk, half teaspoon salt, and pinch of pepper.
5. Add the pork mixture to the eggs, breaking it up into small pieces. Cover the bowl tightly with a sheet of aluminum foil, add 1½ cups of water to your Instant Pot, and set the bowl inside.
6. Place the foil-wrapped tortillas on top.
7. Close the lid and lock it in place. Close the steam release valve and press the manual button, setting the pot to pressure cook for 15 minutes.
8. After that time, allow the steam to gradually release for 10 minutes. Carefully expel any remaining pressure before removing the lid. Use tongs and towels to remove the tortilla package, followed by the bowl of eggs.
9. Assemble the tortillas by adding the egg and sausage mixture, shredded cheese, and the salsa to each. Roll up into a burrito and serve.

Breakfast Fruit Cobbler

Breakfast Cobbler with Plums, Pears and Apples

I love fruit cobbler for dessert but it also makes for a tasty breakfast dish. This recipe calls for honey instead of processed sugar, giving you a healthy twist to an old favorite. Here you'll find directions for both **pressure cooker** preparation and for the **slow cooker** process. The slow cooker only takes an hour, giving you another dish you can prep beforehand, refrigerate, and start cooking when you first wake up.

Yield: 2 servings

Ingredients:

　　1 plum, diced (leave skin on)

　　1 pear, diced (leave skin on)

　　1 apple, cored and diced (leave skin on)

　　2 tablespoons honey

　　3 tablespoons coconut oil

　　¾ teaspoon ground cinnamon

¼ cup shredded, unsweetened coconut

¼ cup pecan pieces, chopped

2 tablespoons salted and roasted sunflower seeds

Whipped cream (optional)

Pressure Cooker Directions:

1. Place the cut fruit into the bowl of your pot. Add the honey and coconut oil, and then sprinkle it with cinnamon.
2. Secure the lid and close off the pressure valve, pressing the steam function and cooking for 10 minutes. Quick-release the pressure at the end of this time.
3. Remove the lid when it is safe and use a slotted spoon to transfer the fruit to a bowl, retaining the liquid.
4. Add the coconut, pecans and sunflower seeds to the pot and select the sauté function. Stir several times to brown the contents on all sides, and then use a slotted spoon to strain out the contents, placing them on top of the fruit.
5. Serve warm, with or without whipped cream.

Slow Cooker Directions:

1. Place the fruit in your Instant Pot, select the slow cooker mode, and cook it on high for one hour.
2. Toast the coconut, pecans, and sunflower seeds in a little butter in a frying pan for about five minutes. Sprinkle atop the fruit before serving.

Build-Your-Own Mini Frittatas

I love to make these when I have morning guests because they can be tailored to the preferences of each individual. I place a variety of ingredient choices in small bowls with spoons and let everyone add what they want. You will need some metal or silicone molds for this recipe.

Here are some ideas for ingredients you can make available:

- Sautéed onions and garlic
- Fried bacon, shredded, or browned sausage

- Sliced green onions
- Sliced green or red peppers
- Dried or fresh herbs
- Parmesan, cheddar, mozzarella, feta, or Swiss cheese, shredded
- Spinach, sautéed in a little olive oil
- Chopped olives
- Green chilies from a can, chopped
- Cooked asparagus, chopped
- Diced tomatoes
- Steamed chopped broccoli

For this recipe you will use the pressure cooking setting.

Individualized frittatas can be cooked in color-coded silicone cups.

Yield: 6 frittatas

Basic Ingredients:

    5 large eggs

    1 tablespoon milk

    Dash of salt and pepper

Directions:

1. In a bowl, whisk the eggs with the milk, salt and pepper.
2. Pour into baking molds about halfway up the mold.
3. Add the additional ingredients, making sure they do not overflow. If the molds are not filled to barely beneath the edge, add a little more egg mixture.
4. Stir each mold with a chopstick to ensure that the ingredients are evenly distributed.
5. Pour one cup of water into the bottom of your Instant Pot, set the molds atop the rack, and insert it into the pot.
6. Select the pressure cooker setting, on manual high pressure, for five minutes. Once the timer goes off, perform a quick release and when it is safe, open the pot, remove the rack holding the molds, and serve.

Chocolate Oatmeal

You can put all the ingredients to this dish in your Instant Pot before you go to bed and turn on the slow cooker function. The scent of chocolate will permeate your home and wake you up in the morning. Once the cooking time is completed, your Instant Pot will switch to warming mode, keeping it ready for anyone who is hungry.

Yield: 4 servings.

Ingredients:

    2 cups old-fashioned oatmeal (don't use the quick type)

    1 cup milk

    6 cups water

    1 teaspoon cinnamon

1 teaspoon vanilla

2½ tablespoons cocoa powder

1 10-ounce bag frozen cherries or strawberries

Mini chocolate chips

Dried apricots or cranberries

Directions:

1. Put the oats, milk, water, cinnamon, vanilla, cocoa powder, and frozen cherries or strawberries in your Instant Pot. Set the lid to "vent" and use the slow cooker setting.
2. Cook for 6½ hours.
3. If the mixture is watery when done, just stir to mix in the liquid. Spoon into bowls.
4. Sprinkle chocolate chips and dried fruit over each serving. Since there is no sugar in the recipe, this will sweeten it.

Country Ham and Egg Casserole

You can use deli ham for this recipe, but I prefer leftover ham roast or steaks. You can include more meat than the recipe calls for, if you like your casserole meatier. I put sour cream on top before serving, but you could just as easily top it with salsa or diced tomatoes.

This is prepared using the pressure cooker setting.

Yield: 4-6 servings

Delicious eggs for Country Ham and Egg Casserole

Ingredients:

    10 large eggs

    1 cup milk

    1 cup chopped ham

    ½ onion, diced

    4 medium-sized red potatoes, skin on, diced

    2 cups cheddar cheese, shredded

    ¼ teaspoon salt

    ⅛ teaspoon pepper

Directions:

1. Use either the insert pan of your Instant Pot or a glass bowl that fits inside. Cover the inside with non-stick spray.
2. Break the eggs into it. Add the milk and whisk everything together.
3. Add the ham, onion, potatoes, cheese, salt, and pepper to the bowl and mix well.

4. Cover the container tightly with foil.
5. Place the steam rack into your Instant Pot and pour in two cups of water. Place the container on top of the rack.
6. Close the lid and select the manual pressure cooking option. Set the timer for 25 minutes and cook.
7. After the pressure has been released, remove the dish, plate individual servings, add toppings, and serve.

Crustless Vegetable Quiche

I love quiche, but sometimes the crust can be difficult to get right. This recipe lets you enjoy your quiche, without the bother of the crust; how's that for a handy solution?

You'll use the pressure cooker option. I prefer using fresh tomatoes over canned, to avoid creating a watery quiche. Likewise, roma tomatoes will provide more tomato and less juice than other varieties. In this case, you'll cook the dish open, without covering it; otherwise the quiche tends to not cook adequately. Before serving, you'll want to dab the top with a paper towel to remove any moisture that has collected on top.

Yield: 6 servings

Ingredients:

½ cup milk

12 large eggs

¼ teaspoon salt

¼ teaspoon pepper

3 green onions, chopped

1 cup fresh roma tomatoes, seeded and diced

3 cups baby spinach, chopped

A few thin tomato slices for garnish on top

¼ cup shredded Parmesan cheese

Directions:

1. Place a trivet in the bottom of your Instant Pot to elevate the baking bowl. Add 1½ cups water to your Instant Pot.
2. In a bowl, whisk together the milk and eggs. Add the salt and whisk well.
3. Add the onions, diced tomatoes, and baby spinach, combining thoroughly.
4. Pour the mixture into a 1½-quart baking dish. Lay the sliced tomatoes on top and sprinkle the top with Parmesan cheese.
5. Place the dish on a sling and lower it into your Instant Pot. Lock the lid, select high pressure, and set the cook time to 20 minutes.
6. When the cooking is finished, turn the pot off and wait 10 minutes before using the quick pressure release.
7. Remove the quiche from your Instant Pot. It should be set but it will not be brown. If you would like to brown it, place it under a broiler for a few minutes until browned.

French Toast Casserole

Here's a quick and easy way to make French toast; it only needs 15 minutes to cook, thanks to our handy pressure cooker setting. I prefer blueberries or raspberries, but you can also use sliced peaches or strawberries in the dish. The fruit cooks down and infuses its sweetness into the bread, so no syrup is needed.

Delightfully Sweet French Toast Casserole

Yield: 4-6 servings

Ingredients:

    1 loaf French or Italian bread, cubed

    ¾ cup milk

    1 cup half and half

    3 eggs

    1 teaspoon vanilla

    1 tablespoon cinnamon

    ½ cup fresh fruit

Directions:

1. Spray a six- to eight-quart baking dish with non-stick spray.
2. Cube the bread and place it in the dish.

3. In a bowl, whisk together the milk, half and half, eggs, vanilla and cinnamon and pour it over the bread cubes. Carefully stir to coat the bread.

4. Sprinkle the fruit on top and cover with foil.

5. Place a trivet in the bottom of your Instant Pot and put one to one and a half cups water in the bottom.

6. Lower the dish to set on the trivet and secure the lid. Cook using the manual pressure cooker setting for 15 minutes, with a natural release.

Fruit and Yogurt

One of the best things about your Instant Pot is its yogurt setting! It easily makes homemade yogurt that is creamy, delicious, and just the way you like it.

I mix my milk when I make yogurt. I use half two percent milk and half whole milk. This gives the yogurt a creamy texture that you just can't get by using all of one or the other. Using all two percent milk yields yogurt that is a little too thin for my taste. However, using all whole milk makes it a little too thick for me. You can experiment until you get the exact consistency you prefer.

Use any kind of fresh or frozen and drained fruit you like or mix the fruit. One of my favorites is to use one cup each of strawberries and blueberries.

For this recipe, you will use a cloth napkin to strain the yogurt and you'll need containers for the finished yogurt. I prefer two-quart glass jars for this purpose, but you can use whatever you want.

You also will need to use commercial yogurt to get all those little microbes for your starter. I use plain Greek yogurt, but you could use any plain yogurt that contains live cultures. You can also use yogurt from one batch as starter for the next batch.

I also use vanilla bean paste for flavoring instead of the usual vanilla extract, because it does not add liquid to the recipe.

Put a *lid* on this jar and you can take your yogurt with you.

Yield: a little less than 1 gallon of yogurt

Ingredients:

½ gallon two percent milk

½ gallon whole milk

½ cup plain Greek yogurt

2 tablespoons vanilla bean paste

2 cups fresh or frozen/drained fruit

1 cup sugar

Directions:

1. Pour the milk into your Instant Pot and secure the lid in place.
2. Press the "Yogurt" button and press the adjust button until it says "boil." The pot should beep after 45 minutes.

3. When it beeps, unplug the pot, take off the lid, remove the liner, and set it on a countertop. Cool until a thermometer reads about 115 degrees F.

4. Put the liner back in your Instant Pot and plug it in again.

5. Use a plastic or silicone whisk to stir in the Greek yogurt and vanilla bean paste.   DO NOT USE A METAL WHISK. The metal can affect the yogurt.

6. Secure the top and press the "Yogurt" button; the timer should say 0:00. Let it count up to eight hours.

7. After 8 hours, strain the yogurt through the cloth napkin and place it into a container, cover, and chill overnight.

8. Boil the fruit and sugar briefly and let the mixture cool to lukewarm before adding the fruit to the yogurt. You can place the fruit in the bottom or spoon it on top.

Peaches and Cream Oatmeal

This recipe uses old fashioned oats and fresh peaches. Do not try to make this with quick oats or frozen peaches; it doesn't work. I hold out a few peach slices to use as garnish, along with a sprinkle of cinnamon.

This recipe is perfect if you have a big family or if you are serving brunch. Leftovers keep well in the refrigerator for a day or two. You can warm them up again after the first day or prepare a half recipe, if you need fewer servings.

You can substitute nectarines, and the oatmeal tastes just as delicious.

Yield: 8 servings

Ingredients:

    4 ripe peaches

    4 cups old fashioned oats

    3½ cups milk

    3½ cups water

    ⅓ cup sugar

    1 teaspoon cinnamon

Directions:

1. Wash and peel the peaches, then cut into thin slices. Save out a sliced half of one peach for garnish. Put the rest in your Instant Pot.
2. Place the oats, milk, water, sugar, and cinnamon in your Instant Pot and stir well.

3. Secure the top and select the multigrain setting, cooking for six minutes.
4. Serve when done, adding extra sugar, brown sugar, milk, and chopped peaches on top.

Sausage Gravy

Here is a new twist to an old recipe using an Instant Pot. You'll want to serve this gravy over baking soda biscuits for a satisfying, stick-to-your-ribs meal. This recipe uses multiple functions on your Instant Pot.

I use sweet Italian sausage because I don't like hot stuff in the morning, but you can use spicy sausage if you desire.

Southern Style Sausage Gravy and Biscuits

Yield: 4 servings

Ingredients:

1 pound bulk Italian sausage

½ teaspoon salt

½ teaspoon ground black pepper, or more to taste

2 cups milk

¼ cup flour

Directions:

1. Set your Instant Pot to sauté and brown the sausage completely.
2. Add the salt and pepper and mix well.
3. Pour in the milk, sprinkle with the flour, and stir into the sausage.
4. Secure the lid on your Instant Pot and seal. Close the vent.
5. Select the manual low pressure function for two minutes. When done, release the pressure.
6. Remove the lid when safe and stir the gravy before serving.

With breakfast thoroughly under our belts, let's explore lunch recipes that include some delectable sandwich fillings and heart-warming soups.

Chapter 2: From Soup to Sandwich, Incredible Lunch Recipes

These lunch recipes consist of sandwich fillings and soups perfect for a family lunch, an individual meal break, or for a group. You'll choose your soup from among traditional chicken and noodles ranging to creamy broccoli and cheese. For sandwiches, you'll find barbeque beef, pulled pork, or can opt for a lovely rustic Italian chicken sandwich. Whatever you choose, it will delight anyone who eats it.

Barbecue Beef Sandwich
The filling for this barbecue beef sandwich is easy to make, using a three-pound beef chuck roast, your favorite barbecue sauce, and a few other ingredients. If you're looking for a way to cut calories, omit the cheese or swap out the bread for a lettuce wrap. The filling is thick and the juice won't run.

You'll use the sauté and pressure cooker functions on your Instant Pot. The first set of ingredients will make much more rub than you need for the recipe. You can put the rest in a bottle and use it to flavor other dishes, since you'll only need one tablespoon for this recipe. This southwestern seasoning goes well with fajitas, tacos or anything that calls for a southwestern flair.

Zesty Barbecue Beef Sandwich

Yield: 6 servings

Ingredients:

For Rub (Southwest Seasoning):

    1 tablespoon chili powder

    ½ teaspoon black pepper

    ½ teaspoon cumin

    1 tablespoon paprika

    1 teaspoon coriander

    ½ teaspoon cayenne pepper

    1 teaspoon garlic powder

    ½ teaspoon red pepper flakes, crushed

    1 teaspoon salt

1½ teaspoons oregano

For Sandwich:

3 pounds beef chuck roast

1 tablespoon olive oil

½ cup beef stock

1½ cups barbecue sauce (divided)

6 slices provolone cheese

6 hamburger buns

Directions:

1. In a bowl, combine all the ingredients for the rub. Remove one tablespoon to use in the recipe and store the rest.
2. Cut the beef roast into four pieces.
3. Set your Instant Pot to sauté and sprinkle the four beef pieces with the southwest seasoning.
4. Pour the olive oil in your Instant Pot and swirl it around the bottom.
5. Use tongs to insert two of the beef pieces, then brown and sear the meat on all sides. Remove to a plate and repeat this process with the remaining pieces of meat.
6. Pour the beef stock into the liner of your Instant Pot; as it heats up, scrape the bottom to loosen any brown bits that are attached.
7. Put the beef pieces back into your Instant Pot and pour one cup of barbecue sauce on top.
8. Cancel the sauté function and put the lid on the pot, securing and sealing it. Press the manual pressure cooker button and set the time to 60 minutes.
9. When the pot beeps, release the pressure manually, and let it decompress for 15 minutes.

10. Remove the beef and place it in a bowl. Shred it with two forks, then add the remaining half cup of barbecue sauce and stir to mix in thoroughly.
11. Place generous amounts of meat on buns, top with a slice of cheese, and serve.

Chicken & Corn Soup With Spinach

This is an unusual soup, but everyone I have ever served it to loves it. If I make it during corn season, I use about four cobs of fresh corn, cutting off the kernels instead of using frozen corn. I always use fresh baby spinach leaves, though. You will use both the sauté and pressure cooker functions on your Instant Pot.

Yield: 4 servings

Ingredients:

1 tablespoon olive oil

3 green onions, chopped (save the dark green tops for garnish, but chop the white and light green parts)

1 large potato, diced

2 medium chicken breasts, thinly sliced

2 tablespoons fresh grated ginger root

4 cups chicken stock, divided

3 cups frozen corn kernels, thawed and divided

2 tablespoons tamari or soy sauce

1 tablespoon fish sauce

2 cloves garlic, diced

½ teaspoon fresh ground pepper

½ teaspoon salt

1 tablespoon cornstarch

4 handfuls of baby spinach leaves

2 eggs

½ fresh lime, juiced

Directions:
1. Select the sauté option on your Instant Pot and set the time to 30 minutes.
2. Place the oil, onions, potato, chicken breast, and ginger root in the pot and sauté for five minutes, stirring occasionally. Select the warm setting.
3. Place one cup of chicken stock in a blender or food processor and add one cup of corn. Process until smooth and creamy.
4. Pour the creamed mixture into your Instant Pot along with the rest of the corn and the chicken stock.
5. Add the tamari, fish sauce, garlic, ground pepper, and salt, stirring to mix.
6. Secure the lid and seal it. Set the pressure function on manual, high pressure, for 15 minutes. After the timer goes off, allow the pressure to release for five minutes. Activate the quick release before opening.
7. Select the sauté mode again and add the spinach, mixing thoroughly.
8. In a small bowl, whisk together the eggs and slowly pour them into the soup, stirring continuously. This will resemble Asian egg drop soup, with threads of egg in the soup. Stir well and turn off the pot.
9. In a small cup, dissolve the cornstarch using a few tablespoons of the soup to make a wet slurry. Pour into the soup and stir. The soup will thicken.
10. Stir in the lime juice, garnish with chopped onion greens, and serve.

Creamy Broccoli and Cheddar Soup

Broccoli and cheddar soup is a popular restaurant menu item. It is rich and velvety and you'll find it easy to prepare in your Instant Pot. Do not use frozen broccoli in this case, because it just won't taste the same as fresh broccoli. This recipe utilizes the pot's sauté and pressure cooker options.

Creamy Broccoli and Cheese Soup

Yield: 4 servings

Ingredients:

- 1 tablespoon olive oil
- 2 cloves garlic, finely chopped
- ½ large onion, finely chopped
- 2 carrots, chopped
- 6 cups broccoli florets
- 4 cups chicken stock
- ¼ cup heavy cream
- 1½ cups grated cheddar cheese
- ½ teaspoon salt
- ¼ teaspoon pepper

Directions:

1. Place the olive oil in your Instant Pot and select the sauté function. Once the pot is hot, add the garlic and onions

and stir for three to five minutes until the onion becomes translucent.
2. Turn off your Instant Pot and add the carrots, broccoli, and chicken stock.
3. Close and seal the lid, then select the manual pressure cooking mode and set the time for four minutes
4. Perform a natural pressure release, waiting for four minutes after the timer beeps before opening the pot.
5. Pour the soup into a blender or into a large container and use an immersion blender. Add cream, salt, and pepper, pureeing until smooth.
6. Add the cheese and let it melt. Stir and serve.

French Dip Sandwiches

There is something fancy about a sandwich that comes with its own flavorful sauce. This recipe makes six sandwiches with accompanying au jus for dipping. You will use the sauté, pressure cooker, and warming settings on your Instant Pot.

Au jus adds elegance to an otherwise plain sandwich.

Yield: 6 sandwiches with au jus.

Ingredients:

- 1 2½-pound chuck roast
- 1 tablespoon olive oil
- 2 teaspoons sea salt
- ¼ teaspoon fresh ground black pepper
- ½ teaspoon garlic powder
- 1 clove garlic, crushed
- 1 medium onion, sliced
- ½ cup red wine
- 1 14-ounce can beef broth
- 1 bay leaf
- 6 Kaiser rolls
- 3 tablespoons butter, melted
- ¼ teaspoon garlic powder
- 1 pinch sea salt
- 6 slices Provolone cheese

Directions:

1. Let the roast set at room temperature for 15 minutes.
2. Place the olive oil in your Instant Pot with the setting on sauté.
3. In a small bowl, mix the salt, pepper, and garlic powder; rub onto the meat.
4. Once the olive oil is hot, sear all sides of the roast and remove to a plate.
5. Add the garlic and onions to your Instant Pot and sauté until softened.
6. Add the red wine and simmer until the liquid reduces by half. Scrape up the brown bits from the bottom while simmering.

7. Add broth and the bay leaf and place the roast back into the pot.
8. Close and seal the lid. Select the Meat/Stew option for pressure cooking and set the timer to 100 minutes.
9. When this time is up, allow the pot to release pressure for 25 minutes, turning the release valve to vent before opening.
10. Remove the meat to a plate and shred using two forks.
11. Strain the liquid and keep it warm in the pot.
12. Preheat your oven to broil and place the open Kaiser rolls on a foil-covered baking sheet, cut side up.
13. Melt the butter in a saucepan; combine the butter, garlic powder and pinch of salt. Brush over the inside of the rolls and toast in the broiler for two to three minutes until golden brown.
14. Place meat on the roll bottoms and top with cheese. Remove the tops of the buns and place the meat-covered bottoms back under the broiler to let the cheese melt.
15. Remove from the oven, place a bun top on each sandwich, pour the liquid into a small bowl, and serve along with the sandwiches.

Hamburger and Cabbage Soup

This soup is simple and delicious; I make it whenever I have a bunch of vegetables in the refrigerator that are past their prime. The recipe calls for onions, celery, carrots, tomatoes, and cabbage, but I have been known to also include potatoes, corn, peas, or green beans. When I do this, I reduce the amount of cabbage by approximately the amount of extra vegetables I'm adding.

You will use the sauté and pressure cooker options on your Instant Pot.

Yield: 10 to 11 cups of soup

Ingredients:

1 pound lean ground beef

1 teaspoon sea salt

¼ teaspoon ground black pepper

½ cup onions, diced

½ cup carrot, diced

½ cup celery, diced

1 28-ounce can crushed tomatoes

4 cups beef stock

5 cups green cabbage, chopped

2 bay leaves

Directions:

1. Select the sauté option on your Instant Pot and spray the liner with non-stick spray.
2. Once the pot is hot, add the ground beef, salt, and pepper, breaking apart the meat and stirring until browned, about five minutes.
3. Add the onion, carrots, celery, and any other vegetables you have included. Sauté for about five minutes.
4. Add the tomatoes, beef stock, cabbage, and bay leaves. Lock and seal the lid and cook on high pressure for 20 minutes.
5. Let the steam release naturally.
6. Remove the bay leaves before serving.

Italian Chicken Sandwich

The Parmesan cheese and basil are what give this chicken sandwich filling its Italian flair. I use this as a sandwich filling, but I also serve it as a salad on top of lettuce, with some cucumbers and tomatoes. The recipe makes three to six sandwiches and I serve the filling on thinly sliced Italian bread or toasted Kaiser rolls. You will use the pressure cooker option on your Instant Pot to prepare this dish.

Kaiser rolls add rustic charm to sandwiches.

Yield: 3-6 sandwiches

Ingredients:

    1 tablespoon olive oil

    2 6-ounce boneless chicken breasts

    1 tablespoon garlic, chopped

    1 tablespoon dried basil

    ½ cup Parmesan cheese, shredded

Directions:

1. Place the oil in your Instant Pot and add the chicken breasts.
2. Crush the garlic, sprinkle it over the breasts, and sprinkle the dried basil on top.
3. Select the pressure cooker option and set it to cook manually for six minutes.

4. When the timer goes off, let the pot vent naturally for about five minutes before performing a quick pressure release.

5. Remove the chicken and shred it with two forks. Place it back into the pot and add the Parmesan cheese.

6. If the chicken is not hot, select the warming option and wait until the cheese melts before serving it up on bread or Kaiser rolls.

Italian Farm-To-Table Vegetable Soup

This rustic soup is something you might find in Tuscany. It uses a variety of delicious fresh vegetables, incorporating a mixture of red chilies, carrots, zucchini, and kale. This is a hearty vegetarian soup that will give you energy for hours. You will use the pressure cooker and the sauté functions on your Instant Pot in its preparation.

Rustic Vegetarian Vegetable Soup

Yield: 4 servings

Ingredients:

- 1 tablespoon olive oil
- 1 medium onion, diced
- 3 cloves garlic, crushed
- ¼ teaspoon sea salt
- ½ long red chili, seeded and chopped
- 2 carrots, julienned
- 2 celery sticks, chopped
- 6 large mushrooms, sliced
- 2 cups kale, stems removed and lightly chopped
- 1 12-ounce can diced tomatoes, drained
- 1 small zucchini, diced
- 4 cups vegetable stock (or chicken stock, if you prefer)
- 1 bay leaf
- Chopped parsley for garnish
- Zest from one lemon

Directions:

1. Select the sauté function on your Instant Pot and let it heat up.
2. Add the olive oil, onion, garlic, and salt, sautéing for two minutes.
3. Add the chili, carrots, and celery; cook for four to five minutes or until the vegetables have become slightly soft.
4. Add the mushrooms, kale, tomatoes, and zucchini, stirring to heat through.
5. Add the stock and the bay leaf; stir to mix.
6. Seal the lid and select the manual high pressure setting, giving it 10 minutes.

7. When the timer goes off, let the pressure release for a couple minutes, and then use the quick release lever to rapidly decompress the pot.

8. Ladle the soup into four bowls; sprinkle with chopped parsley and lemon zest before serving.

New Fashioned Chicken Noodle Soup

This delightful old-fashioned-flavored chicken noodle soup is prepared in a new-fashioned way. Using an Instant Pot it takes only an hour and a half from start to finish. That beats simmering all day on the stove the way grandma made it. You'll use the sauté and pressure cooker options on your Instant Pot.

Chicken noodle soup never tasted so good!

Yield: 8 to 10 delicious cups of soup

Ingredients:

1 tablespoon of olive oil

1 small onion, diced

2 cloves of garlic, minced

2 celery sticks, cut into half-inch pieces

5 carrots, cut into half-inch pieces

1 whole 5-pound chicken, giblets discarded

8 cups water

2 tablespoons soy sauce

2 teaspoons kosher salt

1 teaspoon freshly ground pepper

4 ounces extra wide egg noodles

¼ cup fresh flat leaf parsley, minced

Directions:

1. Use the sauté option on your Instant Pot. Pour in the olive oil when the pot is hot and add the onions. Sauté until the onions soften, for two to three minutes.
2. Add garlic, celery, and carrots, sautéing for two more minutes.
3. Add the whole chicken and pour in the water, soy sauce, salt, and pepper.
4. Lock the lid in place and seal it. Turn to high pressure and time it for 20 minutes in manual mode. The pot will take about 20 minutes to reach high pressure and then will start counting down for 20 minutes.
5. When the timer goes off, flick open the quick release valve.
6. After the pressure is released, carefully open the lid and remove the chicken. Set your Instant Pot to warm so that the soup does not cool.
7. Let the chicken set for a few minutes until you can safely handle it; then remove bones and skin and shred the meat. Place on a plate.

8. Select the sauté option and let the soup come to a boil. Stir in the egg noodles and cook for five to six minutes, until the noodles are cooked.

9. Stir in the shredded chicken and parsley and cook for one to two more minutes before serving.

Philly Cheesesteak Sandwich

This sandwich filling doesn't taste exactly like what you'll find in Philadelphia, but it's pretty close and you'll find it mouth-watering good. It's simple to prepare, too. You'll just dump everything in the pot and use either the pressure cooker option for 40 minutes or the slow cooker function for four to eight hours.

Mouthwatering Phili Cheesesteak

Yield: 6 sandwiches

Ingredients:

    2 cloves garlic, minced

1 onion, sliced

2 green peppers, seeded and sliced in strips

2½ pounds top round, thinly sliced

1 teaspoon salt

½ teaspoon pepper

1 can beef broth

1 envelope dry Italian dressing mix

6 slices provolone cheese

6 hoagie rolls

Directions:

1. Place the garlic, onion, peppers, meat, salt, pepper, beef broth, and Italian dressing mix in your Instant Pot.
2. Attach the lid and seal it.

    Pressure cooking: Activate the pressure cooker on high pressure and set the time for 40 minutes.

    Slow cooking: Set the slow cooker on low for eight hours or on high for four hours.

3. If using the pressure cooker method, let the pot depressurize for 10 minutes, then perform a quick release until it's safe to open the pot.
4. Scoop out the filling and place it on rolls, topping each with a slice of provolone cheese.
5. Set the sandwiches on a broiler pan and broil for two to four minutes until the cheese bubbles and starts to brown.
6. Serve.

Potato and Leek Soup with Kale

Leeks have a mild, pleasant flavor. The only difficulty with leeks is that they need to be cleaned very well. Dirt builds up between the layers and if you don't extract it all, your soup will taste a little too earthy.

You'll use the sauté and pressure cooker options on your Instant Pot for this preparation. Use baby spinach or chard for this recipe. You can also substitute sweet potatoes for the white potatoes; it offers an entirely different flavor.

Leeks look like big green onions but have a milder flavor.

Yield: 4 servings

Ingredients:

2½ tablespoons of butter

2 large leeks, sliced

1 teaspoon salt

3 cups kale leaves

3½ cups white potatoes, diced

3 cloves garlic, chopped

Zest from one lemon

Juice of half a lemon

1 teaspoon Dijon mustard

6 cups vegetable stock

½ teaspoon black pepper

2 cups shredded cheddar cheese

½ lemon, juiced

Zest of ½ lemon

2 tablespoons fresh parsley, chopped

Directions:
1. Select the sauté option on your Instant Pot and melt the butter.
2. Add the leeks and stir, sautéing for about four minutes.
3. Add the kale, potatoes, and salt; stir to mix.
4. Add the lemon zest and its juice, reserving the other half of the lemon for later.
5. Add the Dijon mustard, vegetable stock, and black pepper. Stir and then lock the lid.
6. Set your Instant Pot to manual, high pressure, and set the timer for 12 minutes.
7. When the cooking is done, let the pressure release naturally for five minutes before flipping open the quick release. Make sure all the pressure is released before opening the lid.
8. Add the cheese and allow it to melt, stirring frequently. Add the rest of the lemon juice and its zest.
9. Either use an immersion blender or put the soup in a blender. Once the soup is smooth, add the parsley and spoon it into bowls.

Ramen Noodle Soup
This Asian-inspired soup uses ramen or udon noodles and lots of vegetables. It also requires a whole three to four-pound chicken. You'll want to remove the giblets before cooking and set them aside for future use.

You will use the pressure cooker and the sauté setting for this recipe. The soup includes four soft-boiled eggs, but their use is purely optional. The soup tastes great with or without them.

Yield: 4 bowls of soup

Ingredients:

- 4 eggs (optional)
- 1 tablespoon sesame oil
- 1 teaspoon fresh ginger, grated
- 2 cloves garlic, chopped
- 8 ounces fresh mushrooms, sliced (use any type of mushroom)
- 4 cups chicken stock
- 4 cups water
- 2 tablespoons soy sauce
- Sea salt and pepper to taste
- 1 whole 3- to 4-pound chicken
- 8 ounces ramen or udon noodles
- 1 cup baby spinach, chopped
- 1 carrot, grated

Directions:

1. Place the trivet in your Instant Pot and add a half cup of water. Place four eggs in the pot and seal the lid. Select the manual high pressure cooker setting for three minutes. When three minutes is over, use the quick release lever and remove eggs as soon as it is safe to open the pot. Place the eggs immediately in a bowl of ice water until they are completely cool.
2. Use the sauté function on normal heat, warming the sesame oil first and then sautéing the ginger and garlic for two minutes.
3. Add the mushrooms, chicken stock, water, soy sauce, and sea salt to taste, along with a modicum of pepper.

4. Place the chicken in the pot and cancel the sauté function.
5. Seal the lid of your Instant Pot. Set it to high pressure for 20 minutes in the manual pressure cooker mode.
6. It will take 15 to 20 minutes for the pressure to be fully released. At this point, switch to the warming function and open the quick release valve. After it is safe to open the pot, remove the chicken and set it on a plate to cool for a few minutes.
7. Select the sauté option and allow the broth to come to a boil.
8. Stir in the noodles and cook per the package instructions.
9. Remove the bones and skin from the chicken and shred or cut the meat into bite-sized pieces. Stir in the cooked chicken, spinach, and grated carrots. Adjust the salt and pepper to taste.
10. Ladle into four bowls, toss a whole peeled soft-boiled egg into each bowl, and serve.

Spicy Pulled Pork Sandwich
Pulled pork normally takes a minimum of six hours to cook, but in an Instant Pot it only takes a couple hours. This recipe utilizes the sauté and pressure cooking functions on your Instant Pot. You can also use the warming function to keep the sandwich filling ready for instant use. Instead of serving coleslaw on the side, you'll be adding it atop the meat and serving it as part of the sandwich.

A couple forks are all you need to shred the meat.

Yield: 8 servings

Ingredients:

    1 teaspoon dry mustard

    ½ teaspoon ground cumin

    2 teaspoons paprika

    3 tablespoons light brown sugar, divided

    Kosher salt and pepper to taste

    1 4-pound boneless pork shoulder roast, trimmed of fat and cut into six pieces

    2 teaspoons vegetable oil

    ¾ cup water

    ½ cup apple cider vinegar

    3 tablespoons tomato paste

    8 Kaiser rolls

    Barbecue sauce to taste

Directions:

1. In a small bowl, combine the mustard, cumin, paprika, and a single tablespoon of brown sugar along with salt and pepper to taste.
2. Rub the spice mix into all sides of the six pieces of pork shoulder.
3. Set your Instant Pot to sauté and add the vegetable oil. Once hot, insert three pieces of the pork shoulder and brown them on all sides; this should only take about five minutes.
4. Remove the meat and set it aside, then brown the remaining three pieces. Switch your Instant Pot to the warming function.
5. Whisk the water into the drippings in the pot and add the vinegar, tomato paste, remaining tablespoons of brown sugar, and two more cups of water.
6. Return all the pork pieces to the pot and seal the lid closed. Set the pressure cooker to high for one hour.
7. After an hour, perform a quick release and open the pot when it is safe. Transfer the meat to a large bowl.
8. Select the sauté setting and let the juices simmer until reduced by half (around 15 minutes). Use a ladle to remove any fat that rises to the top. Season the meat to taste with salt and pepper.
9. Use two forks to shred the pork in the bowl. Add three cups of the cooking liquid to the pork and mix it in.
10. Place on buns and serve with extra barbecue sauce.

Now, it is time for some dinner recipes. Let's start with poultry and work our way down to pasta.

Chapter 3: World Class Poultry Recipes

Your Instant Pot saves a lot of time in the kitchen. The time it takes to cook poultry is greatly reduced and dinner will be on the table in less than half the time it normally takes. This is particularly true with large, whole poultry meals like roasted chicken or turkey. You'll want to ensure that your turkey or chicken fits inside your Instant Pot before you set out to cook it. A twelve-pound turkey may not even fit in an 8-quart Instant Pot.

You don't have to keep the chicken or turkey whole to cook it. I've included traditional recipes like chicken and rice as well as chicken and dumplings. You may also want to opt for something Mexican, like green chili turkey chili or an Italian dish like Chicken Cacciatori. Whatever you decide to cook, you can be assured that it will be juicy and delicious when you prepare it in an Instant Pot.

A whole chicken is great, but so are its parts.

Chicken and Brown Rice

This recipe requires frozen, boneless and skinless chicken breasts that are not defrosted before you put them in your Instant Pot. This dish also includes carrots and mushrooms to flavor the rice and create a form of pilaf with shredded chicken mixed in.

Yield: eight servings

Ingredients:

   1 tablespoon olive oil

   2 cloves garlic, minced

   3 green onions, chopped

   3 carrots, chopped

   1 cup mushrooms, chopped

   2 cups chicken broth, divided

1½ cups brown rice, rinsed and drained

2 teaspoons dried thyme

1 teaspoon sea salt

½ teaspoon ground pepper

1 pound frozen chicken breasts, boneless and skinless

Directions:

1. Set your Instant Pot on sauté; as soon as it gets hot, add the oil.
2. Add the garlic, onions, carrots, and mushrooms to the pot. Cook for about four minutes, stirring frequently.
3. Deglaze the pan, using a half cup of the chicken broth and stirring well.
4. Stir in the rest of the chicken broth and the rice.
5. Add the thyme, salt, and pepper, then put in the chicken breasts.
6. Lock the lid and seal it, pressure cooking on manual, high pressure, for 20 minutes. When the cook time has elapsed, activate the quick pressure release, opening the lid carefully after it has completely depressurized.
7. Remove the chicken and shred the meat with two forks, then return it to the pot, stirring to mix it with the rice before serving.

Easy Chicken Adobo

Serve this sweet and spicy chicken dish over cooked rice. This recipe uses the sauté function to brown the chicken first. You'll use the pressure cooker to cook the chicken and then return to the sauté option to make the delectable sauce.

Ingredients:

4 each – chicken legs, thighs, and drumsticks

1 teaspoon sea salt

¼ teaspoon ground black pepper

2 tablespoons olive oil

⅓ cup soy sauce

¼ cup white vinegar

¼ cup sugar

1 large onion, sliced

4 cloves garlic, smashed

2 bay leaves

2 green onions, sliced for garnish

Directions:

1. Place the chicken pieces in a bowl and sprinkle with the salt and pepper. Shake the bowl so that the chicken pieces become evenly seasoned.
2. Select the sauté function and wait until the pot is hot before pouring in the olive oil.
3. Add several of the chicken pieces and brown on all sides, for four to seven minutes. Remove to a plate and repeat the process until all the pieces are browned.
4. Add the soy sauce, vinegar, sugar, onion, garlic, and bay leaves to the pot and stir.
5. Return the chicken to the pot and seal the lid. Set the pressure cooker function on high for eight minutes. Perform a quick release and carefully remove the lid.
6. Turn the setting back to sauté and remove the chicken, setting it in a bowl. Allow the sauce in the pot come to a boil and let it reduce for about 20 minutes. It should be a dark brown and smell heavenly. Remove the bay leaves and pour the sauce over the chicken, garnishing it with green onions and serving with rice.

Fancy Chicken Cacciatore

Chicken Cacciatore is considered a "fancy" or elegant dish that usually takes a great deal of time to make. With an Instant Pot everything is completed in half an hour. Now you can serve your family or friends a fancy dinner in record time.

You'll want to also cook up some rice or noodles for the cacciatore to rest on. I prefer to use egg noodles, but spaghetti will also work well. I've even served it over polenta and found the combination delicious. This recipe will call for the sauté and pressure cooker functions on your Instant Pot.

Serve chicken cacciatore over rice, fetucchini noodles or spaghetti.

Yield: 4 servings

Ingredients:

    4 chicken thighs, deboned and skinless

    1 teaspoon sea salt

    ½ teaspoon ground black pepper

    1 tablespoon olive oil

    ½ cup onion, diced

¼ cup red bell pepper, diced

¼ cup green bell pepper, diced

Half of a 14-ounce can crushed tomatoes

½ teaspoon dried oregano

1 bay leaf

Fresh chopped parsley for garnish

Directions:
1. Season the chicken with salt and pepper on all sides.
2. Select the sauté function on your Instant Pot and let it heat up for a few minutes.
3. Add the olive oil, then insert the chicken and brown it before removing to a plate and setting it aside.
4. Add the onions and bell peppers and sauté for five minutes or until softened.
5. Return the chicken to the pot and pour the tomatoes on top.
6. Sprinkle in the oregano and place the bay leaf in the pot. Stir.
7. Cover with the lid and seal it. Pressure cook on high for 25 minutes, then let it release naturally.
8. Open the lid and remove the bay leaf. Serve over pasta or rice and sprinkle with fresh parsley.

Green Chili Turkey Chili
The flavor of green chili peppers with the black beans and turkey make for a delicious combination. This recipe serves from four to six people and the chili is freezable. Use the sauté and pressure cooker options and if you are making it for a crowd, keep it warm with the warming option of your Instant Pot.

Ingredients:

2 tablespoons olive oil

1 pound ground turkey

3 cloves garlic, minced

1 onion, diced

3 stalks celery, thinly sliced

3 carrots sliced thin

1 green pepper, seeded and diced

1 28-ounce can crushed tomatoes

1 4-ounce can green chilies, drained and chopped

1 15-ounce can black beans, drained and rinsed

½ cup water

1½ teaspoons ground cumin

3 tablespoons chili powder

½ teaspoon sea salt

Toppings may include shredded cheese, sliced green onion, sour cream, or diced avocado.

Directions:

1. Select the sauté function on your Instant Pot and let it heat up for about two minutes. Add the olive oil.
2. Brown the ground turkey, stirring to break it up, until there is no pink. This will take about four minutes.
3. Add the garlic, onion, celery, carrots, and green pepper; stir to cook for about four more minutes.
4. Add the tomatoes, green chilies, black beans, water, cumin, chili powder, and salt; stir to combine.
5. Seal the lid and set the pressure cooker on high for 20 minutes. Activate the quick release valve and open the lid carefully. Stir and taste, adjusting the seasonings per your preference. Serve with toppings of your choice.

Herbed Turkey Meatballs

Serve these meatballs with spaghetti or smother them in barbeque sauce and serve without pasta. They also make a great meatball sandwich. These meatballs are delightfully herb-rich with oregano, garlic, rosemary, and thyme. The sauté and pressure cooker functions are used in this recipe.

Serve turkey meatballs in their own sauce or serve them with spaghetti and sauce.

Yield: 16 golf-ball-sized meatballs

Ingredients:

    1 pound ground turkey

    1 egg

    ¼ teaspoon oregano

    ¼ teaspoon thyme

    ¼ teaspoon rosemary

    ¼ teaspoon garlic powder

    ½ teaspoon sea salt

    ¼ teaspoon ground black pepper

⅛ cup olive oil

1 cup chicken broth

Directions:

1. You'll use the sauté function on your Instant Pot first. Let it preheat for a few minutes while preparing the meatball mixture.

2. In a bowl, combine the turkey, egg, oregano, thyme, rosemary, garlic powder, sea salt, and black pepper. Mix well and roll into balls using about two tablespoons of the mixture for each.

3. Pour the oil into your Instant Pot and brown the meatballs on all sides, for two to three minutes on each side. Transfer to a paper-towel-covered plate to absorb the oil.

4. Pour the chicken broth into your Instant Pot and insert a trivet or a basket, then insert the meatballs. You don't really want the meatballs to sit in the broth, or they'll get soggy and break apart.

5. Seal the lid and set the pressure cooker to five minutes on high pressure. Let it naturally release for five minutes after the timer goes off. Perform a quick release to decompress the pot before carefully removing the lid. Extract the meatballs with a slotted spoon and place them on a platter or in a large bowl.

6. If desired, mix a slurry of cornstarch and water and let the broth come to a boil under the sauté function. Add the cornstarch slurry to the pot and let the broth thicken. Spoon over the meatballs

Holiday Turkey Recipe
It is possible to cook a small turkey in an Instant Pot. An eight-pound turkey should fit vertically in a large Instant Pot and will provide four servings. Use a fresh or defrosted frozen turkey. I will warm you that the turkey skin might not be brown when you finish, but there is a little secret about putting it under a broiler that will make the turkey brown and beautiful. Find that tip at the end of the recipe.

This recipe works just as well for a large whole chicken. The rule of cooking a bird in your Instant Pot is to figure six minutes per pound. An 8-pound turkey takes 48 minutes to cook as you will see in this recipe. If you have a 6-pound chicken, it would only take 36 minutes of cooking time and if you can manage to fit a 12-pound turkey inside your Instant Pot, it would take 72 minutes to cook.

Yield: varies, depending on size of bird

Ingredients:

1 8-pound turkey, defrosted

1 medium onion, quartered

2 cloves garlic, cut in half

1 stalk celery, quartered

1 medium carrot, quartered

1 bay leaf

½ cup water

1 to 1½ teaspoons salt

¼ teaspoon ground pepper

Directions:

1. Use a paper towel to blot any moisture from the turkey.
2. Sprinkle with salt and pepper.
3. Place half the onion and one clove of garlic into the cavity of the turkey.
4. Add the rest of the onion and garlic, the celery, carrots, and bay leaf to the bottom of your Instant Pot.
5. Insert the trivet and add the turkey on top.
6. Set the pressure cooker for a manual 48 minutes. When finished cooking, let it naturally reduce pressure for about 10 minutes, then employ the quick pressure release.
7. Remove the turkey and set it in a shallow baking pan. Baste the bird with a little vegetable oil and some

drippings from your Instant Pot. Set it in your oven and broil for about five minutes, until the skin turns a golden brown.

Latin-inspired Chicken Enchiladas

This chicken enchilada dish is simply scrumptious! It uses the sauté and pressure cooker options of your Instant Pot. You will need to use your stove to prepare the tortillas and the oven to bake the dish a little more, but the extra effort is well worth it.

Yield: 6 servings (2 enchiladas each)

Ingredients:

- 1 tablespoon vegetable oil
- Vegetable oil, for toasting tortillas
- 4 cloves garlic, minced
- 1 cup onion, diced
- 1 jalapeno, seeded and minced
- 2 8-ounce cans tomato sauce
- 1 cup chicken broth
- 1 tablespoon sugar
- 2 tablespoons chili powder
- 1 teaspoon cumin
- 1 teaspoons sea salt
- ¼ teaspoon freshly ground black pepper
- 1½ pounds chicken breasts, boneless and skinless (about three of them)
- 2 tablespoons fresh cilantro, chopped (plus additional for garnish)
- 12 corn tortillas
- 8 ounces Monterey jack cheese, shredded
- 8 ounces sharp cheddar cheese, shredded
- Sour cream

Directions:

1. Select the sauté function on your Instant Pot and let it heat up for a minute or two before adding the vegetable oil to the pot.
2. Sauté the garlic, onions, and jalapeno for about three minutes or until the onions are softened.
3. Add the tomato sauce, broth, sugar, chili powder, cumin, salt, and pepper to the pot; stir to mix.
4. Add the chicken breasts and seal the lid. Set the pressure cooker setting to high pressure, manual mode, for 10 minutes.
5. While cooking, prepare the tortillas and preheat your oven to 400 degrees, Fahrenheit.
6. Brush tortillas with vegetable oil and place on a baking sheet, trying not to overlap them. Place in the preheated oven for five minutes or until warm and pliable.
7. Once the chicken is done, open the quick release valve. Once the pressure is released, remove the chicken to a plate to cool. Shred once it is cool enough to safely handle.
8. Add the cilantro to the sauce in your Instant Pot.
9. Coat a 9 by 13 inch baking dish with non-stick spray.
10. Use a quarter cup measuring cup to scoop out the sauce from your Instant Pot and spread it on the bottom of the dish.
11. Evenly divide half of the cheese, half of the sauce and the chicken among the tortillas, rolling them up and setting them, seam down, in the baking dish. Pour the remainder of the sauce over the rolled up tortillas and sprinkle the rest of the cheese on top.
12. Cover the top of the dish with foil and bake for 20 minutes or until hot and bubbly. Sprinkle with a little fresh cilantro to garnish before serving.

Lemon Chicken Dish

A good lemon chicken dish is a good thing to have in your recipe arsenal. Everyone loves it and it is super easy to make. This particular recipe works well in your Instant Pot using the sauté and pressure cooker options; you can use either thawed or frozen chicken. You'll serve this over noodles or rice, or you can simply pour the sauce over the chicken and serve it by itself.

You can add to the healthfulness factor by using organic chicken and broth and by using ghee instead of butter. I prefer to use arrowroot flour to thicken the lemon sauce because it is delicate; cornstarch or wheat flour would make it a little heavy.

Lemon chicken will tickle your taste buds with delicious citrus flavor.

Yield: 6 servings

Ingredients:

    2 tablespoons butter

3 cloves garlic, minced

1 onion, diced

½ teaspoon paprika

1 teaspoon dried parsley

1 teaspoon salt

½ teaspoon pepper

2 pounds chicken (use all breasts, all thighs, or mix and match)

¾ cup chicken broth

½ cup lemon juice (juice of two lemons)

4 teaspoons arrowroot flour

Directions:

1. Activate the sauté option on your Instant Pot and let it heat up for a few minutes. Once hot, add the butter to melt.
2. Once melted, add the garlic, onion, paprika, and parsley; stir until the onions have softened and the garlic has turned a golden shade.
3. Season the chicken pieces with salt and pepper and while still in sauté mode, brown the chicken on all sides, for three to five minutes.
4. Add the chicken broth and lemon juice to your Instant Pot and stir.
5. Seal the lid of your Instant Pot and set it to high pressure. Cook for seven minutes for thawed chicken and 12-15 minutes for frozen chicken. Let it decompress naturally.
6. Open the pot carefully and remove the chicken to a platter with a slotted spoon. Change the option to sauté and let the juices come to a boil.
7. Gradually stir in the arrowroot flour and continue to stir until the sauce has thickened. Pour over the chicken on the platter and serve with lemon slices as garnish.

Savory Chicken and Dumplings

This is what my mother was making in a pressure cooker when she set our kitchen on fire. I love chicken and dumplings, but after that mishap, we never had it again.

Imagine my delight when I purchased my first Instant Pot and used it to prepare her recipe! That was a taste of home, to be sure. I've simplified the recipe; I've incorporated frozen carrots and peas instead of fresh vegetables my mother used and I've incorporated refrigerated biscuits, because they're quicker and easier to work with.

However, you can still prepare these dumplings using baking soda biscuits. You'll just need to wait until everything is finished and then use the sauté option to bring the chicken to a boil. Add the biscuits and boil this for eight minutes before then covering the pot, still on sauté, and boiling it for another five minutes or so. You'll need to add another half cup of chicken broth to compensate for the evaporation you'll experience with this method.

You'll use the sauté and pressure cooker options to prepare this dish.

Yield: 4-6 servings

Ingredients:

- 1 16-ounce tube refrigerated biscuits
- ½ teaspoon salt
- ½ teaspoon pepper
- 1 teaspoon onion powder
- 1 teaspoon dried oregano
- 1½ pounds chicken breasts
- 1 teaspoon olive oil
- 2 cloves garlic, chopped
- 1 small onion, chopped
- 2 cups chicken broth

1 cup water

1 bay leaf

1½ cups frozen peas and carrots, thawed and drained

Directions:

1. Remove the biscuits from the tube and flatten them on a cutting board, pressing them with your hand until they reach a thickness of one eighth inch. Cut these with a sharp knife into half-inch strips. Set aside
2. In a small bowl combine the salt, pepper, onion powder, and oregano; mix well. Season the chicken breasts on both sides using this mixture, then set aside.
3. Turn your Instant Pot to sauté and let it heat up. Once it is heated, add the garlic and onion and sauté for about three minutes, until softened. Add the chicken breasts and brown on both sides, for about three minutes on each side.
4. Turn off your Instant Pot and add the chicken broth, water, bay leaf, and the thawed vegetables.
5. Stir in the biscuit strips and seal the pot. Set it to manual pressure for 10 minutes. Once the alarm goes off, use the quick release valve to quickly decompress the pot.
6. Open the pot carefully and remove the chicken with a slotted spoon. Let it cool for about five minutes, then use two forks to shred the meat. Remove the bay leaf and discard it.
7. While you shred the chicken meat, turn your Instant Pot to the sauté function and bring the contents nearly to a boil. Add the shredded chicken and heat through, then serve in bowls.

Simple and Delicious Chicken Breasts

This recipe is for the person who works long hours and wants something quick when they get home. The chicken breasts are tender and juicy and taste great served with some buttered egg noodles, or rice. You'll utilize the sauté and pressure cooker options in the preparation of this succulent dish.

Yield: four servings

Ingredients:

½ teaspoon salt

¼ teaspoon pepper

¼ teaspoon dried oregano

⅛ teaspoon dried basil

4 boneless, skinless chicken breasts

1 tablespoon olive oil

1 cup chicken broth

Directions:

1. In a small bowl combine the salt, pepper, oregano, and basil. Mix well and use this to season the chicken breasts.
2. Turn your Instant Pot to sauté and let it heat up. Add the olive oil and place the seasoned chicken breasts in to brown on each side, about four minutes. Remove the chicken from the pot and set aside.
3. Add the chicken broth to the pot and set in the trivet. If you have an 8-quart pot you might want to add an additional 1½ cups of broth.
4. Place the chicken breasts on the trivet, lock and seal the lid, and pressure cook on the manual high setting for five minutes.
5. Allow the pot to naturally release pressure for five minutes, then perform a quick release to bring the pressure down to normal. Remove the chicken from the pot and let it rest for five minutes before serving.

Spicy Butter Chicken

Butter chicken is a dish from India; you'll find this one delicious and spicy. It is served over rice for a reason: to quell the heat. If you need to, however, you can lower the fire factor by reducing the amount of spices. The recipe really does call for eight cloves of garlic. The heavy cream adds depth and richness to the flavor. You'll want to serve this preparation over rice. It utilizes the sauté and pressure cooker functions on your Instant Pot.

Taste the flavors of India in spicy butter chicken.

Yield: 6 servings

Ingredients:

    3 tablespoons unsalted butter (do not use salted butter)

    8 cloves garlic, minced

    2 teaspoons fresh ginger, minced

    2 tablespoons tomato paste

    1 cup tomato puree

    1 tablespoon ground coriander

    3 teaspoons garam masala

1 teaspoon ground cumin

1 tablespoon smoked paprika

1 teaspoon turmeric

1 teaspoon salt

2 pounds boneless, skinless chicken thighs, cut into bite-sized pieces

1 cup water

1 cup whipping cream

2 tablespoons fresh parsley, chopped

Directions:

1. Heat up your Instant Pot on sauté for a few minutes. Add the butter and let it melt.
2. Add the garlic and ginger and sauté for about one minute.
3. Stir in the tomato paste and the tomato puree.
4. Add the coriander, garam masala, cumin, paprika, turmeric, and salt; sauté for three to five minutes.
5. Add the chicken and water and stir. If there is not enough liquid in the pot to cover the chicken, add enough to cover it.
6. Close and seal the lid and set the pressure cooker function on high pressure for five minutes. When the alarm goes off, let the pressure release naturally.
7. Remove the lid from your Instant Pot and select the sauté setting once more. Bring the contents to a boil and add the whipping cream. Turn the heat down to a simmer and let the sauce thicken and reduce for two to three minutes.
8. Serve over rice with parsley sprinkled on top.

Sweet Honey Bourbon Chicken

This chicken dish has a distinctly rich sweet flavor that comes from the bourbon. The sauce is almost sticky but tastes divine. The recipe calls for chicken breasts, but I have used thighs instead and even preferred the results. The rich dark meat paired with the honey bourbon sauce has a stronger chicken flavor.

You'll use the pressure cooker and sauté functions on your Instant Pot and I recommend serving over warm brown rice.

Yield: 4 servings

Ingredients:

- 1 pound chicken breasts, boneless and skinless
- ½ yellow onion, chopped fine
- ¼ cup bourbon
- ¼ cup brown sugar
- ¼ cup soy sauce
- ¼ cup ketchup
- 1½ tablespoons honey
- ¼ cup water
- ½ teaspoon red pepper flakes (omit if you don't like hot stuff)
- ½ teaspoon garlic powder
- 1 dash salt
- 1 dash pepper
- 2 tablespoons cornstarch
- 1 tablespoon water

Directions:

1. Place the chicken and onions in your Instant Pot.
2. In a bowl, combine the bourbon, brown sugar, soy sauce, ketchup, honey, water, red pepper flakes, garlic powder, salt, and pepper; whisk to combine. Pour over the chicken.
3. Place the lid on, lock and seal the pot. Cook on manual for 15 minutes.
4. Perform a quick release and carefully open the lid.

5. Remove the chicken with a slotted spoon and place on a cutting board. Let it rest for five minutes before shredding with two forks. Put the chicken back in the pot and select the sauté function.
6. In a cup, combine the cornstarch and water, then pour this mixture into the pot and stir to combine.
7. Let this cook for two minutes or until the sauce has thickened.
8. Serve over rice and garnish with fresh chopped parsley.

Taco Bowl with Chicken

This is a quick and satisfying dinner, especially if you like Mexican-inspired food. I usually use one packet of taco seasoning, but if you want a more intense flavor, use two. The recipe calls for black beans, but you can use just about any type of bean successfully. This recipe utilizes the pressure cooker and warming features on your Instant Pot.

Yield: 6-8 servings

Ingredients:

3 cups chicken broth, divided

4 or 5 chicken breast halves, boneless and skinless

1 to 2 packets taco seasoning

1 12-ounce bag frozen corn, thawed and drained

1 15-ounce can black beans, drained and rinsed

3 cups uncooked jasmine rice, rinsed

1 15.5-ounce jar of salsa

Shredded cheddar cheese

Sour cream

Cilantro, chopped

Directions:

1. Pour one cup of the chicken broth into the bottom of your Instant Pot and reserve the rest.

2. Place the chicken breasts on top and sprinkle with the taco seasoning.
3. Pour the corn and beans atop the chicken.
4. Pour the salsa on top of everything.
5. Add the uncooked rice and the remaining two cups of chicken broth.
6. Set the pressure cooker option on manual high pressure for 12 minutes. When the alarm goes off, perform a quick release.
7. Open the lid carefully and remove the chicken with a slotted spoon. Place on a cutting board and let it rest for five minutes. Set your Instant Pot on warm while preparing the chicken. Shred the chicken with two forks and return to your Instant Pot to warm through.
8. Serve in bowls topped with cheddar cheese, cilantro, and sour cream, if desired.

Tender Turkey Breast and Gravy
It doesn't have to be Thanksgiving to have a little turkey and gravy. The process doesn't take hours either. You can take a turkey breast out of the freezer and place it directly in the pot. If the turkey is unfrozen, you'll simply reduce the cooking time. You'll use the pressure cooker and sauté options for this dish.

Don't worry about netting on the turkey; you'll cut it off after the meat is cooked.

Yield: 4-6 servings

Ingredients:

- 1 3-pound boneless turkey breast roast
- 1 tablespoon poultry seasoning
- 1 onion, quartered
- 3 stalks celery, quartered
- 4 cloves garlic
- 2 cups chicken broth
- 2 tablespoons butter, cut into several pats
- 2 lemon slices

1 sprig fresh rosemary

2 packets turkey gravy

Directions:

1. Take the turkey out of the packaging and run it under some warm water until you can take the gravy packet from the frozen breast. The netting can stay on the turkey while it is cooking; it won't melt.
2. Pat the turkey breast as dry as you can, using a paper towel; rub the poultry seasoning all over and set the breast aside.
3. Place the onion, celery, garlic, and chicken broth in the bottom of your Instant Pot.
4. Place the trivet in the pot and set the turkey on top.
5. Arrange the butter pats, lemon slices, and sprig of rosemary on the top of the breast.
6. Close and seal the lid, select the high-pressure or poultry setting, and time it for 45 minutes. When finished cooking, let the steam release naturally (about 20 minutes). Carefully open the pot and check the internal temperature of the breast, which should be 170 degrees, Fahrenheit. If necessary, cook for five more minutes before operating the quick release valve.
7. Remove the roast; strain out the vegetables and discard them. Save the broth and return it to your Instant Pot, adding the gravy mix packets. Select the sauté function and whisk the liquid until it starts to boil, then continue to cook for three to five minutes, until the gravy thickens.
8. Cut off the netting, slice the meat, and serve with gravy on the side.

Traditional Chicken and Stuffing

Sometimes you just want an old-fashioned, traditional chicken and stuffing combination for dinner, served with some fresh corn or green beans. This recipe only takes about 30 minutes to prepare. I use stuffing mix and you can use either green beans or corn, cooking everything together.

Yield: 4 servings

Ingredients:

    4 large frozen chicken breasts, skinless and boneless

    1 teaspoon salt

    ½ teaspoon pepper

    ¾ cup chicken broth

    1 6-ounce box stuffing mix

    1 10.5-ounce can cream of chicken soup

    ¼ cup dried cranberries

    1 cup sour cream

    2 cups fresh or frozen green beans or corn

Directions:

1. Season the chicken on all sides with salt and pepper, then set aside.
2. Pour the broth into the bottom of the pot and place the chicken on top.
3. Close and seal the lid and set the manual pressure cooker to 14 minutes for frozen chicken, eight minutes for unfrozen chicken breasts.
4. While chicken cooks, prepare the stuffing by stirring the stuffing mix in a bowl along with the cream of chicken soup and the sour cream. Fold in the cranberries.
5. When the timer goes off, perform a quick pressure release, then turn off your Instant Pot and open the lid. Check the chicken to ensure that it is done. There will be moisture in the bottom of the pot.
6. Pour the green beans or corn on top of the chicken. Set the pot to the manual pressure cooker function for two minutes if using fresh vegetables, four minutes for frozen.

Perform a quick release and extract the chicken and vegetables.

7. Insert the stuffing, reseal the lid, and select the manual pressure cooker function, setting the timer to four minutes. This will heat up the stuffing. (Since the stuffing will absorb the moisture, the pressure cooker won't steam again.)

Now that you have all these delicious poultry recipes under your belt, let's try some equally luscious beef recipes that take mere minutes to prepare in your Instant Pot.

Chapter 4: Mouthwatering Beef Recipes

This chapter gives you a variety of beef recipes that include Asian and Mexican-inspired dishes as well as elegant and casual favorites. Try your hand at preparing some beef and broccoli, Mongolian beef, fajitas, or burritos, just to name a few. Impress your friends with elegant beef Burgundy or creamy beef stroganoff or relax over a down-home meal of meatloaf and mashed potatoes.

These recipes are all prepared in your Instant Pot using primarily the sauté and pressure cooker functions. This means they'll be ready to eat in a fraction of time they would normally require. For example, it usually takes me five hours to create a decent beef stew but with my Instant Pot, I can have a delectable stew on the table in mere minutes.

Asian Beef and Broccoli

This recipe requires a boneless beef chuck roast sliced in strips and served with fresh broccoli. You'll pour over the meat a flavorful brown sauce that includes red pepper flakes, but you can omit these if you can't stand the heat. Serve it over steamed rice and you have a marvelous meal.

Asian beef tastes great with rice or rice noodles.

Yield: 4 servings

Ingredients:

1½ pounds boneless beef chuck roast, trimmed of fat and sliced into thin strips

½ teaspoon sea salt

¼ teaspoon pepper

2 teaspoons olive oil

4 cloves garlic, minced

1 onion, finely chopped

½ cup soy sauce

¾ cup beef broth

⅓ cup brown sugar

2 tablespoons sesame oil

⅛ teaspoon red pepper flakes

1 pound broccoli florets

3 tablespoons water

1 tablespoon cornstarch

Directions:

1. Season the beef with the salt and pepper and set aside.
2. Turn on the sauté function of your Instant Pot and let it heat up. Add the olive oil and brown the meat in batches. Place the browned beef on a plate and set aside.
3. Add garlic and onions to the pot and sauté for one to two minutes.
4. Add the soy sauce, beef broth, brown sugar, sesame oil, and red pepper flakes, stirring until the sugar dissolves.
5. Pour the browned beef back in the pot, close and seal the lid, select the manual, high pressure function and set the cook time for 12 minutes.
6. While the pot is cooking, put the broccoli florets in a microwave safe bowl and add a quarter cup of water. Microwave on high for three to four minutes, until the broccoli is tender. If you're using frozen broccoli, just put the broccoli in a bowl and microwave it on high until it's ready to eat.
7. Use the quick release on your Instant Pot when the timer goes off and carefully lift the lid.
8. Mix the water and cornstarch in a cup until it forms a smooth slurry. Add it to your Instant Pot and stir to combine well.
9. Switch to the sauté function and cook until the sauce thickens. When thickened, dump in the broccoli and heat through.
10. Serve over cooked rice.

Beefy Burritos

These burritos are quite beefy and delicious. They use ground beef and all sorts of tasty ingredients. You can swap out the black beans for pinto beans if you prefer. I use frozen corn kernels that have been thawed and rinsed, but you can use canned corn; just rinse the kernels well to get rid of any added salt. You can provide a variety of toppings for the burritos, such as hot sauce, shredded cheddar, lettuce, olives, and sour cream.

Serve these burritos with tasty sides of refried beans and Spanish rice (Chapter 11).

Yield: 8 burritos

Ingredients:

- 2 tablespoons vegetable oil
- 3 cloves garlic, minced
- 1 onion, diced

- 2 teaspoons ground cumin
- 1 tablespoon chili powder
- 1 cup beef broth, divided
- 1 pound ground beef
- 1 teaspoon salt
- ½ teaspoon pepper
- ¾ cup frozen corn, thawed and rinsed
- 1 15-ounce can black beans, drained and rinsed
- 1 16-ounce can diced tomatoes, with juice
- 1 cup uncooked jasmine rice
- 8 flour tortillas

Directions:

1. Select the sauté function on your Instant Pot and add the oil after letting it heat up. Add the garlic and onion and sauté for about three minutes.
2. Add the cumin, chili powder, and a quarter cup of the beef broth, stirring to combine. Simmer for a minute.
3. Add the ground beef and break it up into smaller lumps. Add the salt and pepper and stir until the beef is evenly browned.
4. Stir in the corn, beans, and tomatoes.
5. Pour the rice on top, but do *not* stir
6. Carefully add the rest of the beef broth around the edges of the pot so as not to disturb the rice.
7. Close and seal the lid and switch the setting to pressure cooker on manual and cook on high for 10 minutes.
8. When timer goes off, perform a quick release and remove the lid. Stir everything all together.
9. You have two options here. First, you can place some of the mixture on a tortilla, add toppings, and roll into a burrito. The other alternative is to omit any sour cream and place the burritos in a greased baking dish with the

seam-side down. Turn on your broiler, sprinkle some cheddar cheese on top and place under broiler for two minutes. This makes the burritos slightly crispy; that's how I prefer them. Of course, you can always add sour cream on top

Braised Beef Short Ribs
This recipe includes a delicious barbeque sauce with a red wine base. You can use this barbecue sauce for chicken and pork, too.

Brown your short ribs to give them that mouthwatering appearance.

Yield: 4 servings

Ingredients:

2 pounds beef short ribs

½ teaspoon sea salt

¼ teaspoon ground black pepper

1½ teaspoons olive oil

1¼ cups onion, diced

1 teaspoon garlic, minced

1 tablespoon brown sugar

½ cup ketchup

½ cup red wine

1½ tablespoons soy sauce

1 tablespoon Worcestershire sauce

1 spring fresh thyme

Directions:

1. Sprinkle the ribs with the salt and pepper and cut into 3-inch segments.
2. Select the sauté function on your Instant Pot and let it heat up.
3. Pour in the olive oil and brown the ribs. Remove, set on a plate, and set aside.
4. Pour in the onions and sauté until transparent.
5. Pour in the garlic and cook for one minute.
6. Return the ribs to the pot.
7. In a bowl, combine the brown sugar, ketchup, red wine, soy sauce, and Worcestershire sauce; whisk together until the sugar has dissolved.
8. Pour the sauce over the ribs and set a sprig of thyme on top.
9. Lock the lid and select the high-pressure function. Set the time for 35 minutes.
10. At the end of the cook time, allow the pressure to release naturally for five minutes before opening the quick release valve.
11. Remove the thyme sprig before serving.

Country Style Cube Steak and Gravy

Cube steaks are the perforated tenderized steaks found on most butcher counters. This recipe calls for a can of condensed soup, in addition to beef broth, to create a delicious gravy. These soups give the gravy its rich flavor without a great deal of fuss. There is no salt and pepper in the ingredients list because you will get plenty in the soups.

Yield: 6 servings

Ingredients:

- 2 pounds cube steak
- ⅓ cup flour
- 2 tablespoons olive oil
- 2 cups beef broth, divided
- 2 onions, sliced
- 1 10.5-ounce can cream of celery soup
- 1 package onion soup mix

Directions:

1. Cut the cube steak into individual serving sizes if it is not already prepared for you.
2. Place flour in a re-closable plastic bag.
3. Drop each serving of steak into the bag and shake to coat with flour.
4. Select the sauté function of your Instant Pot and let it heat up.
5. Add the olive oil and insert the cube steak, in batches, to brown on both sides until crispy. Remove to a plate and set aside.
6. Pour three tablespoons of the beef broth in your Instant Pot to deglaze it.
7. Add the onions and sauté until they become tender
8. Place the cube steak on top of the onions.

9. In a bowl, mix the cream of celery soup, onion soup mix, and the rest of the beef broth. Whisk until combined and pour into your Instant Pot.
10. Select the pressure cooker option on the manual high setting and set the timer for 20 minutes.
11. After the timer goes off, open the quick release valve.
12. Turn off your Instant Pot and let it rest for five minutes to allow the gravy to thicken before opening the pot to serve atop mashed potatoes.

Easy Beef Stroganoff

Beef stroganoff is one of my favorite dishes. The secret to a good stroganoff is a lot of delicious mushrooms and a generous seasoning of high quality paprika and flavorful bay leaves. The sauce often has a pink tinge, due to the paprika. The sour cream should thicken the sauce adequately, along with the flour that was added with the mushrooms. If, however, it fails to thicken, you can dissolve a spoonful of arrowroot flour in a little water and stir this in, just to move the process along. Arrowroot flour, unlike cornstarch, has no flavor and will not alter the natural flavor of the stroganoff.

You can use any mushroom you desire. I prefer baby portabellas because they are meaty and enhance the flavor of the beef. You'll add the noodles last, and they'll cook right in the pot.

Beef stroganoff, Instant Pot style

Yield: 8 servings

Ingredients:

    2 tablespoons olive oil or canola oil

    ½ large onion, diced

    2 teaspoons sea salt, divided

    2 pounds stew meat (beef), cut into 1-inch cubes

    1 teaspoon ground black pepper

    2 cloves garlic, minced

    2 bay leaves

    ½ teaspoon dried thyme

    2 tablespoons soy sauce

    2 tablespoons all-purpose flour

    3 cups fresh mushrooms, chopped

    3 cups beef broth

1 16-ounce package wide egg noodles

1 cup sour cream

1½ teaspoons paprika

Directions:

1. Select the sauté option on your Instant Pot and let it heat up.
2. Add the oil and wait about 30 seconds before adding the onion, along with a half teaspoon of salt. Stir and cook for three minutes or until the onion softens.
3. Season the beef with pepper and a teaspoon of salt; add the meat to the pot in batches, browning thoroughly on all sides for two to three minutes. Remove from the pot to a plate and set aside.
4. Sauté the garlic for about 30 seconds, along with the bay leaves, thyme, and soy sauce.
5. Sprinkle the mushrooms with flour and add to the pot, stirring so the flour is mixed well with the other ingredients. Add the browned meat and stir again to coat it thoroughly.
6. Pour in the broth and the rest of the salt.
7. Close and secure the lid, setting it on high pressure for 15 minutes.
8. Use the quick release method to reduce the pressure before opening the pot. Remove and discard the bay leaves. Add the egg noodles and seal the lid again, selecting the high pressure function and setting the timer for five more minutes.
9. Let the pressure release naturally this time and open the pot. Switch to the sauté function and add the sour cream, stirring it in well. Sprinkle the paprika on top and stir it in.
10. Let the mixture come to almost a boil before turning off the pot to serve.

Elegant Beef Burgundy

This delightful dish is easy to make with an Instant Pot. You'll use a rich red wine for ultimate flavor and serve it up with crusty bread so those enjoying it can sop up all the juices.

A nice Pinot Noir works well in this dish.

Yield: 6 servings

Ingredients:

    2 pounds beef chuck roast, cut into 1-inch cubes

    ¾ teaspoon sea salt, divided

    ½ teaspoon pepper, divided

    3 tablespoons flour, divided

    3 tablespoons olive oil, divided

    3 carrots, diced

    1 small onion, diced

    3 cloves garlic, minced

    1 cup red wine

    1 tablespoon tomato paste

    ½ cup beef stock

    ½ teaspoon dried thyme

    2 bay leaves

Directions:
1. Select the sauté function on your Instant Pot and heat it up.
2. Meanwhile, season the beef cubes with a half teaspoon of salt and a quarter teaspoon of pepper.
3. Sprinkle two tablespoons of the flour over the meat to coat the beef cubes. Shake off any excess.
4. Add two tablespoons of the oil to the hot Instant Pot and brown all sides of the beef cubes in two batches. This should take about five minutes per batch. Remove the meat to a plate or bowl and set aside.
5. Add one tablespoon of olive oil to your Instant Pot and insert the carrots. Sauté for about two minutes before adding the onions.
6. Sauté for two minutes, then add the garlic and sauté for another minute.
7. Add the wine and scrape the bottom of the pot to stir up the brown bits. Let this cook for five minutes, until reduced.
8. Add the tomato paste, beef stock, thyme, bay leaves, and the remaining quarter teaspoon of both salt and pepper.
9. Return the beef to the pot. Close and seal the lid, selecting the high pressure function and a cook time of 40 minutes.
10. Let the pressure lower naturally for 10 minutes and then perform a quick release.
11. Serve while hot.

Fast Meatloaf and Red Potato Mash

Meatloaf is one of those down-home comfort foods many people remember from their childhoods. This meatloaf will create fresh memories for you. The trick is in the honey barbecue sauce and a brown sugar mustard sauce topping that is out of this world. With your Instant Pot, you get to prepare the mashed potatoes right along with the meatloaf. An 8-quart Instant Pot will cook the meatloaf in 25 minutes but if you are using a smaller pot, you'll want to increase the cook time by about 20 minutes. If the meatloaf *still* isn't done, you can always resort to baking it in an oven at 350 degrees Fahrenheit until the center is no longer pink.

Yield: 6-8 servings

Ingredients:

- 3 pounds red potatoes, washed and quartered (do not remove skins)
- 1 cup chicken broth
- 1 cup bread crumbs
- 2 teaspoons garlic powder
- 2 teaspoons dried parsley
- 1 teaspoon salt
- ½ teaspoon pepper
- ¼ teaspoon crushed red pepper flakes
- ½ cup onion, diced
- 2 eggs
- ½ cup honey barbecue sauce
- 2 pounds ground beef
- 2 tablespoons prepared mustard (brown or regular)
- ⅓ cup ketchup
- 2 tablespoons brown sugar
- ¾ cup milk
- 4 tablespoons butter
- ¾ cup sour cream
- ½ to 1 teaspoon salt
- ¼ teaspoon pepper

Directions:

1. Lay the quartered potatoes in the bottom of your Instant Pot in an even layer that is as flat as possible.

2. Pour the chicken broth over this and situate the trivet in so that it lies over the potatoes as flat as possible.
3. In a bowl, combine the bread crumbs, garlic powder, parsley, one teaspoon of the salt, a half teaspoon of pepper, red pepper flakes, onions, eggs, and barbecue sauce; stir until well combined.
4. Add the ground beef and mix with your hands until well combined. Then shape into a loaf.
5. Tear off a piece of tin foil sized to cover the bottom of the meatloaf and rise slightly up the sides, creating a pocket or pan for the meatloaf. The foil should come up the sides so that a minimum of grease will flow into the potatoes. Set this on the trivet.
6. Close the lid and seal it. Cook on high pressure for 25 minutes.
7. Use the quick release method for depressurizing the pot and carefully open the lid. Remove the meatloaf and place it, foil and all, on a shallow-sided baking sheet.
8. Mix together the mustard, ketchup, and brown sugar, then slather this on top of the meatloaf. Place the loaf in your broiler for three to four minutes or until bubbly and brown.
9. Meanwhile, remove the trivet. Add the milk, butter, sour cream, garlic powder, salt, and pepper to the potatoes and use a hand masher to mash them right in the pot. The potatoes may have a few lumps, but they will still be creamy and delicious. Turn your Instant Pot to warm to wait for the meatloaf to finish broiling.
10. Let the meatloaf set for five minutes before cutting into slices and serving along with the red potato mash.

Flank Steak Fajitas

Fajitas are one of my favorite dishes and this one, made with flank steak, is as good as you would get at your favorite Mexican restaurant. Coleslaw mix works wonderfully in Mexican dishes. It consists of julienned or shredded cabbage, carrots, and sometimes other fresh vegetables. It's the coleslaw without the sauce. However, if you would rather chop up cabbage on your own, be my guest.

Flank steak fajitas; use chicken instead for a change of flavors.

Yield: 4 servings

Ingredients:

2 limes, juiced, divided

2 cloves garlic, minced

2 teaspoons olive oil

1 tablespoon taco seasoning

4 tablespoons cilantro, divided

½ teaspoon salt

1 1½-pound flank steak, fat trimmed and cut into half-inch strips

1 14.5-ounce can diced tomatoes with green chilies

1 cup green, yellow, and red bell pepper strips

2 cups coleslaw mix

¼ red onion, cut into thin strips

1½ teaspoons honey

½ teaspoon chili powder

Tortillas

Sour cream

Salsa

Guacamole

Directions:

1. Squeeze the juice of one lime into your Instant Pot and scrape off as much zest as possible into the pot. Add the garlic, olive oil, taco seasoning, two tablespoons of cilantro, and the salt.
2. Add the flank steak and mix so that the liquid in your Instant Pot coats both sides. Let this set for around five minutes to marinate.
3. Add the tomatoes and bell peppers and secure the lid on the pot. Set it on manual high pressure for 12 to 15 minutes. Once the timer goes off, perform a quick release and, when the pressure has returned to normal, open the pot.
4. While cooking the meat, mix in a bowl the coleslaw mix, onions, the rest of the cilantro, the juice from the other lime, honey, and chili powder. Let this set until ready to serve.
5. Warm the tortillas in a skillet and serve by placing some of the meat mixture on a tortilla and topping with some coleslaw mixture and sour cream, salsa, and possibly guacamole.

Italian Beef and Peppers

You'll use a dry package of Italian dressing mix and some jarred Pepperoncini peppers to make this delicious beef dish. Clocking in at less than one hour, this is one of the fastest and simplest of recipes.

Yield: 8 servings

Ingredients:

- 1 tablespoons canola or olive oil
- 1 5- to 6-pound chuck roast
- ½ onion, thinly sliced
- 1 clove garlic, minced
- 1 16-ounce jar sliced pepperoncini peppers, brine retained
- 1 package dry Italian dressing mix
- 1 cup water

Directions:

1. Select the sauté function on your Instant Pot and wait until it's hot. Add the oil.
2. Brown both sides of the chuck roast, taking four to five minutes per side; remove it to a plate, and set aside.
3. Add the onion and garlic to your Instant Pot and sauté for about two minutes, until softened.
4. Pour the brine from the peppers into a large measuring cup and pour a quarter cup of the brine into your Instant Pot, along with half of the peppers. Add in the dry Italian dressing mix and the water.
5. Place the roast back in the pot and secure the lid. Select the manual, high pressure function and assign a cook time of 55 minutes.
6. Perform a quick release and open the lid carefully. Remove the roast (which should fall apart easily) and place this on a cutting board, shredding with two forks.
7. Place the roast on a serving platter or in a large bowl, mix with the rest of the peppers, and serve.

Italian Meatballs for Pasta

This recipe makes 30 meatballs that you can use for sandwiches or in pasta. They need less than a half hour to prepare, so it might even take longer to get the water boiling for the pasta. This recipe usually feeds my family of four.

Serve meatballs with pasta or plop a few on a hoagie bun with Provolone cheese and toast until the cheese bubbles.

Yield: 30 meatballs

Ingredients:

    1 pound lean ground beef

    ¼ cup bread crumbs

    1 teaspoon garlic powder

    1 teaspoon dried oregano

    1 teaspoon onion powder

    2 teaspoons paprika

    ¼ teaspoon celery salt

    ½ teaspoon sea salt

2 teaspoons olive oil

½ onion, sliced

2 cloves garlic, minced

Your favorite spaghetti sauce

Cooked pasta

Directions:

1. Place the ground beef in a large bowl and add the bread crumbs, garlic powder, oregano, onion powder, paprika, celery salt, and sea salt. Mix together well, roll into 2-inch balls, and set aside.
2. Select the sauté option on your Instant Pot. When it is hot, pour in the olive oil and sauté the onions for about three minutes.
3. Add the garlic and sauté it for about a minute.
4. Add a jar of your favorite spaghetti sauce and pour in the meatballs.
5. Put the lid on and secure it. Set the pot to manual, high pressure cooking and set the timer to five minutes.
6. Let the pressure release naturally and perform a quick release before opening.
7. Serve the sauce and meatballs over cooked spaghetti or in buns for sandwiches.

Melt-In-Your-Mouth Beef Stew

Everyone needs a good beef stew recipe in their arsenal; after all, it *is* the ultimate comfort food. This recipe is highly versatile; you can substitute all kinds of vegetables. The recipe calls for a half cup of frozen peas, but you can include lima beans, broccoli, corn, and anything else that is frozen. It also asks for one cup of fresh green beans, but if you have fresh zucchini instead, just cut that up and toss it in. You can use any combination of vegetables; just keep to a half cup frozen and one cup fresh.

If you serve this with crusty bread or crackers and a salad, you'll have a full meal. You'll cook the meat first and add the vegetables later. This makes for beef that is so tender it will dissolve in your mouth.

Yield: 6-8 servings

Ingredients:

2 pounds beef stew meat, trimmed of fat and cut into cubes (I use bottom round or flank steak.)

1 teaspoon garlic powder

1 teaspoon onion powder

½ teaspoon thyme

2 bay leaves

1 teaspoon salt

½ teaspoon pepper

2 cups water

2 cups beef broth

1 onion, chopped

4 stalks celery, chopped

1 cup carrots, chopped

½ cup frozen peas, or other frozen vegetables

5 potatoes, cubed

1 cup fresh green beans or combination of other vegetables

Directions:

1. Place the stew meat, garlic powder, onion powder, thyme, bay leaves, salt, pepper, water, and beef broth in your Instant Pot and secure the lid.
2. Select the manual high-pressure cooker and set the time to 45 minutes.
3. When the cook time is up, let the pressure release naturally for 10 minutes and then perform a quick release.
4. Remove the lid and stir the contents.
5. Stir in all the vegetables.

6. Secure the lid again and select the manual, high-pressure cooker, this time for 10 minutes.
7. Let the pot release its pressure naturally and when done, perform a quick release to ensure the pressure is normal before opening the lid.
8. If the stew is a little runny, switch to the sauté function and mix one tablespoon of arrowroot powder or cornstarch in enough water to make a runny slurry. When the stew starts to bubble, add the slurry and stir it into the liquid. Let this boil a little longer until thickened, and then serve.

Quick Salisbury Steak

Salisbury steak is an old recipe that is deliciously flavored. It used to take hours to prepare this; my grandma always said the longer it cooks on low heat, the better it tastes. Not so with an Instant Pot. This dish is as good as grandma's, but it takes only 20 to 30 minutes to make from start to finish. This dish is traditionally served along with mashed potatoes.

Yield: 4 servings

Ingredients:

1½ pounds lean ground beef

½ cup unseasoned bread crumbs (I used panko and it came out well)

2 teaspoons dry mustard

½ teaspoon garlic powder

½ teaspoon onion powder

½ teaspoon salt

¼ teaspoon pepper

2 tablespoons ketchup, divided

¼ teaspoon Worcestershire sauce, divided

1 tablespoon olive oil

1 onion, thinly sliced

2 cups beef broth

2 teaspoons cornstarch

½ pound mushrooms, sliced

Directions:

1. Place the beef in a large bowl and add the breadcrumbs, dry mustard, garlic powder, onion powder, salt, pepper, one tablespoon of ketchup, and an eighth of a teaspoon of Worcestershire sauce. Mix with your hands until thoroughly combined.
2. Shape into four patties. If they seem too large, split into six patties.
3. Select the sauté function on your Instant Pot and adjust it to medium heat.
4. Add the oil and swirl it to coat the insides of the pot.
5. Add the patties and brown them on both sides. (You might need to do this in batches.)
6. Remove the meat to a plate with a paper towel on it to drain. Set aside.
7. Add the onion to the pot and sauté until softened.
8. Add the beef broth, the remaining ketchup and the rest of the Worcestershire sauce. Scrape up any brown bits from the bottom of the pot.
9. Simmer until the liquid is reduced by about a third.
10. Seal the lid and select the manual high pressure function for five minutes. If you have four large patties, cook for 10 minutes.
11. When the timer goes off, allow the pot to vent for about 10 minutes, then perform a quick release. Open the lid, remove the patties to a plate, and add the mushrooms.
12. Mix the cornstarch with a tablespoon of cold water and stir until there are no lumps. Stir this into your Instant Pot and turn on the sauté function. Let it come to a bubble and stir until thickened.
13. Serve the patties with mashed potatoes and the mushroom gravy on top of it all.

Simple Beef Pot Roast

My mother used to make a pot roast that included wine and coffee; if anyone had seen her in the process, they would have thought her crazy. Coffee and wine? Nonetheless, this gives the roast definition and rich flavor.

I use brown gravy mix instead of fooling around with all the herbs and spices my mother used; it tastes just as savory. You'll want to serve this with potatoes and another vegetable. I recommend also including bread or rolls, with which to sop up all the delicious gravy.

Use brown gravy mix in packets to make an easy pot roast.

Ingredients:

4 1-ounce packets brown gravy mix

3 tablespoons cornstarch

8 ounces red wine

1 cup brewed black coffee

3 tablespoons Worcestershire sauce

½ cup low sodium soy sauce

6 cloves garlic, finely minced

½ teaspoon sea salt

1 teaspoon black pepper

2 tablespoons olive oil

1 3-pound bottom round roast

1 large onion, chopped

1 bag baby carrots, coarsely chopped

2 cups portobello mushrooms, sliced

1 large bag baby carrots, coarsely chopped

1 large sweet yellow onion, coarsely chopped

Directions:

1. Pour the gravy mix in a large bowl along with the cornstarch. Whisk in the red wine and coffee and make sure there are no lumps.
2. Add the Worcestershire sauce, soy sauce, garlic, salt, and pepper; whisk well to combine. Set aside.
3. Select the sauté function on your Instant Pot and once it is hot, add the oil.
4. Sear the roast on all sides. Leave the meat in the pot and turn off the sauté function.
5. Pour the carrots, onions, and mushrooms over the roast. Add the liquid on top and seal your Instant Pot.
6. Set it to manual, high pressure and time it for 105 minutes.
7. Let the pot release manually for 15 minutes and then open the quick release lever.
8. Remove the meat and place it on a cutting board. Either cut or shred the beef. Serve with vegetables and gravy.

Sirloin Tips in Gravy

Sirloin tips in gravy are considered an elegant dish that takes considerable time to make. This recipe is elegant, but it only takes a few minutes in an Instant Pot. It's scaled to feed a large group of people. I serve it over cooked egg noodles, but you can also serve it with potatoes or rice, according to your preference.

Sirloin tips in gravy

Yield: 10 servings

Ingredients:

    3 tablespoons olive oil

    1 5-pound sirloin tip roast, trimmed and cubed

    1 onion, diced

    1½ cups beef broth

    ½ cup red wine

    ½ cup flour

    1½ cups water

Directions:

1. Select the sauté function on your Instant Pot and let it heat up.
2. Add the olive oil and brown the meat in batches, removing it to a bowl when done.
3. Add the onion and sauté for about three minutes, until tender.
4. Place the browned meat back in the pot, along with the onion.
5. Pour in the beef broth and wine, then cover and seal the pot.
6. Set the pressure cooker function to manual high pressure and cook for 15 minutes.
7. While cooking, mix the flour and water to make a slurry.
8. When done, perform a quick release.
9. Open the lid, stir in the flour and water mixture, and select the sauté option. Let it come to a boil and continue boiling, stirring, until the gravy is thick.
10. Add salt and pepper to taste.

Taste-of-the-East Mongolian Beef

This Asian-inspired beef dish is delicious and sweet with brown sugar and ginger but also carries a full-bodied flavor. Serve it over cooked rice for a delicious meal. Use "dark" brown sugar for the touch of molasses mixed in; you need that flavor for this dish to come out right.

Serve over white or brown rice or try some fried chow Mein noodles.

Ingredients:

- 2 tablespoons olive oil or vegetable oil
- 2 pounds flank steak or top sirloin, trimmed and sliced thinly against the grain
- 1 teaspoon fresh ginger, grated
- 2 cloves garlic, minced
- 1 cup low-sodium soy sauce
- 1½ cups dark brown sugar
- ½ cup water
- 2 tablespoons cornstarch
- 3 tablespoons cold water
- 3 to 4 green onions, chopped

Directions:

1. Select the sauté function on your Instant Pot and once it is hot, add the oil.
2. Brown the meat in two to three batches on all sides. Transfer to a bowl and set aside.
3. Place the ginger and garlic in the pot and stir, cooking for one minute.

4. Add the soy sauce, brown sugar, and a half cup of water, and stir.
5. Once the brown sugar has dissolved, add the browned meat to the pot and secure the lid.
6. Set the pot for manual, high pressure and set the timer for 12 minutes.
7. Once the alarm goes off, use the quick release method to release the pressure. Remove the lid and turn off the pot.
8. Combine the cornstarch and water in a small bowl and whisk until completely smooth. Add it to the pot, turning it on to the sauté function and stirring constantly until it thickens.
9. Serve over rice and sprinkle with chopped green onions.

Poultry and beef aren't the only delicious main dishes you can make in an Instant Pot. You can also prepare pork chops, pork roast, pulled pork, and ham using it. A plethora of pork dishes are the focus of the next chapter.

Chapter 5: Sweet and Tender Pork Recipes

Pork is a favorite at our house; we love chops, roasts, and ham dishes. One of my favorites is pulled pork, so I've included two different recipes for this dish. You'll also find several ham recipes that each taste unique and delicious. Pork chops are always economical, and this chapter has a whole bunch of recipes involving them. I hope you'll enjoy these pork recipes as much as my family and friends do.

Autumn Apple Pork Tenderloin
Pork and apples are a delicious combination and you'll find this tenderloin dish is no exception. The pot is sweetened with a little brown sugar and the apples become soft and yummy. The recipe calls for apple cider, but if you can't get your hands on any, you can use apple juice. It isn't the same, but it's still tasty. This dish is great served with warm applesauce or a fresh apple salad.

Yield: 6 servings

Ingredients:

- 2 tablespoons olive oil
- 1 2½- to 3-pound pork tenderloin
- 1 onion, chopped
- 3 apples, chopped
- 2 cups apple cider
- 1 teaspoon salt
- ½ teaspoon pepper
- ½ cup brown sugar

Directions:

1. Activate the sauté setting on your Instant Pot and let it heat up.
2. Add the olive oil and sear both sides of the tenderloin for two to three minutes on each side. Remove to a plate and set aside.

3. Place the onion and apples in your Instant Pot and stir for one minute.
4. Add the apple cider and scrape up any brown bits from the bottom of the pot. Let the mixture come to a boil and continue boiling until it is reduced by half.
5. Season the tenderloin with the salt and pepper. Take a quarter cup of brown sugar and rub it all over the tenderloin. Toss the other quarter cup of brown sugar in the pot and stir before adding the meat.
6. Seal the lid, select the manual, high pressure function, and set the cook time for 22 minutes. Let the pot naturally release pressure for 10 minutes, and then perform a quick release.
7. Let the meat cool for three to five minutes before slicing and serving.

Balsamic Pork Tenderloin

Balsamic vinegar makes for a tasty pork roast, especially when used along with Dijon mustard, garlic, and brown sugar. These ingredients give the tenderloin a sweet and sour flavor that is out of this world. This dish goes well with buttered potatoes and glazed carrots.

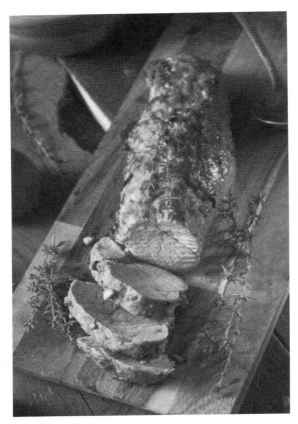

Balsamic vinegar lends a distinctive flavor to pork roast.

Yield: 4 servings

Ingredients:

    1 2½-pound pork tenderloin

    1 teaspoons sea salt

    ½ teaspoon pepper

    2 tablespoons olive oil

    2 cloves garlic, minced

    1 cup chicken stock

    ¼ cup balsamic vinegar

    ½ cup brown sugar

    1 tablespoon Dijon mustard

1 tablespoon Worcestershire sauce

1 teaspoon ground sage

1 tablespoon cornstarch

¼ cup cold water

Directions:

1. Take the pork loin out of the refrigerator 30 minutes before cooking, to bring it up to room temperature. Blot it dry with a paper towel and season with the salt and pepper.
2. Turn on your Instant Pot to sauté and add the olive oil, swirling it around to coat the sides. Once it is hot, place the tenderloin in the pot and brown on all sides, about two minutes per side. Remove to a plate and set aside.
3. Add the garlic and sauté it for one to two minutes.
4. Add the chicken stock, balsamic vinegar, brown sugar, Dijon mustard, Worcestershire sauce, and sage. Stir until the brown sugar is dissolved.
5. Return the tenderloin to the pot, and switch to the manual, high pressure setting, assigning a cook time of seven minutes.
6. When the cooking time is complete, perform a quick release and carefully open the pot, removing the tenderloin to a cutting board. Test with a meat thermometer to ensure the internal temperature is 137 degrees, Fahrenheit. If it's not warm enough, return your meat to the pot for five more minutes before testing again.
7. Extract the tenderloin and cover it with foil to keep it warm.
8. Mix the cornstarch with the water and pour this into the pot, with the sauté function turned on again. Stir the mixture constantly until the liquid bubbles and thickens. Add salt and pepper to taste.

9. Slice the tenderloin into medallions and place on a serving plate. Drizzle the sauce over the meat and serve while warm.

Barbecue Pulled Pork

I really love pulled pork, placed in a lettuce leaf, and rolled up. You can use this with your favorite barbecue sauce and coleslaw recipe. It's great for a football party or anytime.

Serve pulled pork with coleslaw on top for a real treat.

Yield: 8 servings

Ingredients:

- 2 teaspoons paprika
- 1 teaspoon dry mustard
- ½ teaspoon ground cumin
- 3 tablespoons light brown sugar, divided

2 teaspoons sea salt, divided

½ teaspoon black pepper

1 4-pound boneless pork shoulder, trimmed of fat and cut into about six pieces to fit the pot

2 teaspoons vegetable oil

2¾ cups water, divided

½ cup apple cider vinegar

3 tablespoons tomato paste

1 cup barbecue sauce

4 cups coleslaw

Directions:

1. In a bowl combine the paprika, mustard, cumin, one tablespoon brown sugar, one tablespoon salt, and the pepper, stirring to combine thoroughly. Rub this mixture over the pork.
2. Select the sauté setting and let the pot heat up. Add the oil and let it heat as well.
3. Place the pork in the pot in batches and brown on all sides for about five minutes, then remove to a plate.
4. Select the warm setting and whisk the water into the meat drippings.
5. Add the vinegar, tomato paste, remaining two tablespoons of brown sugar and the remaining teaspoon of salt to the pot, along with the remaining two cups of water. Whisk to combine and return the pork to the pot.
6. Secure the lid and set your Instant Pot to manual, high pressure, timing it for one hour.
7. At the end of an hour, perform a quick release and open the pot when it's safe. Transfer the pork to a large bowl and switch the pot to the sauté setting.
8. Simmer the juices until reduced by half – about 15 minutes – ladling off any fat that rises to the top.

9. While it simmers, shred the pork with two forks and remove any fat.
10. Add three cups of the reduced liquid over the pork.
11. To serve, place some shredded pork on a bun, along with a dollop of barbecue sauce and some coleslaw. Yes, the coleslaw is part of the sandwich, not a side dish – at least not this time.

Brown Sugar Ham

This is an old-fashioned brown sugar glazed ham recipe made new. I use a spiral sliced ham or half of a boneless ham. Check before you get going, just to ensure the ham will fit in your Instant Pot. Some hams are too long to fit inside without cutting down to size. This recipe is super simple; it consists of only three ingredients. How's that for a low-stress dinner preparation?

With this recipe, there's no need to limit glazed ham to the holidays.

Yield: 6-8

Ingredients:

1 pre-cooked spiral or boneless ham

3 cups brown sugar

1 20-ounce can pineapple chunks with juice

Directions:

1. Place the ham in your Instant Pot. If it doesn't fit, cut off what doesn't fit and set it on top.
2. Sprinkle the brown sugar evenly over the ham.
3. Do not drain the pineapple chunks. Just pour everything over the top and evenly distribute the pieces atop the ham.
4. Secure the lid and set the pressure cooker to manual, high pressure, for 20 minutes.
5. Let the pressure release naturally.
6. Remove the ham from the pot and let it rest for about five minutes before slicing.
7. Serve with the glaze drizzled over the meat.

Chili Verde with Pork

This recipe gives you a taste of the southwest with tomatillos, poblanos, and other ingredients frequently used south of the border. The fish sauce adds depth to the flavor. You'll find this a real party hit.

Yield: 6-8 servings

Ingredients:

1 4-pound boneless pork shoulder, cut into 2-inch cubes

2 Anaheim or Cubanelle peppers, seeded and chopped

2 poblano peppers, seeded and chopped

2 serrano chilies, chopped

4 tomatillos, husks removed

5 cloves garlic, minced

1 medium onion, chopped

1 tablespoon whole cumin seed, toasted and ground

1 pinch sea salt

    1 tablespoon fish sauce

    ½ cup fresh cilantro leaves

    Corn tortillas

    Limes, sliced

Directions:

1. Place the pork cubes, peppers, chilies, tomatillos, garlic, onion, cumin, and salt into your Instant Pot.
2. Select the manual, high pressure function and set the cook time for 30 minutes.
3. When the timer goes off, let the pressure release naturally for 10 minutes before performing a quick release to return to normal pressure.
4. Remove the pork cubes to a bowl and set aside.
5. Stir the fish sauce and cilantro into the sauce in your Instant Pot.
6. Ladle into a blender and process until smooth. You may need to do this in several batches.
7. Add salt and pepper if needed. Put the pork and the sauce back in your Instant Pot and select the sauté function. Let the dish become hot and bubbly before serving with tortillas and lime wedges.

Chops with Apple Butter
We already know that pork goes well with apples. This recipe combines apple butter and applesauce to make a great dish. Served with a salad and hot vegetables, you'll have a well-rounded meal.

You'll find this one especially tasty in the fall, when apples are ready to harvest. I make my own apple butter, but you can also buy it in most grocery stores. If you have an Amish community nearby, I'd advise you to avail yourself of their most excellent apple butter. I recommend boneless pork chops for this dish so you can get all chop and no bone. It is simply delicious.

There's no bone to pick with this recipe; it's simply great.

Ingredients:

    2½ pounds boneless pork chops

    ½ teaspoon salt

    ¼ teaspoon pepper

    3 tablespoons olive oil, divided

    1 onion, chopped

    3 cloves garlic, minced

    28 ounces of apple butter

    1 cup applesauce

Directions:

1. Salt and pepper your chops.
2. Turn on your Instant Pot to sauté and let it heat up. Add two tablespoons of olive oil and swirl it around the pot.
3. Add the chops and brown them on both sides in batches, removing them to a plate. Avoid overcrowding the meat to ensure even browning.

4. Pour the remaining tablespoon of olive oil into the pot, then add the onion and sauté it for two minutes. Add the garlic and sauté it for another one minute.
5. Place the chops back in the pot and turn off the sauté option. Pour the apple butter and applesauce on top and seal the lid.
6. Select the manual high pressure cooking option and time the pot for 20 minutes. Let the pot release its pressure completely before opening.
7. Serve immediately.

Chops and Rice with Vegetables

This is a simple recipe, but it's oh, so tasty. You'll use frozen mixed vegetables that cook directly in the pot. Basmati rice is preferred for this recipe, partly because of the flavor, but also because it stands up well to high pressure cooking.

Yield: 4 servings

Ingredients:

1 tablespoon olive oil

1 cup onion, chopped

1 teaspoon salt

½ teaspoon pepper

1 cup basmati rice, rinsed

4 thin-cut pork chops with bone in

½ cup frozen mixed vegetables

¾ cup chicken or vegetable broth

Directions:

1. Place the oil in the bottom of your Instant Pot and add the onions. Layer on top the salt, pepper, and rice.
2. Set the pork chops on top of the rice and dump the frozen vegetables over everything.
3. Pour the broth over the veggies.

4. Select the manual high pressure function and set the timer for five minutes.
5. After cooking is complete, allow the pressure to release naturally for about 10 minutes.
6. Open the quick release valve to vent any remaining pressure before opening and serving.

Cranberry Pork Roast

The flavor of cranberries goes just as well with pork as it does with turkey. This recipe uses pork shoulder and whole cranberry sauce to conjure up a delicious main dish. It also calls for apple cider, but you can substitute apple juice if cider is unavailable. Feel free to use this recipe for large family gatherings or parties.

I love the explosion of flavor when I bite into the juicy cooked cranberries in this sauce.

Yield: 15 servings

Ingredients:

    1 4-pound pork shoulder

    ½ teaspoon salt

    ½ teaspoon pepper

- 1 tablespoons minced garlic
- 1 14-ounce can whole cranberry sauce
- 1 cup apple cider, divided
- 1 tablespoon apple cider vinegar
- 1 tablespoon Dijon mustard
- ½ onion, sliced
- 1 tablespoon cornstarch

Directions:

1. Score the fatty top part of the pork roast and place it in your Instant Pot.
2. Sprinkle with salt and pepper.
3. Spread minced garlic on top of the pork.
4. In a bowl, mix the cranberry sauce, a half cup of the apple cider, apple cider vinegar, and Dijon mustard. Whisk together until smooth. Pour over the pork shoulder.
5. Lay the sliced onions on top.
6. Pour the other half cup of apple cider around the sides of the pot.
7. Close and seal the pot. Set it for manual high pressure for 50 minutes.
8. Let the pressure release naturally for about 10 minutes and then perform a quick release. Remove the ham from the pot.
9. To thicken the sauce in the pot, turn on the sauté function. Mix the cornstarch with enough cold water to make a thin slurry. Pour into the pot while stirring. Continue to stir and let the sauce bubble until thickened.
10. Serve the sauce over the pork roast.

Cuban-Style Pulled Pork

Most pulled pork recipes are simply barbeque recipes, but Cuban pulled pork is a little different. The spices are heavier and include citrus juice. The meat will have a fresher flavor. Serve on buns, wrap in a tortilla or wrap in a lettuce leaf and eat. You do use the broiler in your oven to make the pork a little crispy, but it makes the pulled pork excel in flavor. This large recipe is perfect for a party or a large dinner.

Yield: 16 servings

Ingredients:

- 2 teaspoons salt
- 1 teaspoon pepper
- 1 teaspoon dried oregano
- 1 teaspoon ground cumin
- 1 4-pound pork shoulder
- 6 cloves garlic, minced
- 2 bay leaves
- ½ cup fresh orange juice (2 oranges)
- ¼ cup fresh lime juice (2 limes)
- ¾ cup vegetables stock
- Fresh cilantro for garnish

Directions:

1. In a small bowl, whisk together the salt, pepper, oregano, and cumin, rubbing it into all sides of the pork roast.
2. Place the roast in the bottom of your Instant Pot.
3. Sprinkle the garlic over the top and add the bay leaves.
4. Pour in the orange juice, lime juice, and vegetable stock, then seal the lid.
5. Set the pot to manual high pressure and the cook time for 60 minutes.
6. After the cook time is finished, let the pot release for 10 minutes before performing a quick release. Carefully remove the lid.
7. Preheat the broiler.
8. Extract the pork and shred it with two forks, getting rid of any fat in the process. Place on a couple shallow-sided baking sheets.

9. Strain the cooking liquid and drizzle it over the pork.
10. Place the baking sheets under the broiler for four to five minutes to let the edges of the pork turn brown and crispy.
11. Sprinkle with fresh cilantro, if desired, and serve while hot.

Finger-Lickin'-Good Pork Ribs

These country style ribs are flavored with a dry rub consisting of brown sugar, paprika, and other magically tasty ingredients. No more do you need to boil the ribs first; your Instant Pot takes care of tenderizing them under high pressure.

A flavorful rub makes for flavorful ribs.

Yield: 4 servings

Ingredients:

1 tablespoon brown sugar

1 teaspoon paprika

1 teaspoon onion powder

1 teaspoon garlic powder

1 teaspoon salt

½ teaspoon pepper

½ teaspoon cumin

¼ teaspoon cayenne pepper

3 pounds country style pork ribs

¾ cup beef broth

½ cup barbecue sauce

Directions:

1. Whisk the brown sugar, paprika, onion powder, garlic powder, salt, pepper, cumin, and cayenne pepper in a small bowl.
2. Spread these spices over both sides of the ribs and rub or massage them into the meat.
3. Pour the broth into the bottom of your Instant Pot and then set the ribs on top.
4. Top with the barbecue sauce.
5. Secure the lid and select the manual, high pressure function, setting a cook time of 45 minutes. Let the pressure release naturally for 15 to 20 minutes.
6. Remove the ribs and serve with additional barbecue sauce on the side.

Ginger Pork, Japanese Style

This delicious pork recipe comes from Japan. It combines ginger, miso, sake, and other ingredients which, combined, make a lovely, fragrant sauce. One ingredient, mirin, is a Japanese wine used in cooking. It provides some of the unique flavor associated with Japanese cuisine.

This recipe is usually served with white rice. If you want something with fewer carbs, you can serve the dish over zucchini noodles.

Yield: 4 servings

Ingredients:

- ¼ cup ginger root, grated
- 2 cloves garlic, minced
- 1 tablespoon white miso paste
- ¼ cup sake
- ¼ cup mirin
- 2 tablespoons soy sauce
- ½ cup water
- 1 2-pound pork shoulder
- 1 teaspoon salt
- ½ teaspoon pepper
- 2 tablespoons peanut oil
- ½ cup green onions, chopped

Directions:

1. In a glass measuring cup, combine the ginger root, garlic, miso, sake, mirin, soy sauce, and water; mix well and set aside.
2. Select the sauté option on your Instant Pot and let it heat up.
3. While the pot is warming, season the pork shoulder with the salt and pepper.
4. Pour in the peanut oil and brown the meat on all sides, sautéing for five minutes on each side. Remove to a plate and set aside.
5. Add the onions to the pot and sauté them for one minute, then turn off the pot.
6. Cut the meat into half-inch thick strips.
7. Dislodge all the brown bits on the bottom of the pot and pour the sauce into a heat-tolerant container.

8. Place the pork slices in the pot with any juice that has accumulated and secure the lid.
9. Set your Instant Pot on manual, high pressure, then cook for 12 minutes, letting the pot release the pressure naturally.
10. Open the pot when the pressure has returned to normal and serve over rice.

Green Beans, Potatoes, and Ham

This is a down home southern dish that I absolutely love. The smoky flavor of the ham infuses the vegetables with mouthwatering goodness This recipe will bring back the savory taste of home.

Yield: 6 servings

Ingredients:

1½ cups chicken stock

½ teaspoon salt

¼ teaspoon pepper

¼ teaspoon red pepper flakes

¼ teaspoon garlic powder

¼ teaspoon liquid smoke

3 ham shanks

½ onion, chopped

1½ pounds fresh green beans, trimmed and snapped in half

8 small red potatoes, halved or quartered (do not peel)

1 tablespoon butter, divided

Directions:

1. Pour the chicken stock into your Instant Pot and add the salt, pepper, red pepper flakes, garlic powder, and liquid smoke.

2. Put the ham shanks on top, secure the lid, and set it to manual, high pressure for 10 minutes. Perform a quick release and open the pot.
3. Add the onions and scatter half the green beans and half the potatoes on top.
4. Add half of the butter to the pot and then layer the remaining green beans and potatoes, placing the rest of the butter on top of everything.
5. Seal the lid and select the manual, high pressure function; time it for five minutes.
6. Let the pressure release naturally and carefully open the lid.
7. Spoon out the vegetables into a bowl.
8. Place the ham shanks on the cutting board and cut off or shred the meat from the bones. Add the shredded meat to the vegetables, stir to combine, and then spoon the cooking broth over the top before serving.

Ham and Beans

Ham and beans is an earthy dish that you either love…or don't. I happen to love it. I always use a leftover ham bone with quite a bit of meat on it. I also prefer great northern beans.

This recipe calls for dry beans. It is important to soak them and then sort out any blackened or bad beans. The best thing about this recipe is that it only takes about an hour to prepare, not the all-day ordeal required when you cook it on the stove or in a Crock-Pot.

Cornbread is the perfect accompaniment to ham and beans.

Yield: 8 servings

Ingredients:

    2 cups shredded ham, plus 1 ham bone or 3 ham hocks

    4 tablespoons dried minced onions

    1 teaspoon salt

    1 teaspoon pepper

    32 ounces dry northern or pinto beans, soaked overnight and rinsed

    Water

Directions:

1. Place the ham and bone, minced onion, salt, and pepper in the bottom of your Instant Pot.

2. Add the rinsed and drained beans and about two inches of water.
3. Set your Instant Pot to manual, high pressure and set the timer to 15 minutes.
4. Once the cook time is completed, perform a quick release and the dish is ready to serve.

Honey Chops

Use boneless pork chops to make this sweet dish that doesn't contain any sugar, but instead uses honey and maple syrup. Please don't use anything but real maple syrup because it will not taste good without it. The fresh ginger, cinnamon, and cloves along with the Dijon mustard give this this dish a real punch.

Honey Glazed Pork Chops

Yield: 4 servings

Ingredients:

    2 pounds boneless pork chops

    ½ teaspoon sea salt

¼ teaspoon black pepper

½ tablespoon maple syrup

2 tablespoons Dijon mustard

¼ cup honey

½ teaspoon fresh ginger, minced

¼ teaspoon ground cloves

½ teaspoon ground cinnamon

½ cup water

Directions:

1. Select the sauté option and let it heat up.
2. Sprinkle the boneless pork chops with salt and pepper and place into your Instant Pot.
3. Brown the chops on both sides.
4. In a small bowl combine the maple syrup, mustard, honey, ginger, cloves, cinnamon, and water. Whisk well to combine and pour over the chops.
5. Seal the lid, select the manual, high pressure function, and set the cook time for 15 minutes.
6. Once the timer goes off, let the pressure release for five minutes. Perform a quick release to remove the remaining pressure.
7. Carefully open the lid and remove the chops to a serving plate.
8. Turn on the sauté function and let the sauce bubble and thicken for a few minutes.
9. Pour this over the chops before serving.

Honeyed Ham

Honey and ham go together well. The honey gives the ham a natural sweetness that can't be beat. I prefer a bone-in spiral cut pre-cooked ham, because the slices are very thin, and the honey creates a little crispy crust on the very edges while keeping the rest of the slice moist and juicy.

A spicy honey glaze might be just the thing your ham needs.

Ingredients:

¼ cup water

1 5- to 6-pound spiral cut, bone in, pre-cooked ham

½ cup honey

¾ cup brown sugar

2 teaspoons Dijon mustard

½ teaspoon ground cinnamon

¼ teaspoon ground ginger

⅛ teaspoon ground nutmeg

1 pinch ground cloves

Directions:

1. Pour the water into the bottom of your Instant Pot.
2. Insert the ham, sliced side down. If your ham is too large to fit, trim off as necessary and insert it where there's space in the pot.

3. In a bowl, mix the honey, brown sugar, mustard, cinnamon, ginger, nutmeg, and cloves; whisk together well. Pour over the ham in the pot.
4. Secure the lid and select the manual, high pressure setting, with a cook time of 10 minutes.
5. When cooking is finished, let the pressure release naturally for 10 minutes before performing a quick release.
6. Remove the ham with tongs to a platter, sliced side up, and let it rest for at least 10 minutes.
7. Turn on the sauté function of your Instant Pot and let the liquid bubble, reducing the sauce until thick. Pour over the ham and serve.

Old Fashioned Ham and Potatoes with Asparagus

This is a one-pot meal recipe. You will use a steamer basket for the vegetables and will use an oven to keep the vegetables warm, as well as a brief shot under a broiler right at the end.

Yield: 6 servings

Ingredients:

    2 tablespoons olive oil

    1 onion, chopped

    5 to 6 slices of ham, cut into chunks

    1 cup water

    5 russet potatoes, thinly sliced

    1 8-ounce bag frozen asparagus

    2 tablespoons butter

    2 tablespoons flour

    1 cup milk

    1 16-ounce bag shredded cheddar cheese

Directions:

1. Select the sauté function on your Instant Pot and let it heat up.

2. Add the olive oil and onions, sautéing for two to three minutes before turning off the pot.
3. Add the ham pieces and the water.
4. Place the sliced potatoes in the steamer basket and set it on top of the ham and onions.
5. Cut the frozen asparagus into pieces and place on top of the potatoes.
6. Set the pot for manual, high pressure and set the timer for 12 minutes.
7. As soon as the cooking time is finished, perform a quick release and remove the basket with the asparagus and potatoes. Dump them into a non-stick sprayed baking pan and place them in a low-temperature oven, just to keep them warm.
8. Turn on the sauté function again and remove the ham from the pot, placing it in a bowl.
9. Add the butter and flour to the pot and stir until it bubbles.
10. Stir in the milk and sauté, stirring constantly, until the sauce thickens, for about two minutes.
11. Stir in the cheese until melted.
12. Turn off the pot, stir in the ham chunks, and spoon the mixture over the vegetables.
13. Broil the dish for two to three minutes, until slightly brown, before serving.

Smothered Pork Chops

This is traditionally a Southern dish, but you don't have to live in the South to enjoy its creamy deliciousness. The recipe is laden with heavy cream, butter, and other items that only add to its richness.

Yield: 4 servings

Ingredients:

- 1 tablespoon paprika
- 1 teaspoon salt

1 teaspoon onion powder

1 teaspoon garlic powder

½ teaspoon pepper

¼ teaspoon cayenne pepper

4 boneless pork chops

2 tablespoons olive oil

½ medium onion, sliced

6 ounces mushrooms, sliced

1 tablespoon butter

½ cup heavy cream

1 teaspoon cornstarch

1 tablespoon fresh parsley

Directions:

1. In a bowl, mix the paprika, salt, onion powder, garlic powder, black pepper, and cayenne pepper with a whisk and set aside.
2. Wash off the pork chops and pat them dry with a paper towel.
3. Sprinkle one tablespoon of the spice mixture on each side of the chops. Rub in the seasoning and reserve the rest of the spice mixture.
4. Select the sauté setting on your Instant Pot and let it heat up.
5. Add the oil and brown the chops for about three minutes on each side. Remove to a plate and set aside.
6. Place the onion in the pot and sauté it for about two minutes, then add the mushrooms and sauté them for another two minutes.
7. Turn off the sauté function and place the browned chops on top of the onion and mushrooms.
8. Secure the lid on your Instant Pot and select the manual, high pressure function, with a cook time of 25 minutes.

9. When the cook time is completed, let the pressure release naturally for about 10 minutes, then finish with a quick release.
10. Remove the chops and place on a serving plate, covering with foil to keep them warm.
11. Select the sauté function again. Whisk the remaining spice mixture into the pot and stir in the butter and heavy cream. Let it become nice and bubbly.
12. Mix the cornstarch with some of the liquid in the pot and whisk out any lumps. Pour this in and stir as the sauce thickens. This will take only a few minutes and the gravy will continue to thicken as it cools.
13. Serve the pork chops with the gravy poured on top and sprinkled with fresh parsley. Mashed potatoes on the side wouldn't hurt, either.

Sunday Pork Roast with Vegetables and Gravy

This dish uses a pork tenderloin or pork loin roast. The tenderloin will cook faster than the roast, so add 10 minutes to this recipe when using a roast. The internal temperature should be around 145 degrees F when done. This recipe will make eight servings of pork roast and vegetables fit for a family dinner.

Sunday pork roast is just as tasty on any other day of the week.

Ingredients:

- 1 2-pound pork loin roast
- 1 teaspoon sea salt
- ½ teaspoon pepper
- 2 tablespoons butter
- ½ onion, diced
- 3 cloves garlic, minced
- 2 stalks celery, chopped
- 2 carrots, chopped
- ½ cup chicken or vegetable broth
- 2 tablespoons Worcestershire sauce
- 1 teaspoon Dijon mustard
- 1 tablespoon brown sugar
- 1 teaspoon dried rosemary
- ½ teaspoon dried oregano
- ½ teaspoon dried thyme
- 1 tablespoon cornstarch
- ¼ cup water

Directions:

1. Season the pork with salt and pepper.
2. Select the sauté function and let the pot heat up. Add the butter and melt.
3. Add the pork roast and sear all sides to a golden brown. Remove and set on a plate.
4. Add the onions and sauté for two minutes. Add the garlic and sauté for another minute.
5. Add the celery, carrots, broth, Worcestershire, mustard, brown sugar, rosemary, oregano, and thyme.
6. Return the meat to the pot and select the manual, high pressure cooker, timing it for 15 minutes.

7. At the end of this time, perform a quick release, open the pot, and check the internal temperature. If the meat is less than 145 degrees, Fahrenheit, reseal the pot and pressure cook for another 10 minutes before checking the temperature again.
8. As soon as the meat is hot enough, remove it from the pot and cover it to keep it warm. Let it rest for 15 minutes before slicing.
9. Meanwhile, turn your Instant Pot back on to the sauté function and mix the cornstarch with the water. Whisk this mixture into the pot and simmer, stirring until thickened.
10. Taste test the sauce, adjust salt or pepper as needed, and serve over the sliced pork roast.

The next chapter offers lamb dishes from all over the world. Here you'll find Irish stew next to Moroccan lamb, lamb curry, and other enticing recipes.

Chapter 6: Tasty Lamb Recipes From Around The World

Lamb is not frequently eaten in the United States, but other parts of the world consume massive quantities. Lamb contains plenty of protein and is a great source of iron. Its high concentration of vitamin B12 is a boost to nervous system health. It also contains Omega three fatty acids. Besides, lamb just tastes pretty good!

Cabbage and Chops

Lamb chops and cabbage mix well along with the flavor of fennel. For best results, you'll want to use chops that are about three quarters of an inch thick.

Ingredients:

- 4 lamb chops
- 1 teaspoon salt
- ½ teaspoon pepper
- 1 teaspoon fennel seed
- 1 small cabbage (a little less than a pound)
- 1 tablespoon olive oil
- ¾ cup beef stock
- 2 teaspoons flour

Directions:

1. Sprinkle the chops with salt, pepper, and fennel seed before setting aside.
2. Slice the head of cabbage in half and remove the core. Cut into ¾-inch slices and set aside.
3. Turn your Instant Pot on to the sauté function and let it heat up. Add the oil and brown only one side of the chops. Do this in batches if necessary. Turn off the sauté option.
4. Remove the chops from the pot, replacing them with the cabbage. Set the chops on top with their browned sides up. It is okay to overlap them.

5. Add any juice from the chops and then pour the stock around the edges into your Instant Pot.
6. Select the manual, high pressure function, and set the timer for 10 minutes.
7. At the end of that time, let the pressure release naturally for five minutes and then perform a quick release.
8. Carefully open your Instant Pot, remove the cabbage and lamb chops to a serving platter, and turn on the sauté option. Let the liquids in the pot start to bubble, then whisk in the flour. This will allow the gravy to thicken.
9. Pour the gravy over the chops and serve.

Easy Irish Lamb Stew

Lamb stew usually takes hours of simmering, but with an Instant Pot you need less than 30 minutes! If you can remove the bone from the chops, do so, but leave the bone in the pot to lend its flavor to the stew.

If you can't remove the bone, don't worry. Just put cut up most of the chop and add the bone with some meat still on. The meat will easily strip off after it is cooked.

Irish Lamb Stew – hearty, filling, and delicious

Yield: 4 servings

Ingredients:

- 4 lamb shoulder chops (2 to 3.5 pounds, total), cubed
- 2 teaspoons olive oil
- 3 large onions, thinly sliced
- 8 carrots, cut into rounds
- 6 large or 8 small red potatoes with skins on, halved
- 1 teaspoon salt
- 1 teaspoon pepper
- 2 cups water
- 1 sprig of fresh thyme
- 2 tablespoons cornstarch
- 1 tablespoon fresh parsley, chives, or both, chopped

Directions:

1. Select the sauté function and let the pot heat up.
2. Add the oil, then the meat, and brown on all sides. Do this in batches and remove to a plate when done.
3. Add the onions and sauté for about two minutes, then add the carrots and sauté for four minutes. Add the potatoes and sauté for two more minutes.
4. Remove the vegetables to a bowl and add water to the pot to deglaze the bottom.
5. Turn off the sauté function and add the sprig of thyme to the pot.
6. Layer meat and vegetables alternately, sprinkling a little salt and pepper on each meat layer.
7. Seal the lid and set the pot to manual, high pressure for 11 minutes.
8. Allow the pressure to reduce naturally for 12 minutes and then perform a quick release before opening.
9. Combine the cornstarch with a little of the pot juices, to form a runny mixture. Stir this mixture into the pot.

Activate the sauté function and continue to stir while the stew bubbles and thickens.
10. Sprinkle with parsley before serving.

Elegant Lamb Shanks in Wine Sauce

This is an elegant supper for two that is ready in under an hour. You'll use meaty lamb shanks and chicken stock with delicious port wine to prepare this dish. The rich butter, olive oil, and other flavorings make all the difference.

Yield: 2 servings

Ingredients:

- 2 pounds lamb shanks
- 1 teaspoon salt
- ½ teaspoon pepper
- 1 tablespoon olive oil
- 6 cloves garlic, whole
- ½ cup port wine
- ½ cup chicken stock
- 1 heaping tablespoon tomato paste
- 1 teaspoon dried rosemary
- 1 tablespoon unsalted butter
- 1½ teaspoons balsamic vinegar

Directions:

1. Trim the shanks of any excess fat and sprinkle with the salt and pepper.
2. Turn your Instant Pot on to the sauté function and let it heat up. Pour in the olive oil and brown the shanks on both sides. Remove to a plate.
3. Add the garlic and sauté until it turns a light golden brown.
4. Add the port, stock, tomato paste, and the rosemary, stirring until the paste has dissolved.

5. Add the meat. Switch to manual, high pressure function and set the cook time for 30 minutes.
6. When finished cooking, let the pressure release naturally for about 15 minutes, then perform a quick release, to remove any lingering pressure before opening.
7. Remove the shanks from the pot and select the sauté function again. Let the liquid come to a boil and reduce for four to five minutes, or until thickened.
8. Add in the butter, whisk to combine, then stir in the vinegar.
9. Serve this delicious sauce over the meat.

Flavorful Lamb Curry

Lamb curry has been enjoyed around the world for centuries; now it has arrived in your kitchen. This recipe includes fresh ginger, coconut milk, and lime, items that are a little exotic but are easily found in the grocery store. Ghee may be a little more difficult to locate; it's most often found in health food stores, but it is worth hunting for. Traditionally, curry is served with lamb or goat meat, but you can substitute beef or chicken if you wish.

The meat will need to marinate for at least 30 minutes, but it can marinate for up to eight hours, something you can set up in the morning to have on hand when you're ready to start cooking later.

Serve lamb curry with bread and end with plain yogurt to cool the palate.

Yield: 6 servings

Ingredients:

    1½ pounds lamb stew meat

    1-inch piece of fresh ginger, grated

    4 cloves garlic, minced

    Juice of ½ lime

    ½ cup coconut milk

    ¼ teaspoon sea salt

    1 pinch black pepper

    1 tablespoon ghee (or butter)

    1 14-ounce can diced tomatoes

    1 tablespoon yellow curry powder

1 medium onion, diced

3 medium carrots, sliced

1 medium zucchini, diced

Parsley for garnish

Directions:

1. In a big bowl, combine the lamb, ginger, garlic, lime juice, coconut milk, salt, and pepper. Mix well, cover, and marinate for 30 minutes, minimum, up to eight hours.
2. Place the meat mixture in your Instant Pot.
3. Add the ghee, tomatoes and their juice, curry powder, onions, and carrots to the pot, sealing the lid.
4. Set the pressure cooker to manual, high pressure and set a cook time of 20 minutes. Let the pressure release naturally for 10 to 15 minutes, then perform a quick release.
5. Open the lid and activate the sauté function.
6. Add the zucchini and simmer until the sauce thickens and the zucchini is tender, about six minutes.
7. Garnish with parsley and serve.

Harvest Lamb Stew

This lamb stew contains acorn squash and green beans. There is absolutely no sautéing involved this time; you just dump everything in and pressure cook it. The stew comes out perfect as it is; no need for thickening.

The recipe calls for vegetable stock, but I have successfully used both beef and chicken broth with equal success.

Yield: 4 to 5 servings

Ingredients:

1 acorn squash

2 pounds lamb stew meat, cut into 1-inch cubes

3 large carrots, cut into coins

1 large onion, chopped

4 cloves garlic, minced

1 cup fresh green beans, ends cut off and snapped in half

1 sprig fresh rosemary or ½ teaspoon dried rosemary

1 bay leaf

¼ cup vegetable broth

Salt and pepper to taste

Directions:

1. Set the squash in the microwave and cook on high for one minute. This will make it easier to cut. Peel the squash, seed it, and cut the flesh into bite-sized cubes.
2. Place the squash, stew meat, carrots, onions, garlic, green beans, rosemary, bay leaf, vegetable broth, salt, and pepper in your Instant Pot and seal the lid.
3. Select the manual, high pressure function and set the cook time for 35 minutes.
4. When finished cooking, let the pressure reduce naturally for 15 minutes, and then perform a quick release before opening and serving the tasty stew.

Lamb and Sweet Potato Stew

This stew tastes slightly sweet and spicy, thanks to the sweet potatoes, the cumin, and the other spices that are included. These bring out the best of the lamb's flavor and make for a sumptuous dish. If you cannot find bone broth, you can substitute chicken broth.

Lamb and Sweet Potato Stew

Yield: 4 servings

Ingredients:

    1½ teaspoons salt

    ½ teaspoon pepper

    1 teaspoon cumin

    1½ teaspoons ground coriander

    1 1½-pound lamb shoulder, cut into 2-inch cubes

    1 teaspoon olive oil

    1 onion, diced

    4 cloves garlic, minced

    2 inches of ginger root, minced

    1 tablespoon tomato paste

    1 cup bone broth

    1 cinnamon stick

2 large sweet potatoes, cut into 1-inch cubes

Fresh parsley for garnish

Directions:

1. Combine the salt, pepper, cumin and coriander in a small bowl. Rub these over all sides of the lamb, place the meat on a plate, and set it aside.
2. Activate the sauté function on your Instant Pot and let it heat up. Add the olive oil and brown the lamb on all sides, in batches. Return the meat to the plate and set aside again.
3. Add the onion to the pot and sauté for three to five minutes. Add the garlic, ginger, and tomato paste, sautéing for one minute and stirring constantly.
4. Pour in the broth, drop in the cinnamon stick, then add in the lamb with any juices the meat has released.
5. Seal the pot and set it on manual, high pressure, for 25 minutes.
6. Let the pressure release naturally, then open the pot to add the sweet potatoes.
7. Select the manual, high pressure cooker function and cook for 10 more minutes, then perform a quick release immediately.
8. Stir to combine, garnish with chopped parsley, and serve.

Lamb Pot Roast with Potatoes

This pot roast is great for a sit-down dinner. I prefer to use a boneless leg of lamb, just because it is easier to slice before serving. There are no vegetables included in this dish, but you can certainly add some onions and carrots to the pot. If so, add a few minutes to the cooking time.

Dried cranberries are an optional addition to roast lamb.

Yield: 4-5 servings

Ingredients:

    2 tablespoons olive oil

    1 5- to 6-pound boneless leg of lamb

    1 teaspoon marjoram

    1 teaspoon sage

    1 teaspoon sea salt

    ½ teaspoon ground black pepper

    1 bay leaf, crushed

    1 teaspoon dry ginger

    1 teaspoon dry thyme

    3 cloves garlic, minced

    2 cups chicken or vegetable broth

    2½ pounds white potatoes, cut into 2-inch pieces

    2 tablespoons cornstarch

Water

Directions:
1. Select the sauté function on your Instant Pot and wait for it to heat up before adding the olive oil.
2. Once the oil is hot, add the lamb and brown it on all sides. Turn off the sauté function.
3. In a small bowl, combine the marjoram, sage, salt, pepper, crushed bay leaf, dry ginger, and dry thyme. Sprinkle over the lamb.
4. Sprinkle the garlic on top.
5. Pour in the broth around the edges of the pot, then seal it.
6. Select the manual, high-pressure cooker and set the time to 50 minutes. Let the pot release its pressure naturally for 10 minutes, before performing a quick release and carefully opening the lid.
7. Insert the potatoes and seal the lid again. This time, set the high-pressure cooker for 10 more minutes.
8. Perform a quick release when the cook time is done and open the lid. Remove the potatoes with a slotted spoon and set aside. Remove the lamb and set it on a serving plate. Add the potatoes around it.
9. Mix the cornstarch with enough water to make a runny slurry and stir into the pot after turning on the sauté function. Stir until the sauce thickens. Pour it over the lamb and serve.

Lamb Stew with Dates and Cinnamon

This stew has a Middle East-meets-the-Mediterranean flair. Dates give it some sweetness and dried cranberries lend added pizzazz.

Yield: 4 servings

Ingredients:

1 teaspoon ground cumin

1 teaspoon turmeric powder

1 teaspoon ground coriander

1 teaspoon salt

½ teaspoon pepper

1 2-pound boneless leg of lamb

1 tablespoon coconut oil

1 red or purple onion, sliced

4 slices fresh ginger root, minced

7 dried dates, pitted and cut into half

⅛ cup dried cranberries

6 cloves garlic

1 cinnamon stick

1 cup chicken stock

2 bay leaves

1 tablespoon tomato paste

1 tablespoon red wine vinegar or lemon juice

1 tablespoon cornstarch

Cooked rice

Directions:

1. Combine the cumin, turmeric, coriander, salt and pepper in a small bowl.
2. Rub the mixture into the leg of lamb.
3. Turn your Instant Pot on to the sauté function and let it heat up. Add the coconut oil and let it melt.
4. Brown all sides of the lamb, for about three minutes on each side and remove to a plate when done.
5. Add the onion and ginger and cook for two minutes.
6. Turn off the sauté function and add the dates, cranberries, garlic, cinnamon stick, chicken stock, bay leaves, tomato paste, and red wine vinegar, stirring to combine. Place the lamb in the pot and seal it.
7. Select the manual, high pressure cooker function and set the cook time for 80 minutes.

8. At the end of the cooking time, let the pressure release naturally for 10 minutes before performing a quick release. Open the pot and remove the lamb to a cutting board.
9. Select the sauté function and let the liquid come to a boil while slicing the meat. Let the liquid bubble for two to three minutes.
10. Dissolve the cornstarch into enough water to make a thin slurry and pour it into the liquid. Stir until it thickens.
11. Set the lamb back in the pot and let it warm up.
12. Serve over rice.

Middle Eastern Lamb Stew

Many people in the Middle East love to eat lamb (although sometimes it is replaced with goat meat). This lamb stew is a little different from the others. It includes chickpeas and instead of dates, the recipe calls for dried apricots and honey. The spices are the traditional cumin, coriander, and turmeric. The quinoa base is a suggestion. You can use rice or nothing if you prefer; however, I like it with quinoa.

Yield: 4 servings

Ingredients:

2 tablespoons ghee or olive oil

1 onion, diced

5 cloves garlic, minced

1½ pounds lamb stew meat, cut into 1-inch cubes (I prefer a shoulder cut)

1 teaspoon salt

1 teaspoon pepper

1 teaspoon coriander

1 teaspoon turmeric

1 teaspoon cumin

1 teaspoon ground cinnamon

½ teaspoon chili pepper or red pepper flakes

½ cup red wine vinegar

2 tablespoons honey

2 tablespoons tomato paste

1¼ cups chicken stock

1 15-ounce can chickpeas, rinsed and drained

¼ cup dried apricots, chopped

2 tablespoons raisins or dried currants

2 cups cooked quinoa

Directions:

1. Select the sauté function on your Instant Pot and let it heat up.
2. Add the ghee or olive oil and sauté the onions for four minutes. Add the garlic and sauté it for two more minutes.
3. Combine the salt, pepper, coriander, turmeric, cumin, cinnamon, and chili flakes in a small bowl.
4. Add the lamb to the pot, dump in the spices, and brown the cubes on all sides, for about five minutes. Turn off the pot.
5. Pour in the red wine vinegar, honey, tomato paste, stock, chickpeas, apricots, and raisins; stir together.
6. Cover and seal the lid, set the pressure cooker option to manual, high pressure, and set the timer to 60 minutes.
7. At the end of the cook time, let the pressure release naturally for 20 minutes before performing a quick release.
8. Open the lid. The lamb should fall apart.
9. Serve over quinoa with a garnish of fresh chopped parsley.

Roman Lamb

"When in Rome, do as the Romans do." At least, so goes the saying. You may not be in Rome, but if Romans eat lamb like this, we should *all* do as the Romans do! This recipe includes the herbal flavors of thyme and rosemary, the saltiness of anchovy fillets, and the freshness of green peas and leeks. You can't go wrong with this one.

This dish does require marinating for 30 minutes up to 8 hours, but the longer the better, in my estimation.

Yield: 6 servings

Ingredients:

3½ pounds boneless lamb shoulder, trimmed and cut into bite-sized pieces

3 cloves of garlic, grated

4 cloves of garlic, left whole

1½ teaspoons sea salt

½ teaspoon pepper

4 sprigs rosemary

6 sprigs thyme

2 tablespoons olive oil, divided

2 medium-sized leeks, white and light green parts, chopped

1 cup dry white wine

5 oil-packed anchovy fillets, chopped

1 pinch red pepper flakes, crushed

1 cup frozen peas, thawed and drained

1 tablespoon fresh tarragon, chopped

2 green onions, thinly sliced

2 tablespoons fresh mint, chopped, for garnish

Directions:

1. Place the lamb pieces in a large bowl along with the grated garlic, salt, pepper, and the sprigs of rosemary and thyme. Cover and set in the refrigerator, from 30 minutes to eight hours.

2. Remove the rosemary and thyme sprigs from the lamb and set them aside.
3. Turn on the sauté function of your Instant Pot and let it heat up. Add one tablespoon of olive oil and let it heat up.
4. Add the lamb and brown it on both sides, for five to seven minutes per side. Transfer to a plate. Do this in batches if necessary.
5. Add the remaining olive oil to the pot and let it heat up. Add the leeks and sauté them for about five minutes, until golden. If the pot gets too hot, turn it off to prevent the leeks from overcooking. Then turn it back on to the sauté function for the steps that follow.
6. Add the wine and scrape up the brown bits from the bottom of the pot. Let the liquid simmer until it reduces by half, about two minutes, then turn it off.
7. Add the anchovies and red pepper flakes.
8. Return the lamb to the pot, along with the reserved sprigs of rosemary and thyme.
9. Seal the lid of your Instant Pot and select the manual, high pressure setting; set the timer for 50 minutes.
10. Allow the pressure to release naturally.
11. When it is safe, remove the lamb to a serving platter with a slotted spoon.
12. Spoon the fat off the top and discard it. If the sauce is thin, turn on the sauté function and allow it to boil until it thickens a little.
13. Add the peas and tarragon and simmer for about two minutes before ladling the sauce over the lamb.
14. Sprinkle with green onions and mint, then serve.

Savory Leg of Lamb

A leg of lamb is an Easter tradition for many households, but it is delicious at any time of the year. If you use a bone-in leg, make sure it will fit into your Instant Pot before buying. I've had success using up to 5½-pound legs.

I do use herbs de Provence, but some people take issue with a spice mix that includes lavender, thinking it'll remind them too much of soap. If you encounter this objection, you can substitute a combination of rosemary and thyme, with just a hint of nutmeg.

Cooking a leg of lamb roast fills the house with a delicious aroma

Yield: 8 servings

Ingredients:

    1 5-pound leg of lamb, with or without the bone

    1 to 1½ teaspoons Herbs de Provence

    1 teaspoon garlic powder

    1 teaspoon onion powder

    1 teaspoon sea salt

    ½ teaspoon pepper

    2 tablespoons olive oil

1 onion, chopped

2 cloves garlic, minced

3 carrots, chopped

2 cups vegetable broth (or chicken broth)

5 large potatoes, sliced

Directions:

1. Blot the lamb with paper towels.
2. Mix the Herbs de Provence, garlic powder, onion powder, salt, and pepper in a small bowl and rub into the leg of lamb. Cover and refrigerate for one hour.
3. Select the sauté function on your Instant Pot and let it heat up. Add the olive oil and brown all sides of the lamb, five minutes on each side. Remove to a plate and set aside.
4. Add a little more oil to the pot if necessary and add the onions. Sauté for about three minutes, then add the garlic and sauté for two more minutes.
5. Add the carrots and sauté for another two minutes. Remove the onions, garlic and carrots to a bowl and set them aside.
6. Pour the broth into the pot and scrape the bottom to loosen the brown bits.
7. Turn off the sauté function and place the trivet in the pot.
8. Set the leg of lamb on the trivet. Add the potatoes around the roast, then lay the carrots, garlic, and onions on top. Seal the lid in place.
9. Set the pot for manual, high pressure for 35 minutes. When the cook time is finished, let the pressure release naturally.
10. Open the pot and serve.

Tasty Lamb Ragout

Ragout is a tomato-laden stew packed with herbs. It has a big flavor that combines well with lamb.

Yield: 8 servings

Ingredients:

- 1 tablespoon olive oil
- 1½ to 2 pounds lamb stew meat, cut into bite-sized pieces
- 1 onion, chopped
- 2 celery stalks, diced
- 2 carrots, sliced
- 4 cloves garlic, minced
- 1 teaspoon sea salt
- ½ teaspoon pepper
- 1 teaspoon dried rosemary
- 1 teaspoon dried oregano
- 2 cups tomato puree
- 1 cup chicken stock
- 2 bay leaves
- Cooked pasta

Directions:

1. Set your Instant Pot to the sauté function and allow it to heat up.
2. Add the oil and let it heat up. Add the lamb and brown all sides in batches, transferring to a bowl when browned.
3. Add the onion, celery, and carrots to the pot and sauté for about eight minutes, stirring frequently to prevent burning.
4. Add the garlic, salt, and pepper, sautéing for another couple minutes, scraping the brown bits from the bottom of the pot.

5. Add the rosemary and oregano, then stir in the tomato puree, the chicken stock, and the bay leaves. Let it come to a simmer and turn off the pot.
6. Seal the lid and select the manual, high pressure function, setting the timer for 45 minutes.
7. At the end of the cook time, perform a quick release and open the pot.
8. Using a slotted spoon, remove the lamb to a serving bowl and turn on the sauté function again.
9. You can shred the meat with two forks or leave it in chunks. It should come apart very easily.
10. Let the sauce come to a boil and reduce to a thick and chunky consistency, stirring frequently.
11. Serve over cooked pasta.

Tender Lamb Chops
Sometimes you just want a quick and easy dinner. Here's a recipe that takes less than an hour to prepare.

It can be hard to fit a rack of lamb into an Instant Pot, but chops are no problem.

Yield: 4-6 servings

Ingredients:

    2 teaspoons sea salt

    1 teaspoon pepper

    1 teaspoon dried oregano

    1 teaspoon dried rosemary

    1 teaspoon garlic powder

    3 pounds of lamb chops

    1 teaspoon olive oil

    2 tablespoons unsalted butter

    1 tablespoon tomato paste

2 green onions, chopped

1 cup beef broth

Directions:

1. Mix the salt, pepper, oregano, rosemary, and garlic powder in a small bowl and sprinkle it over both sides of the lamb chops.
2. Turn on the sauté function of your Instant Pot and let it heat up. Pour in the olive oil and the butter, letting it heat up.
3. Brown the lamb chops on both sides in in batches, allowing four to five minutes per side. Remove to a plate and set aside.
4. Add the tomato paste and green onions to the pot and cook for two minutes, stirring frequently to prevent scorching.
5. Pour in the beef stock and deglaze the pot.
6. Return the lamb chops to the pot and seal the lid. Switch to manual, high pressure for 20 minutes.
7. At the end of the cook time, perform a quick release before opening the lid.
8. Serve with mashed potatoes, rice, or noodles.

Seafood comes out delicious in an Instant Pot. In the next chapter you'll be free to explore all sorts of fish as well as other seafood – ranging from shrimp to shellfish and lobster. The Instant Pot simplifies the preparation of these luscious dishes and shortens the preparation time considerably.

Chapter 7: Incredible Seafood Recipes

Using your Instant Pot to make seafood is an almost perfect situation. Crab legs and other sea food must be steamed; your Instant Pot is an ideal steamer. The only caution: never boil a live lobster or crab in an Instant Pot; the water doesn't heat up enough to instantly kill these animals, making for a messy situation. Otherwise, your Instant Pot is a great tool for preparing seafood and keeping it warm. It is fine to cook mussels and clams in an Instant Pot because the water will heat up enough with the sauté setting to humanely kill them.

Buttery Mussels

Mussels are one of those shellfish that you can prepare in an Instant Pot because the sauté setting is hot enough to kill them instantly. Before cooking, place the mussels in a colander and rinse them off, checking to be sure they are shut tight. If they are open, tap them on the countertop; if they do not close, discard them. Also discard any mussels that are cracked. If the beard is not already removed, use tweezers or a sharp knife to cut or pull it off.

Mussels cook quicker, using an Instant Pot.

Yield: 4 servings

Ingredients:

- 2 tablespoons butter
- 2 shallots, chopped
- 4 cloves garlic, chopped
- ½ cup white wine
- ½ cup vegetable or chicken broth
- 2 pounds mussels, cleaned
- 1 lemon

Directions:

1. Select the sauté function on your Instant Pot and let it heat up.
2. Add the butter and let it melt.
3. Add the shallots and sauté until they are translucent, for two to three minutes.
4. Add the garlic and sauté for another minute.
5. Add the wine and broth and let it heat up before turning off the pot.
6. Add the mussels, seal the lid, and select the manual, high pressure function for five minutes.
7. Let the pressure release naturally before opening the pot.
8. Serve the mussels with fresh lemon slices.

Clams Steamed in White Wine with Garlic Butter

You check clams just like you do mussels. Rinse them off in a colander and discard any cracked or open shells. I use unsalted butter in this recipe, but if all you have is salted butter, use it and omit the salt.

Yield: 4 servings

Ingredients:

- 5 pounds of clams
- 1 pound red potatoes, quartered

1 stick unsalted butter

1 teaspoon sea salt

2 cloves garlic, minced

1 cup white wine

1 pinch Old Bay seasoning

1 lemon

½ cup fresh parsley, chopped

Directions:

1. Wash and check all clams and let drain.
2. Quarter the potatoes and set aside
3. Heat up your Instant Pot on the sauté option. Add half the butter and salt and sauté the potatoes for about five minutes, in batches. Remove to a bowl when done.
4. Add the garlic and sauté for one minute.
5. Pour in the wine and bring to a boil. Reduce for about five minutes.
6. Add the clams and Old Bay seasoning.
7. Seal the lid and select the manual, high pressure function, cooking for two minutes. Let pressure release naturally.
8. Using a slotted spoon, remove the clams to a bowl.
9. Turn on the sauté function again, simmering the juices for five minutes.
10. Add the rest of the butter, the juice from half the lemon (slice the other half to serve with the clams) and the parsley. Mix and pour this sauce over the clams, then serve.

Coconut Curry Tilapia

This spicy fish dish is good with tilapia or any white fish. I have used cod, halibut, and whitefish and the dish came out great every time. It includes a variety of flavors, from coconut milk to mustard seed and other spices. The ginger-garlic paste and curry leaves are commonly found where Indian food is sold. You can make your own by grinding a half inch of peeled ginger root with three cloves of garlic. For the curry leaves, substitute basil leaves. It really does cook in three minutes.

Yield: 4 servings

Ingredients:

    1 tablespoon olive oil

    ½ teaspoon mustard seed

    10 curry leaves (or 5 basil leaves)

    1 tablespoon ginger-garlic paste

    ½ medium onion, thinly sliced

    ½ medium green bell pepper, chopped

    ½ medium orange or yellow pepper, chopped

    ½ teaspoon turmeric powder

    ½ teaspoon chili powder

    1 teaspoon cumin powder

    1 teaspoon garam masala

    1 teaspoon salt

    2 teaspoons ground coriander

    1 can coconut milk

    1 pound tilapia fillets, cut into 2-inch pieces

    3 sprigs cilantro

    6 mint leaves

    ½ teaspoon lime juice

Directions:

1. Select the sauté function of your Instant Pot and let it heat up. Add the oil and let it heat up.
2. Add the mustard seeds and stir. When the seeds start to sputter, throw in the curry leaves and ginger-garlic paste. Sauté for 30 seconds.

3. Add the onion and bell peppers, sautéing for about a minute.
4. Add the turmeric, chili powder, cumin, garam masala, salt, and coriander powder; sauté for 30 seconds.
5. Pour in the coconut milk, bring it to a simmer, and let it simmer for one minute.
6. Lay the tilapia in the pot along with the cilantro and stir to coat the fish.
7. Place the mint leaves on top and seal the pot. Set it to manual, high pressure and assign it to cook for three minutes.
8. As soon as the cook time has elapsed, perform a quick release and open the pot.
9. Stir in the lime juice and serve over white or brown rice.

Crab Legs in an Instant Pot

Your Instant Pot is the perfect tool to prepare crab legs. It is so easy you will want to make them all the time. You can serve any number of people with this recipe. Since it only takes two minutes to cook (and you always want your crab legs freshly cooked), it's a simple matter to prepare multiple batches as they are needed.

Crab legs are scrumptuous, dipped in melted butter.

Yield: 4 servings

Ingredients:

- 2 pounds frozen crab legs
- ¾ cup water
- 4 tablespoons butter, melted
- Lemon juice

Directions:

1. Place the frozen crab legs in the Instant Pot's steamer basket.
2. Pour in the water and seal the lid
3. Select the high pressure function and set the time for two minutes.
4. At the end of two minutes, perform a quick release.
5. Open the pot and ensure that the crab legs are a bright pink,
6. Mix the butter with a squirt of lemon juice and serve.

Easy Lobster Tails

Yes, you can make lobster tails in an Instant Pot. I suggest using frozen lobster tails, unthawed. If I only need two, I reduce the cook time to two minutes. This recipe will serve four lobster tails. Remember: never put a live lobster in your Instant Pot because it doesn't heat up enough to kill the lobster instantly.

Cutting down the center of the shell butterflies the lobster tail and makes it easier to get at the meat.

Yield: 2 servings

Ingredients:

    4 frozen lobster tails

    1 cup water

    1 tablespoon Old Bay seasoning

    1 cup butter, divided

    2 teaspoons lemon juice

    1 teaspoon garlic, minced

    1 teaspoon dill

    ½ teaspoon salt

    ½ teaspoon pepper

Directions:

1. Use kitchen shears to cut a line down the center of the lobster tail. Separate the lobster from the shell at the top middle and hold the tail with the shell up. Insert the shears and just cut down the center of the shell. This butterflies the lobster tail before it is cooked. It is hard to do this when the lobster is hot. Leave the shell on the lobster tail and set aside.
2. Put the water in your Instant Pot.
3. Add the Old Bay Seasoning and stir to mix.
4. Place the trivet in the bottom of your Instant Pot and lay the lobster tails on top, shell-side down.
5. Seal the lid and select the manual, high pressure function, setting the timer to four minutes. Because the tails are frozen, it will take about 10 minutes for the pot to actually heat up and start to cook. That is fine.
6. While cooking, make the butter sauce by placing half the butter in a frying pan on the stove, then letting it melt and start to turn brown.
7. Add the rest of the butter, the lemon juice, garlic, dill, salt, and pepper, sautéing until everything is melted. Remove from the heat and set aside.
8. When the cook time is finished, perform a quick release and use tongs to remove the tails.
9. Serve the lobster tails with butter sauce in small bowls on the side.

Fish in Parchment

Putting fish in parchment allows it to steam and retain its moisture. You'll want to measure carefully to ensure the packages you create will fit inside your Instant Pot. You want to keep one inch of space free around the sides of the pot.

This recipe requires very thin pieces of potato and onion. Use a mandolin or a food processor to cut them.

Yield: 4 servings

Ingredients:

2 tablespoon olive oil, divided

3 small potatoes, thinly sliced

Salt and pepper to taste

4 grouper fillets (thawed and drained)

4 sprigs of fresh thyme

4 sprigs fresh parsley

1 onion, shaved into thin rings

2 lemon slices

2 cups water

Directions:
1. Lay out four rectangles of parchment paper on a flat surface.
2. Swirl some of the olive oil onto each piece.
3. Place a single layer of potato slices in the middle of the paper.
4. Add some salt and pepper to each package.
5. Place a fish fillet on top and put another swirl of olive oil on top.
6. Place thyme and rosemary sprigs on top of each fillet.
7. Arrange onion rings on top of each.
8. Add a few lemon slices, another pinch of salt, and a swirl of olive oil
9. Fold the parchment paper in on the short sides and bring the long sides up and over the fish, rolling the parchment down to contain the fish in a package.
10. Cut off some aluminum foil and enclose each package securely inside the foil.
11. Pour the water into the bottom of your Instant Pot.
12. Insert the trivet into your Instant Pot and place two of the foil-wrapped packages on top.
13. Set the steamer basket on top of the two foil wrapped packages. Set the remaining packages in the steamer basket.

14. Seal the lid, select the manual, high pressure function, and set the time for 10 minutes.
15. Let the pressure release naturally for five minutes and then perform a quick release.
16. Remove the foil wrapped packages with tongs. Let them set for three to five minutes before unwrapping them carefully from the foil.
17. Use kitchen shears to cut open the parchment and serve the fish onto a plate just before eating.

Flavorful Fish Tacos

Fish tacos are popular and no wonder! They are delicious and easy to make in an Instant Pot. You can use either fresh or frozen fish for this recipe. That's handy for me, because sometimes I forget to defrost something for dinner. This recipe lets me simply pull out some fish fillets from the freezer and pop them into my Instant Pot. I'll have dinner on the table in less than an hour.

Serve fish tacos with a little lemon or lime and some sour cream.

Yield: 4 servings

Ingredients:

1 cup water

2 large cod fillets (frozen or fresh)

1 tablespoon Old Bay seasoning

2 tablespoons olive oil

½ cup shredded cheese

Toppings like lettuce, sour cream, salsa, guacamole, onions, tomatoes, etc.

Taco shells

Directions:

1. Place the water in the bottom of your Instant Pot.
2. Season both sides of the fillets with the Old Bay seasoning and set them in the steamer basket inside your pot.
3. Close and seal the lid. Select the manual, high pressure function and cook for six minutes if the fillets are frozen, three minutes if fresh.
4. When the timer goes off, let the pot release its pressure naturally for a few minutes before performing a quick release.
5. Remove the fish from the pot and divide it among the taco shells. Add toppings and serve.

Garlic Butter Salmon

This is another package recipe because foil is used to contain all the ingredients for the salmon dish. This makes the salmon flavorful and flakey. This recipe makes enough for three people and includes a vegetable. The ingredients are divided between the three foil-wrapped packages.

Yield: 3 servings

Ingredients:

1 pound medium-sized fresh asparagus stalks

1 1-pound salmon fillet (cut into three equal pieces)

2 cloves garlic, minced

¼ cup lemon juice

Salt to taste

¼ cup butter, cut into four pats

1½ cups water

Directions:

1. Tear off three large pieces of foil and place them on a flat surface with the shiny side down. Fold up the edges, to prevent liquid from spilling out.
2. Divide the asparagus equally and place it in the center of each piece of foil.
3. Divide the minced garlic and rub it on both sides of each piece of salmon. Set the salmon on top of the asparagus.
4. Sprinkle a tablespoon of lemon juice over each fillet. You should have one more tablespoon left. Set it aside.
5. Sprinkle a little salt over each of the fillets.
6. Place one pat of butter on top of each package, giving you one tablespoon left over. Set it aside.
7. Seal the foil tightly, so no steam will escape from the package while cooking.
8. Pour the water into the bottom of your Instant Pot and place the trivet inside.
9. Stack the three foil-wrapped packages on top of the trivet and seal the pot.
10. Select the steam option and set it to cook for four minutes.
11. While cooking, put the remaining tablespoon of butter in a saucepan with the leftover tablespoon of lemon juice and melt to make a sauce.
12. Turn off your Instant Pot and remove the foil packages from the pot with tongs.
13. Open the foil packages and set the contents on individual plates. Pour a little of the butter lemon sauce on top and serve.

Lime Shrimp and Rice

Use frozen, deveined shrimp for this recipe. It must be frozen when it goes into the pot or it will overcook. The lime flavor mixes with the garlic, shrimp, and cilantro to make a delightful combination.

Yield: 4 servings

Ingredients:

¼ cup butter

2 tablespoons garlic, minced

Salt and pepper to taste

1 cup long grained white rice

1½ cups vegetable broth or water

1 can black beans, rinsed and drained

1 pound frozen shrimp (can be raw or cooked)

Juice of half a lime

½ teaspoon lime zest

¼ cup cilantro, chopped

Directions:

1. Select the sauté function on your Instant Pot and let it heat up.
2. Add the butter and let it melt.
3. Add the garlic, salt, and pepper, sautéing until fragrant.
4. Add the rice and cook until it becomes slightly brown.
5. Pour in the broth or water and the beans.
6. Add the frozen shrimp and seal the lid.
7. Select the manual, high pressure function and set the cook time for five minutes.
8. As soon as the time is up, perform a quick release and serve, garnished with cilantro and a slice of lime.

Mediterranean Cod

This fish dish is super easy to make. You just throw everything in the pot and in 15 to 20 minutes, you have dinner on the table. You can use either frozen or fresh cod.

Tomatoes cook into the fish, adding delightful flavor.

Yield: 6 servings

Ingredients:

    3 tablespoons butter

    1 onion, sliced

    1 clove garlic, minced

    1 teaspoon salt

    ½ teaspoon pepper

    1 teaspoon oregano

    6 pieces frozen or fresh cod (about 1½ pound)

    1 28-ounce can diced tomatoes

Directions:

1. Select the sauté function on your Instant Pot and let it heat up.
2. Add the butter and let it melt.
3. Sauté the onion in the butter for about two minutes, until fragrant.
4. Add the garlic and sauté for one more minute.
5. Sprinkle the cod with salt, pepper, and oregano, then set it in the pot.
6. Sauté the fish in the sauce for eight minutes, stirring to coat the fish.
7. Add the diced tomatoes and seal the pot.
8. Select the manual, high pressure function and set the time to three minutes for fresh fish and five minutes for frozen.
9. At the end of the cook time, immediately perform a quick release, stir, and serve.

New England Clam Chowder
This is an easy way to prepare a traditional clam chowder that rivals the old-fashioned method for sheer deliciousness! The flavor and consistency of the chowder is exceptional.

Serve clam chowder with a sprinkling of chives or parsley and a little crispy bacon.

Yield: 6 servings

Ingredients:

- 3 6.5-ounce cans chopped clams (reserve the juice)
- Water
- 4 slices bacon, chopped
- 3 tablespoons butter
- 1 onion, sliced
- 2 stalks celery, diced
- 2 sprigs fresh thyme or ¼ teaspoon dried thyme
- 2 cloves garlic, minced
- 1 teaspoon sea salt
- ¼ teaspoon pepper
- 4 cups potatoes, diced (If using red potatoes, do not peel)
- 1½ cups heavy cream
- Chopped chives for garnish

Directions:

1. Drain the clams into a 2-cup measuring cup and set the clams aside. Add enough water to the juice to make two cups of liquid. Set aside.
2. Turn on the sauté function on your Instant Pot and allow it to heat up.
3. Add the bacon and cook it, not until crispy but just enough to render the fat.
4. Add the butter, onion, celery, and thyme sprigs. Scrape the bottom to loosen up the tasty brown bits.
5. When the onion is translucent and the celery has softened, add the garlic, salt, and pepper. Sauté for another minute.
6. Add the potatoes and the clam juice, stirring well to mix.
7. Secure the lid and select the manual, high pressure function, setting the cook time for five minutes.

8. When the cook time is completed, let the pot rest for three minutes and then perform a quick release.

9. Stir the contents of the pot and use a potato masher to lightly mash the potatoes.

10. Select the sauté function and add the clams and heavy cream. Heat through, but do *not* bring the contents to a boil.

11. If the chowder requires thickening, add a tablespoon cornstarch to two ladles of chowder in a small bowl. Mix thoroughly and whisk back into the chowder. As the chowder warms, it should thicken.

12. Ladle the chowder into bowls and garnish with chives.

New Tuna Noodle Casserole

Tuna Noodle Casserole is an old standby in almost every household. When there is nothing else in the house, just break out a box of mac and cheese and a can of tuna and you have a meal.

This recipe is a bit more elevated. Instead of using cream-of-something soup, you use chicken stock and heavy cream. Frozen peas and fresh celery add texture, along with butter-flavored crackers. Elbow macaroni stands up well to pressure cooking; the pasta cooks right along with everything else in the pot.

This recipe is even more elegant because I've done away with the cans of tuna. Instead, fresh tuna is called for. If you invite some friends over for gourmet tuna noodle casserole and then serve this, they'll be delighted.

Yield: 8-10 servings

Ingredients:

4 tablespoons butter, divided

1 cup onions, chopped

1 cup celery, chopped

1 teaspoon salt

½ teaspoon black pepper

2 cups elbow macaroni

3½ cups chicken stock

8 ounces fresh tuna

3 tablespoons flour

¼ cup heavy cream

1 cup frozen peas (do not thaw)

1 cup butter-flavored crackers, finely crushed

1 cup shredded cheddar cheese

Directions:

1. Select the sauté function on your Instant Pot and let it heat up. Once heated, melt one tablespoon of the butter.
2. Add in the onion, celery, salt, and pepper; sauté for about three minutes.
3. Pour in the uncooked macaroni and the chicken stock.
4. Put the tuna on top and seal the lid.
5. Select the manual, high pressure function and set the timer for five minutes.
6. Meanwhile, place the remaining three tablespoons of butter in a saucepan over medium heat on the stove.
7. When melted, stir in the flour and keep stirring until the slurry turns slightly brown. This will take about two minutes, giving you a roux that will thicken the sauce. Remove it from the heat and set aside.
8. As soon as the Instant Pot is finished cooking, perform a quick release and carefully remove the lid.
9. Extract the tuna with a slotted spoon or tongs and set aside.
10. Add the roux to the pot and turn on the sauté function. Stir until the roux is well mixed in and there are no lumps. The sauce will thicken.
11. As soon as the liquid thickens, turn off your Instant Pot and stir in the heavy cream until thoroughly combined.
12. Add the frozen peas and mix well.

13. Return the tuna to your Instant Pot. Sprinkle the crackers on top and cover with cheese.
14. Put the lid back on and let the pot set for five minutes to allow the peas to thaw and the cheese to melt. Then serve to your admiring public.

Non-Traditional Seafood Boil

Traditionally, a seafood boil occurs outdoors. The water is boiled in a pot over an open flame. This nontraditional method takes place in the comfort of your own home using your Instant Pot.

The method is fast and super easy. While boiling in a pot over a fire might take an hour or more, this recipe is on your table in less than 30 minutes. It's patterned on the lowcountry boils of Louisiana with andouille sausage and shrimp thrown in. You can add clams, mussels, or other seafood; just keep it to around one pound in total weight.

Traditional sea food boils include lobster, cray fish or shrimp, clams, mussels, corn and potatoes

Yield: 6 servings

Ingredients:

1 large onion, chopped

4 cloves of garlic, quartered

6 small red potatoes, skins on, cut into six wedges

3 ears of corn, shucked and cut into 6 pieces each

1½ pounds fully cooked andouille sausage, cut into 1-inch pieces

1 pound frozen shrimp (or combination of shrimp, clams, mussels, or other seafood)

1½ tablespoons Old Bay seasoning

2 cups chicken broth

1 lemon cut into wedges

½ cup fresh parsley for garnish

Directions:

1. Lay down a layer of onions in the bottom of your Instant Pot and sprinkle the garlic on top.
2. Add the potato pieces in an even layer and put the corn on top.
3. Add the sausage pieces and the seafood.
4. Sprinkle with Old Bay Seasoning.
5. Pour in the broth around the sides of the pot.
6. Squeeze the lemon wedges on top of everything and discard the rinds.
7. Lock the lid in place and select the manual, high pressure function for five minutes.
8. When the cooking time is completed, let the pressure reduce naturally for about five minutes, then perform a quick release.
9. Set everything out on a platter and garnish with sprigs of fresh parsley.

Oyster Stew

This recipe calls for oysters in a jar, juice included. It also calls for heavy cream, although coconut milk can be used as a dairy-free alternative. The butter in the recipe can be substituted with coconut oil, if you wish.

Oyster stew is sheer richness in a bowl.

Yield: 4 servings

Ingredients:

    2 tablespoons butter

    2 tablespoons green onion, minced

    1 cup celery, minced

    2 cloves garlic, minced

    2 10-ounce jars shucked oysters with their liqueur

    1 pint heavy cream

    1 cup vegetable broth

    ½ teaspoon sea salt

    ½ teaspoon white pepper

    2 tablespoons fresh parsley, chopped, for garnish

Directions:

1. Select the sauté function and let your Instant Pot heat up.

2. Add the butter and let it melt.
3. Add the green onions and celery and sauté for about three minutes.
4. Toss in the garlic and sauté for another minute.
5. Add the oysters, juice included, along with the cream and broth.
6. Seal the lid and select the manual, high pressure setting for five minutes.
7. Perform a quick release and add the salt and pepper, stirring to combine.
8. Ladle into bowls and sprinkle with parsley.

Quick Honey Balsamic Salmon

This recipe takes three minutes to cook, so if you need make more than two servings, you can easily repeat the process, while keeping the cooked salmon warm. For such a simple recipe, the salmon tastes great, thanks to the sweet and sour juxtaposition of honey and balsamic vinegar.

Refrigerate fresh salmon, tightly wrapped, for less than two days before cooking.

Yield: 2 servings

Ingredients:

    Salt and pepper to taste

    2 5-ounce salmon fillets

    1 cup water

    2 tablespoons balsamic vinegar

    2 tablespoons honey

Directions:

1. Sprinkle salt and pepper to taste on both the fillets. Set aside.
2. Pour the water into the bottom of your Instant Pot and set the trivet inside.
3. Mix the vinegar and honey in a small bowl and brush it on both sides of the salmon fillet before setting it atop the trivet, skin side down. Set aside the rest of the vinegar and honey sauce.
4. Secure the lid and set the pot on manual, high pressure, with a cook time of three minutes.
5. When the cook time is completed, let the pressure release naturally for a couple minutes and then perform a quick release. Open the pot and lift out the salmon, setting it on a serving plate
6. Brush the salmon with additional sauce and garnish with fresh parsley before serving.

Shrimp and Bow Ties

This is a delicious pasta and shrimp dish made with chicken stock and white wine. It is super easy to make, and the bow-tie pasta is easy to pick up on a fork along with the shrimp. You'll want to cook and drain the pasta before starting to prepare the rest of the dish, but this can be done well beforehand, if you wish.

It's easy to see where bow-tie pasta got its name.

Yield: 4 servings

Ingredients:

- 2 tablespoons olive oil
- 2 tablespoons butter
- 2 cloves garlic, chopped
- ½ cup chicken stock
- ½ cup white wine
- 2 pounds raw shrimp (shelled and deveined)
- 2 cups uncooked bow-tie pasta, prepared beforehand
- 1 tablespoon fresh lemon juice
- Parsley for garnish

Directions:

1. Turn on the sauté function of your Instant Pot and let it warm up.
2. Place the oil and butter in the pot and stir until the butter melts.
3. Add the garlic and sauté until fragrant.
4. Pour in the chicken stock and white wine, then deglaze the pot.
5. Turn off the sauté setting.
6. Add the shrimp to the pot and seal the lid.
7. Select the manual, high pressure cooker and set the timer for two minutes.
8. Once the timer goes off, let your Instant Pot release naturally for five minutes.
9. Perform a quick release, then open the lid and stir in the cooked bow-tie pasta.
10. Add the lemon juice, sprinkle with parsley, and serve.

Shrimp and Sausage Jambalaya

This is a real taste of New Orleans. You can substitute Kielbasa for the smoked sausage if you can't find Andouille sausage. The minute it starts to cook, it lets loose a wonderful aroma that will attract neighbors to your door. You'll soon discover it tastes even better than it smells.

Jambalaya is a combination of French and Spanish cuisine (Cajun) from the Bayou and contains seafood and sausage with rice and vegetables

Yield: 6 servings

Ingredients:

- 1 tablespoon olive oil
- 1 medium onion, diced
- 3 stalks celery, diced
- 1 red pepper, seeded and diced

3 cloves garlic, minced

1 pound smoked sausage, cut diagonally into half-inch pieces

½ teaspoon salt

½ teaspoon black pepper

1 teaspoon Cajun seasoning

¼ teaspoon cayenne pepper or 3 to 6 dashes Tabasco sauce

1¼ cups uncooked long grain white rice, rinsed

1 14.5-ounce can petite diced tomatoes with juice

¾ cup chicken stock

1 pound medium shrimp; peeled, de-headed and deveined

2 green onions, chopped, for garnish

Directions:

1. Select the sauté function on your Instant Pot and let it heat up.
2. Add the olive oil and sauté the onion, celery, and red pepper for three to four minutes.
3. Add the garlic and sauté for another minute.
4. Add the sausage, salt, pepper, Cajun seasoning, and Cayenne pepper; stir for another two to three minutes.
5. Rinse the rice, drain it, and add it to the pot to sauté for one minute.
6. Pour in the tomatoes with their juice and the chicken stock.
7. Add the shrimp and seal the lid.
8. Select the manual, high pressure setting and set the timer for four minutes.
9. Allow the pressure to release naturally for five minutes, then perform a quick release before opening the pot.
10. Fluff the rice with a fork and serve with green onions sprinkled over the top.

Shrimp Risotto

I love risotto and especially enjoy preparing it in my Instant Pot. Risotto can come out either watery or like paste, but with the Instant Pot, it comes out perfect every time. You'll want to use Arborio rice, the traditional rice used in risotto. Stovetop preparation of the rice alone is a long labor-intensive process, but the Instant Pot.

Arborio rice, with its rich creaminess, is one key to a perfect risotto.

Yield: 4 servings

Ingredients:

    4 tablespoons butter, divided

    1 small onion, chopped

    2 cloves, garlic, minced

    1½ cups dry Arborio rice

2 tablespoons dry white wine

4½ cups chicken stock, divided

Sea salt and pepper to taste

1 pound large shrimp, deveined

¾ cup Asiago cheese, grated

¼ cup fresh parsley, chopped

Directions:
1. Select the sauté function on your Instant Pot and melt two tablespoons of the butter.
2. Sauté the onion in the butter for about two minutes.
3. Add the garlic and sauté for another minute.
4. Add the rice and stir for yet one more minute.
5. Pour in the wine and cook for about 30 seconds, letting the alcohol evaporate.
6. Add three cups of chicken stock and season with the salt and pepper to taste.
7. Secure the lid and select the manual, high pressure cooker, timed for nine minutes.
8. Perform a quick release and remove the lid. Select the sauté function again and add the shrimp, along with the remaining broth. Cook until the shrimp are opaque, for three to five minutes.
9. Stir in the cheese and remaining butter, letting them melt and turn into a creamy sauce.
10. Sprinkle in the parsley, stir, and serve.

Spicy Honey-Flavored Mahi-Mahi

The spiciness of this dish comes from ginger and sriracha sauce. I add citrus flavor, to give you a taste of Polynesia on a plate. Because the lime juice must be chilled, refrigerate it for about an hour before using. If you want a sweeter flavor, substitute mango-orange juice for the straight orange juice. This recipe uses fish that is not frozen.

Yield: 2 servings

Ingredients:

- 2 mahi mahi fillets
- Sea salt and pepper to taste
- 2 cloves garlic, minced
- 1 1-inch piece of fresh ginger, grated
- ½ lime, juiced and refrigerated
- 2 tablespoons sriracha sauce
- 2 tablespoons honey
- 1 tablespoon orange juice
- 1 cup water

Directions:

1. Sprinkle the fish with sea salt and pepper to taste and set aside.
2. Mix the garlic, ginger, chilled lime juice, sriracha sauce, honey, and orange juice in a bowl. If it is too spicy, you can add more honey or orange juice.
3. Pour the water into the bottom of your Instant Pot and insert the steam rack in the bottom, with the handles up.
4. Place the mahi mahi on the rack in a single layer and pour the sauce over the top.
5. Secure the lid and select the manual, high pressure function for five minutes.
6. Perform a quick release, open the pot, and serve.

Tasty Instant Pot Sea Scallops

Gear up for Mediterranean style scallops, prepared in the blink of an eye. The wine, lemon, garlic, and tomatoes add extra flavor. Serve over buttered angel hair pasta.

Yield: 4 servings

Ingredients:

- 2 tablespoons olive oil
- 1 tablespoon unsalted butter

½ cup onion, chopped

3 teaspoons garlic, chopped

16 ounces raw sea scallops

¾ cup dry white wine

½ lemon, squeezed (use the juice)

6 plum tomatoes, chopped

½ teaspoon dry oregano

Salt and pepper to taste

Directions:

1. Select the sauté function on your Instant Pot and let it heat.
2. Add the olive oil and butter and let it melt.
3. Sauté the onion for about three minutes, then add the garlic and sauté for another minute.
4. Introduce the scallops and let them brown on both sides, but do not cook through.
5. Turn off the sauté function and add the wine, lemon juice, tomatoes, oregano, salt, and pepper.
6. Seal the lid and select the manual, high pressure function for two minutes.
7. Perform a quick release and serve over pasta.

We've used pasta in many of these dishes already, but there are so many ways to prepare pasta that I decided it deserves its own chapter.

Chapter 8: The Best Pasta Recipes

Pasta dishes prepared in an Instant Pot come out perfect. They are never sticky or slimy. Most pasta recipes only take a few minutes to cook in an Instant Pot, so you can have dinner on the table in record time.

Broccoli, Sausage, and Pasta

This is a whole meal prepared in a single pot and it is simply delicious. You'll sauté some of the ingredients, dump the rest in, set the pot to cooking, and you are done before the table can be set.

Yield: 6 servings

Ingredients:

1 tablespoon olive oil

1 pound loose sausage (sweet, mild, or hot)

2 tablespoons water

1 pound penne pasta

1 tablespoon tomato paste

1 teaspoon salt

3 to 4 more cups of water

4 cups fresh broccoli florets

2 cloves garlic, minced

1 teaspoon paprika for garnish

Directions:

1. Select the sauté function on your Instant Pot and heat it up.
2. Add the oil; when it is hot, pour in the sausage and stir while browning. It should brown in about five minutes.
3. Remove the sausage and set it aside. To remove any excess grease from your pot, turn off the unit and carefully extract the inner pot, pouring out the grease as needed.

4. Add two tablespoons of water to the pot and scrape up any brown bits on the bottom.
5. Place the uncooked pasta in the bottom of the pot with the tomato paste and the salt. Mix and smooth into a layer.
6. Pour in just enough water to cover the pasta.
7. Add the broccoli florets on top, stem sides down.
8. Secure the lid and set to manual, high pressure for three minutes and let it do a natural pressure release at the end.
9. Open the pot and stir in the sausage, then select the sauté function and use it to warm up the sausage.
10. Sprinkle with paprika before serving.

Chicken Alfredo Pasta with Spinach

The sauce for this dish is super creamy and flavorful. The recipe calls for penne pasta, but you can also experiment with bow ties, linguini or spaghetti. This kid-friendly pressure cooker pasta meal is perfect for busy weeknights.

Chicken Alfredo is a delightful alternative to spaghetti sauce.

Yield: 4 servings

Ingredients:

- 1 teaspoon olive oil
- 2 boneless chicken breasts
- 1 teaspoon sea salt
- ¼ teaspoon pepper
- 3 to 4 garlic cloves, minced
- 3 cups unsalted chicken stock, divided
- 1 pound penne pasta
- 1 cup heavy cream
- 2 tablespoons unsalted butter
- 1 ounce Parmesan cheese, grated
- 2 cups baby spinach

Directions:

1. Select the sauté function on your Instant Pot and let it heat up.
2. Put in the olive oil.
3. Season the chicken with salt and pepper and put inside your Instant Pot. Brown on both sides, for 1½ minutes per side, and remove to a plate. Set aside.
4. Add the garlic and sauté for about a minute. Remove the garlic to a stainless-steel bowl that fits inside your Instant Pot.
5. Deglaze the pot by pouring in a half cup of the chicken stock and scraping the bottom of the pan. Turn off the pot.
6. Place the pasta in the bottom of your Instant Pot and pour in the rest of the chicken stock to submerge the pasta.
7. Place the chicken breasts on top of the pasta.
8. Pour the heavy cream into the bowl, along with the garlic, and then drop in the unsalted butter. Place the bowl on top of the chicken inside your Instant Pot.

9. Select the manual, high pressure function and set the timer for four minutes.
10. When the cook time is completed, let the pressure release naturally for two minutes before performing a quick release.
11. Remove the bowl carefully (it will be hot) and take out the chicken meat underneath, transferring it to a dish.
12. Melt one half ounce of Parmesan cheese into the ingredients in the bowl, whisking with a fork. When melted, add the other half ounce and whisk again.
13. Taste to see if it needs more salt or pepper and adjust accordingly.
14. Turn on the sauté function of your Instant Pot and wait until it is hot.
15. Add the Alfredo sauce to the pasta in your Instant Pot and stir to coat the pasta.
16. Turn off the pot and stir in the spinach, just long enough for it to wilt before serving.
17. Place some of the pasta on each plate, slice the chicken breasts and divide them evenly among the plates, sprinkling additional Parmesan cheese on top.

Chicken Parmesan Pasta

This dish contains all the flavors of Chicken Parmesan, in the shape of a pseudo-casserole. This recipe says to just spread the butter and breadcrumb mixture atop the finished product and serve it directly, but I prefer to spoon everything into a casserole dish at the end, spreading the breadcrumb mixture on top and placing it under the broiler for a few minutes to increase the crunchiness factor by browning the breadcrumbs.

Yield: 4-5 servings

Ingredients:

2 tablespoons olive oil

½ onion, diced

2 cloves garlic, minced

2 skinless, boneless chicken breasts, cut into bite-sized pieces

1 teaspoon salt

½ teaspoon pepper

1 teaspoon dried Italian seasonings

1 24-ounce jar spaghetti sauce

2 cups water

2 cups pasta, (elbows, bow ties, or rigatoni)

1 cup mozzarella cheese, shredded

½ cup unseasoned bread crumbs

2 tablespoons butter, melted

½ cup Parmesan cheese

Directions:

1. Turn on the sauté function of your Instant Pot and let it heat up.
2. Add the oil to the pot, then add the onion, sautéing until translucent, for about three minutes.
3. Add the garlic and sauté for another minute.
4. Sprinkle the salt and pepper over the chicken pieces and place them in the pot to brown. Cook for two minutes, stirring constantly.
5. Pour in the spaghetti sauce and water; stir to combine.
6. Add the pasta and use a wooden spoon or silicone spatula to push it down until the pasta is covered by liquid.
7. Select the manual, high pressure function, and set the cook time for 10 minutes.
8. When the timer goes off, perform a quick release.
9. Stir in the mozzarella cheese. If you're using the broiler, this is the time to transfer everything to a casserole dish.
10. Place the bread crumbs in a small bowl and add the melted butter. Mix well and spread over the top of the chicken mixture.

11. Sprinkle the parmesan cheese on top. Serve immediately or pop it into the broiler to crisp up the crumbs and melt the cheese before offering it up for consumption.

Creamy Tortellini Alfredo

You can find frozen or refrigerated tortellini in your local grocery store. This recipe also calls for pancetta, which can usually be found in the deli section of most grocery stores. If you cannot locate any, you can use salami, although it has a harsher flavor than pancetta, so you may wish to use less.

Tortellini are delightful morsels stuffed with cheese or meat.

Yield: 4 servings

Ingredients:

   3 tablespoons salted butter

   1 green onion or shallot, diced

5 ounces pancetta, diced

½ teaspoon garlic powder

½ teaspoon pepper

⅛ teaspoon nutmeg

2½ cups water

15 to 20 ounces fresh tortellini

1 10-ounce box frozen peas

¾ cup Parmesan cheese, grated

¾ cup half and half

4 ounces cream cheese, cubed

Directions:

1. Select the sauté function on your Instant Pot and let it heat up.
2. Add the butter and let it melt.
3. Add the shallot or onion and sauté for about two minutes.
4. Add the pancetta and sauté for another two minutes
5. Add the garlic powder, pepper, and nutmeg, stirring to combine.
6. Pour in the water, followed by the tortellini. Cover the tortellini as much as possible by pressing it down with a spatula.
7. Secure the lid, select the manual, high pressure function, and set the timer for four minutes.
8. When the cook time has elapsed, perform a quick release.
9. Switch to the sauté mode and add the frozen peas. They should thaw in one or two minutes. Stir and sauté for at least one minute.
10. Add the parmesan cheese, half and half, and cream cheese; stir gently until everything has melted, for two to three minutes.
11. Turn off the pot and let it set a few minutes to thicken and cool, then serve.

Easy Carbonara

Carbonara is a cream sauce flavored with ham or bacon. It makes a classic dish, rich with heavy cream and parmesan cheese. In this recipe I throw in some frozen peas for good measure...and to provide a pop of color.

Peas brighten your carbonara.

Yield: 6 servings.

Ingredients:

    6 slices thick bacon, cut into small pieces

    1 medium onion, chopped

    3 cloves garlic, minced

    16 ounces dry spaghetti or fettuccini, broken to fit in the pot

    4 cups water

    8 ounces Parmesan cheese, grated

    3 eggs

    ¼ cup heavy cream

½ cup frozen peas

Directions:

1. Turn on your Instant Pot to the sauté setting and let it heat up.
2. Add the bacon pieces, cooking until they are golden brown. Then remove to a paper towel-covered plate to drain.
3. Add the onions to the pot and sauté for one to two minutes, until softened.
4. Add the garlic and sauté for another minute.
5. Break the pasta to fit into the pot and cover it with water.
6. Seal the lid, select the manual, high pressure setting and cook for five minutes.
7. While cooking, whisk half of the Parmesan cheese into the eggs.
8. As soon as the cook time is completed, perform a quick release, open carefully, and stir in the egg mixture along with the heavy cream. Stir constantly until the pasta is well coated.
9. Pour in the frozen peas along with half the bacon and stir well. It should take only a minute to thaw and cook the peas.
10. Sprinkle the rest of the Parmesan cheese and the bacon on top, then serve.

Easy Spaghetti and Meatballs

Here is a quick and simple meal you can prepare in about 15 minutes with jarred spaghetti sauce. The meatballs are delicious. I add onion and green or red pepper to my meatballs, but if you don't want them, just leave them out. This recipe makes enough for four to five people.

Spaghetti and meatballs is a staple of the American dinner table.

Yield: 4-5 servings

Ingredients:

- ¼ cup unseasoned breadcrumbs
- 1 teaspoon Italian seasoning
- 1 clove garlic, minced
- ½ onion, minced
- ½ green or red bell pepper, minced
- ½ teaspoon salt
- ¼ teaspoon pepper
- ¼ cup milk
- 1 egg
- 1 pound ground beef

1 jar of spaghetti sauce

Water

8 to 10 ounces of pasta

Directions:

1. In a bowl, combine the breadcrumbs, Italian seasoning, garlic, onion, bell peppers, salt, pepper, and milk.
2. Add the egg and mix everything together.
3. Add the beef and mix in well.
4. Turn on the sauté function of your Instant Pot and let it heat up.
5. Pour the sauce in the bottom of the pot.
6. Pour two sauce jars full of water into the pot.
7. Add the pasta and cover it with as much liquid as possible.
8. Roll the meat mixture in the bowl into golf-ball-sized meatballs and set them on top of the pasta. You should be able to make up to 10 meatballs.
9. Seal the lid of the pot and select the manual, high pressure function, with a cook time of 11 minutes.
10. Let the pressure release naturally for eight minutes before performing a quick release.
11. Open the pot, stir, and serve.

Fajita Pasta with Chicken

The only thing missing from this fajita recipe is the flour tortillas, but you'll never miss them because of the pasta. You may never want regular chicken fajitas again, because this dish is so delicious.

Yield: 4-6 servings

Ingredients:

2 tablespoons olive oil

1 pound boneless, skinless chicken breasts, cut into bite-sized strips

3 tablespoons dry fajita seasoning

1 medium onion, diced

2 bell peppers, diced

5 cloves garlic, minced

1 10-ounce can tomatoes with green chilies or fire-roasted tomatoes

2½ cups chicken broth

8 ounces uncooked penne pasta

½ teaspoon black pepper

Directions:

1. Select the sauté function on your Instant Pot and let it heat up.
2. Add the olive oil, half the chicken strips, and half the fajita seasoning. Sauté until the chicken turns white, then remove to a plate. Do the same with the rest of the chicken and seasoning.
3. Add a little more olive oil to the bottom of the pot if it is dry. Sauté the onions and bell peppers together for two to three minutes, until softened.
4. Add the garlic and sauté for another minute.
5. Return the chicken to the pot and pour the tomatoes, juice and all, into the pot, followed by the chicken broth.
6. Drop in the uncooked pasta and use a spatula to force it underneath the liquid.
7. Seal the lid and select the manual, high pressure function with the timer set for six minutes.
8. When the timer goes off, let the pot release pressure naturally for about five minutes, and then perform a quick release.
9. Add black pepper, stir, and serve.

Instant Pot Bolognese

Bolognese is another pasta sauce. What sets it apart from other red sauces is that it is primarily meat – beef, pork, or both, with a little tomato sauce added. This particular recipe adds a bit of milk and wine at the end to boost the richness of the dish. If you prefer not to use wine, you can substitute beef stock.

Bolognese sauce is a meaty pasta sauce.

Yield: 6 servings

Ingredients:

    1 tablespoon olive oil

    1 onion, finely chopped

    3 stalks celery, finely chopped

    2 carrots, finely chopped

    2 cloves garlic, minced

    1 6-ounce can tomato paste

    2 pounds lean ground beef, pork, or a combination

    1 teaspoon salt

    1 teaspoon pepper

    1½ teaspoons dried thyme

    1 teaspoon dried oregano

    1 teaspoon dried basil

    1 28-ounce can crushed tomatoes

1 cup whole milk

1 cup dry red wine

Directions:
1. Select the sauté function on your Instant Pot and let it heat up.
2. Add the olive oil to the pot and sauté the onions, celery, and carrots for three to four minutes, until the onion becomes translucent and the other vegetables soften.
3. Add the garlic and sauté for another minute.
4. Add the tomato paste and stir into the vegetables.
5. Add the ground beef. Break it apart and let it brown.
6. Add the salt, pepper, thyme, oregano, and basil.
7. Pour in the crushed tomatoes. Stir to combine thoroughly.
8. Add the milk and wine, stir, and seal the lid.
9. Select the manual, high pressure setting for 20 minutes. Let the pot depressurize naturally for 10 minutes and then perform a quick release.
10. Turn on the sauté function and stir the sauce. Let it sauté for five minutes, then ladle over cooked pasta to serve.

Lasagna in an Instant Pot

You can make lasagna in an Instant Pot, but you will need a six- or seven-inch springform pan that fits inside. In this version of lasagna, you begin with dry noodles. You will break them to fit into the pan. Make two long, folded strips of foil to use as a sling. These will lie, crisscrossed, beneath the springform pan to make it easier to safely lift out at the end. The finished dish will be heavy, so make sure your foil strips are strong enough to hold up under the weight.

If you like mushrooms in your lasagna, sauté some slices along with the vegetables.

Yield: 6 servings

Ingredients:

- 1 tablespoon olive oil
- 1 onion, chopped
- 2 cloves garlic, minced
- 1 pound lean ground beef
- 8 ounces ricotta cheese
- 1 cup shredded mozzarella cheese, divided
- 1 cup grated Parmesan cheese, divided
- 1 egg
- 1½ teaspoons Italian seasoning
- ¼ teaspoon salt
- ¼ teaspoon pepper
- 1 package oven-ready lasagna noodles
- 1 20-ounce jar spaghetti sauce

Directions:

1. Set your Instant Pot to the sauté function and let it heat up.
2. Place the oil in the pot and add the onions. Sauté for three minutes, then add the garlic and sauté for another minute.
3. Add the ground beef and brown the meat. Turn off your Instant Pot. Scoop everything out into a bowl and set it aside.
4. In another bowl, mix the ricotta cheese, a half cup each of the mozzarella and Parmesan cheeses, the egg, Italian seasoning, salt, and pepper. Set aside.
5. Break the lasagna noodles in pieces to cover the bottom of the springform pan.
6. Spoon a layer of sauce over the noodles (about a third of the jar).
7. Add half the ground beef.
8. Lay down half of the cheese mixture.
9. Add another layer of dry noodles.
10. Layer another third of the sauce.
11. Put the rest of the ground beef on top.
12. Place the rest of the cheese mixture on top of that.
13. Top with more broken noodles and the rest of the tomato sauce spread over them.
14. Sprinkle the remaining mozzarella and Parmesan cheese over the sauce.
15. Set the trivet in the bottom of the pot and add 1½ cups of water.
16. Cover the springform pan loosely with foil and prepare your foil slings.
17. Place the slings, crisscrossed, on top of the trivet and set the pan on top.
18. Seal the lid and Select the manual, high pressure function with the timer set for 20 minutes.
19. At the end of the cook time, let the pressure release naturally for 10 minutes, then perform a quick release.

20. Carefully extract the pan using the slings (it will be hot). Set it under a broiler just long enough to brown the cheese.
21. Let it set for three minutes, cut, and serve.

Mac N Cheese

Who doesn't like a creamy macaroni and cheese with crunchy breadcrumb topping and the flavor of bacon? This recipe is chock-full of really good stuff. I use mild and sharp cheddar for this dish but feel free to experiment with your favorite cheeses.

Macaroni and cheese is a beloved American comfort food.

Yield: 4-6 servings

Ingredients:

    1 pound uncooked elbow macaroni

    4 cups water

    3 tablespoons butter, cut into 3 pieces

1 teaspoon salt

1 cup shredded sharp cheddar cheese

1 cup shredded mild cheddar cheese

½ teaspoon dry mustard

1 cup whole milk

½ cup cooked crispy bacon, broken into small pieces

Directions:
1. Place the pasta, water, butter, and salt into your Instant Pot. Select the manual, high pressure setting and cook for four minutes.
2. At the end of the cook time, let the pressure release naturally for 10 minutes and then perform a quick release.
3. The liquid should be absorbed, but pour out anything that remains.
4. Stir the pasta and select the sauté function.
5. Mix the two cheeses and dry mustard in a small bowl.
6. Pour the mixture into the pot and stir to mix.
7. Add the milk and stir well.
8. Let the macaroni and cheese begin to bubble, then sprinkle the bacon on top.
9. Serve immediately.

Better-Than-Kids' Mac and Cheese
This is a slightly elevated macaroni and cheese with multiple levels of flavor, including spicy. Garlic powder, hot sauce, and a variety of cheeses are used to form this marvelous creation. I crumble bacon on top and serve with sliced green onion, but those are simply additions to an already wonderful dish. This recipe serves six to 8.

Ingredients:
4 cups chicken broth
1 teaspoon hot sauce
2 tablespoons butter
1 teaspoon garlic powder

½ teaspoon salt
½ teaspoon pepper
16 ounces uncooked elbow macaroni
2 cups shredded Monterey Jack cheese
1 cup shredded Mozzarella cheese
1 cup shredded Parmesan cheese
½ to 1 cup milk

Directions:
1. Pour the chicken broth, hot sauce, butter, garlic powder, salt, and pepper into your Instant Pot and stir to combine.
2. Add the macaroni and make sure it is mostly submerged.
3. Secure the lid and select the manual, high pressure cooker, for five minutes.
4. When the timer goes off, perform a quick release.
5. Stir in the cheeses and the milk; stir until smooth. Taste and add salt or pepper as needed.
6. Serve with crispy bacon and slices of green onion on top.

Pad Thai In An Instant Pot
Pad thai is an Asian dish that uses rice noodles and shrimp with vegetables; I've found it quite delicious. It is also easy to prepare in an Instant Pot and will quickly become a favorite.

Rice noodles and bean sprouts make pad thai special.

Yield: 4 servings

Ingredients:

    8 ounces rice noodles, cooked per package instructions

    4 tablespoons vegetable oil, divided

    ⅓ cup brown sugar

    3 tablespoons rice vinegar

    3 tablespoons fish sauce

    2 tablespoons soy sauce

    2 cloves garlic, minced

    4 green onions, chopped, divided

    2 carrots, julienned

    3 large eggs, beaten

2 cups fresh bean sprouts

1 pound uncooked shrimp, deveined

1 lime

⅓ cup cilantro

¼ cup peanuts, crushed

Directions:
1. Prepare the noodles per the package instructions and drain well. Place in a dish, add one tablespoon of the vegetable oil, and toss to coat. This will prevent them from sticking together. Set the dish aside.
2. Combine the brown sugar, rice vinegar, fish sauce, and soy sauce. Whisk to mix and set aside.
3. Select the sauté function on your Instant Pot and let the pot heat up.
4. Add the rest of the vegetable oil, the garlic, and half of the green onions. Sauté for two minutes.
5. Add the carrots and sauté for two more minutes.
6. Push everything to the sides of your Instant Pot.
7. Add the beaten eggs to the middle and scramble until cooked through.
8. Stir in the sprouts and cook for one more minute.
9. Add the shrimp and stir everything back together in the pot so the ingredients are well combined.
10. Secure the lid and select the manual, high pressure, setting the cook time for two minutes.
11. As soon as the cook time has elapsed, perform a quick release and open the pot. Do not turn off the pot. It should revert to warming mode.
12. Add the noodles and sauce and toss all together. Replace the lid, but do not lock it down. Just keep it warm.
13. When it starts to bubble, squeeze the lime juice in and stir it in. Serve with cilantro, peanuts, and green onions on the side.

Pasta Faggioli Soup

A friend of mine used to make this soup when she was cleaning out the refrigerator. We dreamed of that day! Her mom came from Italy, so her recipe was authentic. Unfortunately for us, she kept the recipe a family secret. However, this recipe comes pretty close to the real thing; I think you'll enjoy it.

The soup is full of ditalini (literally, "tiny thimbles") pasta and all kinds of yummy beans. If you want fiber, this is a good way to get it. Regarding the bulk sausage, you can use the hot variety if you wish; I just happen to prefer the mild sausage.

I like a lot of beans in my soup and this is a *lot* of beans. This recipe includes instructions for cooking your own beans. Because the process does take a couple hours, including the time needed to pressurize the pot and decompress it at the end, I recommend cooking the beans one or more days ahead of time. Or, you can wimp out like I often do and use three cans of already cooked beans. Yes, instructions for using canned beans are also included below.

Ditalini pasta is essential to pasta Faggioli.

Yield: 4-6 servings

Ingredients:

½ cup dry pinto beans

½ cup dried cannellini beans

½ cup dry red kidney beans

5 cups water

4 cloves garlic, sliced

2 tablespoons olive oil

1 tablespoon salt

1 tablespoon olive oil

½ onion, chopped

2 stalks celery, diced

1 large carrot, chopped

2 cloves garlic, chopped

1 pound Italian bulk sausage

4 cups chicken broth

1 15-ounce can diced tomatoes with juice

1 15-ounce can tomato sauce

1 teaspoon salt

½ teaspoon black pepper

1½ teaspoons dried Italian seasoning

¼ teaspoon red pepper flakes, crushed

1 cup ditalini pasta, cooked al dente

Parmesan cheese and fresh basil for garnish

Directions:

1. Rinse the beans (all kinds) and cull out any bad ones.
2. Place the beans in your Instant Pot and pour in the water.
3. Add the sliced garlic (adjust the amount to your taste), two tablespoons of olive oil and a tablespoon of salt.
4. Select the high pressure cooker function and a cook time of 45 minutes.
5. When the cook time is completed, let the pot decompress naturally; this may take 15 to 20 minutes. Remove the beans and set them aside.
6. Alternatively, drain and rinse three cans of beans thoroughly. You'll add these to the pot when you pour in the chicken stock.

7. Set your Instant Pot to sauté and let it heat up.
8. Add the olive oil and let it heat up.
9. Add the onion, celery, and carrots to your Instant Pot and sauté until softened, three to four minutes
10. Add the garlic and sauté it for another minute.
11. Add the sausage and brown it well. If too much grease settles in the bottom of the pot, turn off the pot and drain some off before continuing.
12. Add the broth, beans, diced tomatoes, tomato sauce, salt, pepper, Italian seasoning, and red pepper flakes.
13. Seal the lid and select the manual, high pressure function, cooking for 10 minutes.
14. Let the pot release pressure naturally for four minutes and then perform a quick release.
15. Open and stir in the cooked pasta.
16. Serve in bowls with a grating of Parmesan cheese and a sprig of basil as garnish.

Pasta in Cream Sauce with Sausage

This recipe is made with Italian sausage. I use the mild version because I feel the mild sausage blends a little better with the cream sauce in this recipe, but you can use hot and spicy sausage if you wish. I use seashell pasta, but penne can also be used.

Yield: 6 servings

Ingredients:

1 tablespoon olive oil

½ cup onions, chopped

2 cloves garlic, minced

1 pound Italian sausage

½ cup dry white wine

1 cup bell peppers, chopped

1 tablespoon sugar

1½ teaspoons dried basil

1 teaspoon oregano

1 teaspoon salt

¼ teaspoon black pepper

1½ cups water

1 28-ounce can crushed tomatoes

½ pound dry pasta

½ cup heavy cream (or half and half, if you must)

Fresh shredded Parmesan cheese for garnish

Fresh chopped parsley for garnish

Directions:

1. Select the sauté setting on your Instant Pot and let it heat up.
2. Add the oil and onions and sauté for three minutes.
3. Add the garlic and sauté for another minute
4. Add the sausage and brown well.
5. Pour in the white wine to deglaze the pot and cook until it's almost evaporated.
6. Turn off the pot.
7. Add the bell peppers, sugar, basil, oregano, salt, and pepper. Stir together.
8. Add the water, tomatoes with juice included, and pasta; again, stir to combine.
9. Seal the lid, select the manual, high pressure function, and set the cook time for five minutes.
10. When the cook time is completed, perform a quick release and open the lid.
11. Select the sauté function again.
12. Add the cream and simmer for two to three more minutes to absorb the remaining liquid in the pot.
13. Sprinkle each serving with Parmesan cheese and parsley.

Penne In Vodka Sauce

I always thought vodka sauce was hard to make because you paid so much for it at a restaurant. That light pink sauce tasted so elegant. However, it is incredibly easy to prepare; you can make it in about 30 minutes in your Instant Pot.

Vodka sauce comes out a pretty pink color with great taste.

Yield: 4 servings

Ingredients:

- 1 tablespoon olive oil
- 1 onion, diced
- 6 cloves garlic, minced
- 1 teaspoon red pepper flakes, crushed
- ½ cup vodka
- 1 28-ounce can tomato puree
- 1 pound penne pasta
- 1 teaspoon salt
- 2 cups water
- ½ cup heavy cream
- ¼ cup grated Parmesan cheese

Fresh parsley, chopped, for garnish

Directions:

1. Select the sauté function on your Instant Pot and let it heat up.
2. Pour in the olive oil and onions. Sauté for three to four minutes or until the onions become translucent.
3. Add the garlic and red pepper flakes and sauté for one more minute.
4. Pour in the vodka and let it cook down for two minutes.
5. Add the tomato puree, pasta, salt, and water; stir to combine. Make sure most of the pasta is under the liquid.
6. Seal the lid and select the manual, high pressure function with a cook time of four minutes.
7. Let the pressure reduce naturally for two minutes before performing a quick release and opening the lid.
8. Pour in the cream and Parmesan cheese and stir until everything has melted.
9. Serve with chopped parsley sprinkled on top.

Satisfying Cheeseburger Pasta

Kids love this recipe and most adults also enjoy it. I prefer the fun shape of wagon wheel pasta, but you can use anything you want, from seashell pasta to bow ties. This is a sizeable dish you're making; it's great for feeding large groups but it can also be frozen for future use. Feel free to change up the meat; sausage and ground turkey work just as effectively as the original ground beef. Regarding the hot sauce, just use what you're comfortable with.

Yield: 10 servings

Ingredients:

1 tablespoon olive oil

1 tablespoon butter

1 onion, chopped

1 clove garlic, minced

1 pound ground beef

1 teaspoon salt

½ teaspoon ground pepper

1 tablespoon ground mustard

3 tablespoons ketchup

3 drops hot sauce

1 pound pasta

3 cups beef broth or water

1 cup milk

1 cup Monterey Jack cheese, shredded

2 cups sharp cheddar cheese, shredded

Directions:

1. Turn your Instant Pot to sauté and let it heat up. Add the olive oil and butter and let the butter melt.
2. Add the onion and sauté for two minutes.
3. Add the garlic and sauté for one minute.
4. Add the ground beef and stir to break it up in the pot. Let it set for a few minutes before stirring to make sure it browns.
5. Add the salt, pepper, mustard, Ketchup, and hot sauce, mixing well.
6. Turn off the pot and add the pasta.
7. Pour in the broth and milk and make sure the pasta is mostly submerged.
8. Seal the lid of the pot, select the manual, high pressure function and set the cook time to about five minutes or half of the cook time stated on the pasta box.
9. Let the pot release its pressure naturally for three minutes before performing a quick release.
10. Stir in the cheeses and let them melt.
11. Serve while hot.

Smooth and Cheesy Taco Pasta

This dish is great for a football party or any time you want some Mexican-inspired food. This one is so good you'll find it hard to believe that it took only a half hour to make and didn't cost hardly anything.

Yield: 8 servings

Ingredients:

- 1 teaspoon olive oil
- 1 pound lean ground beef
- 1 package dry taco seasoning
- 1 16-ounce jar of salsa
- 4 cups chicken broth
- 1 12-ounce box of small pasta shells or rotini
- 2 cups shredded Monterey Jack cheese

Directions:

1. Select the sauté function on your Instant Pot and let it heat up. Add the olive oil.
2. Brown the ground beef until it is almost cooked through.
3. Pour in the taco seasoning and salsa; and stir well to combine.
4. Add the chicken broth and bring the pot to a simmer.
5. Add the pasta and submerge it under the liquid.
6. Secure and seal the lid and select the manual, high pressure function with a cook time of four minutes (or half the regular cooking time for the pasta).
7. At the end of the cook time, perform a quick release and open the pot. Stir and add the cheese.
8. Stir again before serving.

Vegan Pasta Puttanesca

Puttanesca sauce is sometimes called prostitute sauce and there is a reason for that. It is said to have been invented by a prostitute in Naples. She didn't have much money, so she made it using what she had in the cupboard: pasta, tomatoes, olives and a few other ingredients. I'm not sure how true that story is, but I know Puttanesca sauce is pretty tasty.

Puttanesca sauce traditionally contains olives and capers, mixed with tomato sauce.

Yield: 4 servings

Ingredients:

    1 teaspoon olive oil

    3 cloves garlic, minced

    4 cups pasta sauce

    3 cups water

    4 cups dry pasta (elbows or penne)

    ¼ teaspoon red pepper flakes, crushed

    1 tablespoon capers

    ½ cup Kalamata olives, pitted and sliced

    Salt and pepper to taste

Directions:

1. Turn on your Instant Pot to the sauté function and let it heat up.

2. Add the olive oil and garlic and sauté for about a minute. Turn off your Instant Pot.
3. Add the pasta sauce, water, pasta, red pepper flakes, capers, and olives; stir to mix.
4. Seal the lid and select the manual, high pressure function and a cook time of five minutes.
5. Let the pressure release naturally before opening the lid.
6. Stir the pasta and add salt and pepper if desired.

This vegan dish reminds me: I have a whole chapter of vegetarian dishes coming up. I think you'll like them, even if you aren't a vegetarian.

Chapter 9: Healthy and Tasty Vegetarian Recipes

Your Instant Pot is perfect for making vegetarian dishes because it allows vegetables to cook through without getting soggy and often without losing the bulk of their nutrients. I try to eat at least two meatless entrees every week; some of these recipes are my very favorites.

Baked Beans with Mushrooms
Baked beans are an American standard, but this recipe is completely vegetarian. I prefer dried porcinis, but I have also used shitake mushrooms. In this case you must use dried mushrooms because the soaking liquid adds ever so much more flavor to the dish.

The recipe calls for dried beans soaked overnight, but I have been known to use canned beans that are rinsed well and drained. This recipe will require about two 15-ounce cans. Use whatever bean you like.

Serve beans with a little Brown Bread

Yield: 4-6 servings

Ingredients:

    1½ cups dry cannellini beans

    Water

    1 teaspoon salt

    1 ounce dried porcini or shitake mushrooms

    1 cup warm water

    2 tablespoons olive oil

    1 medium onion, diced

    1 medium carrot, diced

    ¼ teaspoon salt

2 cloves garlic, minced

1 14.5-ounce can tomato puree or diced tomatoes

1 tablespoon ketchup

1 tablespoon soy sauce

2 tablespoons brown sugar

2 tablespoons dry onion soup mix

1½ teaspoons paprika

½ teaspoon allspice

2 bay leaves

Directions:

1. Place the dried beans in a bowl and cover them with water. Add salt and soak overnight or for a minimum of eight hours. Drain and rinse before using. If using canned beans, you'll wait until later to add them to the pot.
2. Soak the mushrooms in warm water for 10 minutes until they are rehydrated.
3. Select the sauté function on your Instant Pot and let it heat up.
4. Add the olive oil, onions, and carrots; sauté for five minutes.
5. Add the salt and garlic and sauté for one minute
6. Remove the mushrooms from the water but reserve the water. Chop the mushrooms and sauté them for five minutes.
7. Add the drained and rinsed beans, along with the reserved mushroom liquid and stir to combine.
8. Add the tomatoes, ketchup, soy sauce, brown sugar, dry onion soup mix, paprika, allspice, and bay leaves; stir well.
9. Lock the lid, select the manual, high pressure function, and set the cook time for 12 minutes.
10. At the end of the cooking time, let the pressure release naturally for 15 minutes before performing a quick release. Open the pot and stir.

11. Serve over toast or rice.

Curried Sweet Potatoes, Chickpeas, And Spinach

This is a highly spiced dish. In fact, it contains more herbs and spices than anything else; you can consider it a wake-up call for your senses. It is made with sweet potatoes, but I also have prepared this dish substituting fresh pumpkin and found it equally delicious. This is a small recipe, but it is easily doubled; you only need to add a few minutes to the cook time.

Yield: 2 servings

Ingredients:

1 teaspoon olive oil

½ teaspoon cumin seeds

¾ cup onion, chopped

1 inch fresh ginger, chopped

3 cloves garlic, chopped

1 teaspoon dried coriander

½ teaspoon curry powder

½ teaspoon turmeric

¼ teaspoon cinnamon

¼ teaspoon black pepper

¼ teaspoon cayenne pepper

2 fresh tomatoes, chopped

1 15-ounce can chickpeas, drained

1 to 1½ cups sweet potato, chopped

2 cups water

½ teaspoon salt

2 cups fresh baby spinach

1 teaspoon lemon juice

Directions:

1. Select the sauté function on your Instant Pot and let it heat up.
2. Add the oil and cumin seeds sautéing for a minute, until the seeds change color and start to let loose some fragrance.
3. Add the onion and ginger and sauté for three minutes. Add the garlic and sauté for another minute.
4. Add the coriander, curry, turmeric, cinnamon, black pepper, and cayenne pepper; stir to combine.
5. Add the tomatoes, chickpeas and sweet potato, sautéing for three more minutes.
6. Add the water and salt, stir, and seal the lid.
7. Select the manual, high pressure function for eight minutes.
8. At the end of the cook time, perform a quick release and open the lid. Add the baby spinach and lemon juice and stir until the spinach wilts.
9. Serve immediately.

Garlic Flavored Quinoa with Mushrooms and Cherry Tomatoes
This dish is flavored with cherry tomatoes, carrots, onions, and mushrooms. You'll use finely chopped onions and parsley to garnish the dish and to add additional freshness to the flavor.

Quinoa is a nutritious Middle Eastern grain

Yield: 3 servings

Ingredients:

    3 tablespoons olive oil

    1 onion, sliced

    1 carrot, sliced into coins

    2 cups fresh mushrooms, sliced

    2 tablespoons fresh lemon juice (a whole lemon)

    Zest from half a lemon

    ¼ teaspoon black pepper

    1 teaspoon sea salt

    4 cloves garlic, diced

    1 cup quinoa (red or white)

1 cup vegetable stock

10 cherry tomatoes

Directions:
1. Use the sauté function on your Instant Pot and let it heat up.
2. Add the onions and carrots and sauté for four to five minutes, until softened and the onion is translucent.
3. Add the mushrooms, lemon juice, zest, pepper, sea salt, and garlic; sauté for a few minutes.
4. Add the quinoa and stir.
5. Pour in the stock and scrape down the sides of the pot.
6. Place the cherry tomatoes on top and seal the lid.
7. Select the manual, high pressure function and set the cook time for 10 minutes.
8. At the end of the cook time, let the pressure release naturally for five minutes, then perform a quick release.
9. Garnish and serve.

Lentil Tacos

Lentils have an earthy flavor and that you'll either love...or not. They are a great source of protein and therefore, a staple of the vegetarian diet. Cooked lentils can be made to look somewhat like ground beef, making them a natural when it comes to food like tacos. Its earthy flavor enhances the seasonings in this dish.

Because I am not truly a vegetarian myself, I do add dairy products like sour cream and shredded cheese to my lentil tacos, but this dish is still delicious without them. Maybe you'll want to top it with guacamole or salsa instead. This recipe makes four servings.

When cooked, lentils look much like ground beef in a taco.

Yield: 4 servings

Ingredients:

    4 cups water

    4 ounces tomato sauce

    2 tablespoons taco seasoning

    2 cups dry lentils

    ½ cup onions, chopped

Directions:

1. Place the water, tomato sauce, and taco seasoning in the pot and stir to combine.
2. Add the dry lentils and the onions.
3. Seal the lid and select the manual, high pressure function, setting a cook time of 15 minutes.

4. At the end of the cook time, allow the pressure to release on its own before opening the pot. Let it set for three to five minutes before making up the tacos.

Note: I use taco shells for this dish and I spread a little salsa inside before inserting the lentil mixture. I sprinkle a little lettuce on top along with a dollop of guacamole before serving. I have also added cooked brown rice and hot sauce on occasion.

Mexican-Inspired Quinoa Dish with Lime Sauce
This delicious recipe does need meat at all. I like to use red quinoa because it has a little more crunch than the white type, but suit yourself. The sauce includes vegan mayonnaise, which you can swap out for guacamole, if you prefer.

Yield: 3-4 servings

Ingredients:

1 cup quinoa (dry)

3 cups water

2 tablespoons olive oil

1 red bell pepper, diced

1 medium onion, chopped

1 stick celery, diced

½ long red chili, seeded and minced

1½ teaspoons salt, divided

3 cloves garlic, diced, divided

1 teaspoon red pepper flakes, crushed

1 teaspoon dried oregano

1 teaspoon paprika

1 teaspoon ground cumin

1 teaspoon coriander seed

Half of a 14.5 ounce can of diced tomatoes

1 cup frozen corn kernels

½ cup frozen peas

⅛ cup water

2 tablespoons fresh cilantro, chopped

2 tablespoons vegan mayonnaise (or regular mayonnaise, if you're not vegan)

1 tablespoon fresh lime juice

Directions:

1. Place the quinoa in a bowl and cover it with the three cups of water. Let this soak for at least one hour before draining.
2. Select the sauté function on your Instant Pot and let it heat up.
3. Pour in the olive oil, bell pepper, onion, celery, and the red chili, along with a teaspoon of salt. Sauté until the vegetables are softened, about four minutes.
4. Add two cloves of garlic, the red pepper flakes, oregano, paprika, cumin, coriander, and another half teaspoon of salt; sauté for one to two minutes.
5. Add the tomatoes, corn, peas, and ⅔ cup of water, stirring to combine.
6. Secure the lid and select the manual, high pressure function for four minutes. Let the pressure reduce naturally.
7. While your Instant Pot is cooking, prepare the cilantro sauce by combining the cilantro, a minced garlic clove, the mayonnaise, and the lime juice in a blender. Blend until smooth.
8. Open the lid of your Instant Pot and dish out the quinoa mixture into bowls, drizzling a little sauce on top before serving.

Moroccan Sweet Potato & Lentil Stew

This is a sweet and delicious dish that is best served over cooked brown rice or quinoa to give it added bulk. The sweetness comes not just from the sweet potatoes, but also from the raisins.

Yield: 4-6 servings

Ingredients:

- 1 tablespoon olive oil
- 2 medium onions, chopped
- 5 cloves garlic, minced
- 1 teaspoon turmeric
- 1 teaspoon cinnamon
- 2 teaspoons cumin
- 2 teaspoons paprika
- 2 teaspoons coriander
- ½ teaspoon ground ginger
- 1 teaspoon black pepper
- 1 pinch ground cloves
- 1 pinch red pepper flakes
- 2 sweet potatoes, peeled and cut into one-inch cubes
- 2 celery stalks, chopped
- 4 carrots, diced
- ¼ cup raisins
- 1 cup red lentils
- 2 14.5-ounce cans diced tomatoes, with juice
- 2 cups vegetable stock
- 2 handfuls chopped greens

Directions:

1. Select the sauté function and let your Instant Pot heat up.
2. Pour in the olive and onions and sauté for two to three minutes.
3. Add the garlic and cook for one more minute.

4. In a bowl, mix the turmeric, cinnamon, cumin, paprika, coriander, ginger, pepper, cloves, and pepper flakes. Add half of this mixture to your Instant Pot.
5. Add the sweet potatoes, celery, carrots, and raisins to the pot and stir, sautéing for two minutes.
6. Stir in the lentils, tomatoes and vegetable stock and seal the lid.
7. Select the manual, high pressure function on your Instant Pot and set the cook time to 10 minutes.
8. At the end of the cook time, allow the pressure to reduce naturally.
9. Open the pot and stir in the chopped greens. Serve over rice or quinoa.

Quick Pea Risotto

Risotto is one of my favorite dishes, but when it is bad, it is *really* bad! It can be sticky and gooey, and impossible to work with. Yet, I have never had bad risotto with this recipe. In my Instant Pot, it always comes out fine.

The secret to a fine risotto is the proper preparation of Arborio rice. This rice contains some extra starch which, when prepared correctly, adds to the creamy goodness of the dish. If you like risotto, you'll love this recipe.

Only use Arborio rice when making risotto.

Yield: 2-3 servings

Ingredients

    2 tablespoons butter

    1 medium onion, diced

    2 stalks celery, diced

    ½ teaspoon sea salt

    ½ teaspoon black pepper

    2 cloves garlic, minced

    1 cup Arborio rice, dry

    1 cup frozen green peas

    Zest of one lemon

    2 cups vegetable stock

    1 ounce Parmesan cheese, grated

    2 tablespoons lemon juice

Directions:

1. Select the sauté function on your Instant Pot and let it heat up. Add the butter and let it melt.
2. Add the onion, celery, salt, and pepper, sautéing for three to four minutes, or until the vegetables soften.
3. Add the garlic and sauté it for another minute.
4. Pour the rice and peas into your Instant Pot and stir to combine.
5. Pour in the vegetable stock and add the lemon zest.
6. Scrape everything off the sides of your Instant Pot to submerge it all under the liquid in the pot.
7. Secure the lid and select the manual, high pressure function, setting the cook time for five minutes. At the end of cooking, let the pressure reduce naturally for five minutes before performing a quick release.
8. Open the lid and stir in the Parmesan cheese until it melts, then drizzle with the lemon juice, stir lightly, and serve.

Ratatouille in an Instant Pot

This is a very pretty dish. You layer the vegetables, alternating them to create a snail shape in the bottom of a round pan. It makes for a very impressive presentation, but it also tastes delicious.

Yield: 4 servings

Ingredients:

    1 tablespoon dry thyme

    1 teaspoon sea salt

    ½ teaspoon black pepper

    1 red onion, thinly sliced

    2 medium tomatoes, thinly sliced

1 large zucchini, sliced in circles or half moons

1 medium eggplant, sliced into thin circles or half moons

2 cloves garlic, diced

2 tablespoons olive oil

1 tablespoon aged balsamic vinegar

1 cup water

Directions:

1. Mix the thyme, salt, and pepper in a small bowl.
2. Slice all the vegetables and place them in a large bowl. Sprinkle them with half of the thyme mixture
3. Take up a 6- or 7-inch springform pan that fits into your Instant Pot and line it with foil, so the juices will not escape.
4. Sprinkle the bottom of the pan with half the minced garlic and start layering vegetable slices in the pan. I start with the onion, then add tomato, zucchini, and eggplant, overlapping them around the outer edge of the pan. Keep working inward until the whole bottom is covered with a spiral, snail shape.
5. Sprinkle the top with the rest of the garlic and the thyme mixture.
6. Drizzle with olive oil and balsamic vinegar.
7. Pour the water in the bottom of your Instant Pot and set down the trivet inside. Place the springform pan on top.
8. Lock the lid in place and select the manual, high pressure function, setting the cook time to six minutes.
9. At the end of the cook time, allow the pressure to release naturally, but perform a quick release at the end to be safe before opening the lid.
10. Remove the springform pan with tongs and let it cool for a few minutes before removing the sides and serving your ratatouille on a platter.

Savory Vegetarian Stew

This stew is very hearty and is filled with good things like beans, tomatoes, and corn. It also packs a punch, with cumin and chili powder for spices.

The recipe calls for 15-ounce cans of pinto beans, instead of soaking dry beans overnight and then cooking them for what? Two hours? This recipe will use three cans, mixed or matched, of any type of bean you want to use.

Vegetarian stew is perfect for cold winter nights.

Yield: 6 servings

Ingredients:

   1 tablespoon olive oil

   1 onion, sliced

   2 cloves garlic, minced

   1 bell pepper, diced

   1 fresh jalapeno pepper, seeded and minced

   1 14.5-ounce can diced tomatoes

   4 cups cooked and drained pinto beans

   1 cup frozen or fresh corn kernels

   1½ teaspoons ground cumin

   1 tablespoon chili powder

   1 cup fresh cilantro, chopped

    1½ cups vegetable broth

Directions:

1. Select the sauté function on your Instant Pot and let it heat up
2. Pour in the olive oil, then the onions, and sauté for three minutes or until the onions become translucent.
3. Add the garlic and sauté for a minute.
4. Add the bell pepper and jalapeno and sauté another minute.
5. Add the diced tomatoes with their juice, the beans, corn, cumin, chili powder, cilantro, and the vegetable broth to the pot.
6. Secure the lid and select the manual, high pressure function, setting the cook time to four minutes. Let the pressure release naturally and at the end, release the lid and serve immediately.

Spicy Vegan Chili

This recipe makes massive servings of chili. I usually freeze half of it for later and when I thaw and reheat the chili, it tastes just as good as when I first made it. This chili is spicy enough to clear your sinuses nicely. The Masa flour, commonly used to make tamales, adds a special flavor and texture so don't use anything else. You can find it in any Hispanic food store.

Yield: 12 servings

Ingredients:

    1 tablespoon olive oil

    1 onion, chopped

    1 red bell pepper, diced

    1 green bell pepper, chopped

    2 cloves garlic, minced

    8 ounces fresh mushrooms, chopped

    2 cups water

½ teaspoon garlic powder

½ teaspoon black pepper

1 teaspoon oregano

1 teaspoon chili powder

1 teaspoon paprika

1 15-ounce can pinto beans, drained and rinsed

1 15-ounce can kidney beans, drained and rinsed

1 8-ounce can tomato sauce

1 15-ounce can diced tomatoes with juice

1 6-ounce can tomato paste

2 tablespoons masa flour

Directions:

1. Select the sauté function on your Instant Pot and let it heat up.
2. Pour in the olive oil and sauté the onions and bell peppers for three to five minutes, until vegetables are softened.
3. Add the garlic and sauté it for another minute.
4. Add the mushrooms, water, garlic powder, pepper, oregano, chili powder, paprika, and beans; stir to mix.
5. Add the tomato sauce and diced tomatoes on top; do *not* stir.
6. Select the manual, high pressure function on your Instant Pot, setting the cook time for 10 minutes.
7. At the end of the cook time, let the pressure release naturally for 10 minutes before performing a quick release.
8. Add the tomato paste and masa flour, letting it rest for 10 minutes but stirring occasionally. Serve.

Vegan Posole

Posole is a spicy Mexican dish made from hominy and other items. This recipe calls for red chili puree and jackfruit, which are readily available in most Hispanic grocery stores.

Yield: 8 servings

Ingredients:

- 1 tablespoon olive oil
- 1 medium onion, chopped
- 6 cloves garlic, minced
- 1 14-ounce can of red chili puree
- 2 20-ounce cans jackfruit
- 6 cups vegetable broth
- 2 25-ounce cans hominy

Garnishes: lime juice, cilantro, or thinly sliced radishes

Directions:

1. Select the sauté function on your Instant Pot and let it heat up.
2. Add the oil and onions and sauté them for four minutes
3. Add the garlic and sauté it for one more minute.
4. Pour in the chili puree and cook for another minute.
5. Add the jackfruit and cook for two minutes. Use a potato masher to break up the jackfruit.
6. Add the vegetable broth and secure the lid.
7. Select the manual, high pressure function on your Instant Pot, setting the cook time for 10 minutes. At the end of that time, let the pressure release naturally for 20 minutes before performing a quick release.
8. Remove the lid and pour in the hominy. Again, select the high pressure cooker, this time for one minute.
9. Allow the pressure to release naturally before opening carefully. Season the dish with salt to taste, garnish, and serve.

Veggie Chow Mein

This is a tasty vegetarian chow mein recipe that uses rice or ramen noodles that you must bury under the water to cook. Your taste buds will be very happy with the delicious spices.

Add bamboo shoots, mushrooms, and water chestnuts to this dish for something really special.

Yield: 4 servings

Ingredients:

    2 tablespoons olive oil

    1 onion, sliced

    1 inch fresh ginger, chopped or grated

    4 carrots, sliced

    4 stalks celery, sliced

    1 small leek, cleaned and sliced

2 cloves garlic, minced

1 tablespoon Worcestershire sauce

2 tablespoons soy sauce

2 tablespoons Chinese five spice powder

1 tablespoon oriental seasoning

1 teaspoon coriander

1 teaspoon parsley

Salt and pepper to taste

1 pack rice or ramen noodles

Directions:

1. Select the sauté function on your Instant Pot and let it heat up.
2. Add the olive oil, onion, ginger, carrots, and celery; sauté for about five minutes.
3. Add the leeks and garlic. Sautéing for another minute or two.
4. Add the Worcestershire sauce, the soy sauce, five spice powder, oriental seasoning, coriander, parsley, salt, and pepper; stir to combine.
5. Add the water and stir again.
6. Place the noodles in the pot and carefully bury them under the liquid and the vegetables.
7. Seal the lid and select the manual, high pressure function for 13 minutes.
8. Let the pressure release naturally for 10 minutes before performing a quick release.
9. Open the lid, stir, and serve.

Not all bean, rice, and grain dishes are vegetarian. The next chapter will explore ways to use grains to prepare delectable dishes in your Instant Pot, including the making of quick breads.

Chapter 10: Amazing Grain and Breads Recipes

Your Instant Pot is perfect for making recipes using grains like quinoa and rice, so this chapter takes advantage of that quality. We've already seen that the Instant Pot can cook beans successfully; now we get to explore the world of breads. This chapter includes plenty of additional grain dishes, but it also contains a group of tasty bread recipes, ranging from crusty bread, to quick breads like pumpkin and zucchini. The sky is the limit with an Instant Pot; this chapter reinforces that point.

Baked Beans and Ham

As kids, baked beans were a favorite for my family. We looked forward to summer parties where baked beans were as common as the ever-present watermelon. This recipe contains the smoky flavor of bacon and garlic, as well as the sweetness of maple syrup and molasses. Even the ham carries pleasant summer memories, left over from a glorious ham dinner. You can serve this dish any time of the year, but for me, it will always evoke the ambiance of summer.

Yield: 6 servings

Ingredients:

    1 pound navy beans

    6 cups water

    6 slices thick bacon, chopped

    1 onion, chopped

    4 cloves garlic, minced

    ¼ teaspoon sea salt

    ¼ teaspoon pepper

    2 cups water

    ¼ cup pure maple syrup

    ½ cup molasses

¼ cup ketchup

½ cup barbecue sauce

1 tablespoon prepared honey mustard

1 teaspoon balsamic vinegar

⅓ cup brown sugar

1 cup leftover ham, diced

Directions:

1. Soak the beans in six cups water overnight, drain and rinse. Set aside.
2. Select the sauté function on your Instant Pot and let it heat up. Add the bacon and cook until almost done.
3. Add the onion and sauté for about three minutes.
4. Add the garlic and sauté for another one minute.
5. Add the salt, pepper, water, syrup, ketchup, molasses, barbecue sauce, mustard, and vinegar and stir to combine. Let this come to a simmer.
6. Pour in the beans, brown sugar, and ham, stirring to combine.
7. Seal the lid and select the manual, high pressure function on your Instant Pot, with a cook time of 30 minutes. Let pressure release naturally for 20 minutes afterwards, then perform a quick release.
8. Sample the beans; if they are not quite done, reseal the pot and cook for 10 more minutes on high pressure, using the quick release immediately afterward.
9. If the beans come out watery, select the sauté function and let them simmer with the lid open, stirring frequently for 10 minutes or so. They will thicken as they cool.

Banana Bread in an Instant Pot

A good way to use up aging bananas before they attract flies is to make banana bread. You'll love the results! This bread will come out so moist you'll never want to bake it in an oven again. For this recipe, you will need a six or 7-inch springform pan that fits inside your Instant Pot.

The recipe is quite versatile. For my friends who can't eat nuts, I often make this bread with raisins instead; sometimes I make it plain. I often play with spices as well, adding ginger, nutmeg, a hint of cloves, or other sweet spices.

The best tool to mash bananas with is a plain old fork.

Yield: 1 loaf

Ingredients:

    1 stick butter, room temperature

    ½ cup sugar

    2 eggs

    2 cups all-purpose flour

    ½ teaspoon salt

    1 teaspoon baking soda

    3 bananas, mashed

    ½ cup chopped nuts, dates, or raisins (optional)

    1 cup water

Directions:

1. Prepare the springform pan by buttering the inside.
2. Beat the stick of butter with an electric mixer.
3. Cream the sugar and butter, then add the eggs and beat well until all combined.
4. In another bowl, mix the flour, salt, and baking soda. Gradually stir this mixture into the moist ingredients until just combined.
5. Add the bananas and stir in by hand.
6. Gently fold in any of the optional ingredients.
7. Pour the batter into the pan.
8. Set the trivet in the bottom of your Instant Pot and pour in the water.
9. Take two strips of aluminum foil and fold lengthwise to make a sling that rests, crisscross, beneath the pan but over the trivet. When the cooking process is finished you will be able to grab the ends of the sling and safely extract the pan.
10. Seal the lid and select the manual, high pressure function, setting the cook time for 50 minutes.
11. At the end of the cooking process, let the pressure reduce naturally for 10 minutes, then perform a quick release.
12. Extract the pan and let it cool for 10 minutes or longer before releasing the springform pan, slicing, and serving.

Bean and Beef Stew

This stew will stick to your ribs and give you enough protein to get through your day. At the same time, it is delicious.

Four types of beans are represented here: kidney beans, black-eyed peas, navy beans, and black beans. This recipe shows you how to soften dry beans in your Instant Pot without having to soak them overnight. If you're *really* in a hurry though, you can use canned beans (1½ cups of each), instead; just drain and rinse well before adding.

I prefer round or flank steak for this recipe, giving it a much different texture from chili. One day, I added a jar of roasted red peppers when it was close to the expiration date; I enjoyed the results so much that they've become a standard part of the recipe. The stew freezes well, so don't be intimidated by its massive size.

To fully satisfy your hunger, fill up on bean and beef stew.

Yield: 12 servings

Ingredients:

- ½ cup dry small red kidney beans
- ½ cup dry navy beans
- ½ cup dry black-eyed peas
- ½ cup dry black beans
- 2 tablespoons vegetable oil, divided
- 6 cups water, divided
- 1 onion, sliced
- 2 cloves garlic, minced
- 1½ pounds beef, cut into bite-sized cubes

½ teaspoon salt

¼ teaspoon pepper

1 14.5-ounce can diced tomatoes

1 14-ounce can tomato sauce

1 cup roasted peppers, either canned, fresh, or frozen

1 teaspoon dried parsley

½ teaspoon dried marjoram

½ small cabbage, sliced

2 cups baby carrots

Directions:

1. To soften the beans, pour the dry beans, one tablespoon of vegetable oil and five cups of water into your Instant Pot. Seal and select the manual, high pressure function; set the time for 25 minutes.
2. At the end of the cook time, perform a quick release and pour beans and liquid into a large bowl and set aside.
3. Rinse and dry your Instant Pot before proceeding.
4. Select the sauté function on your Instant Pot and let it heat up.
5. Pour the remaining tablespoon of vegetable oil into the pot along with the onion and sauté for about three minutes. Add the garlic and sauté for another minute
6. Season the beef pieces with salt and pepper and brown them in the pot for about 10 minutes.
7. Add the roasted peppers, diced tomatoes, tomato sauce, and the remaining cup of water. Seal the lid, select the manual, high pressure function, and set the cook time for 20 minutes. At the end of the cook time, perform a quick release.
8. Open the lid, add the roasted peppers, parsley, marjoram, cabbage, and baby carrots.
9. Reseal the lid. Select the manual, high pressure function and set the time for 10 minutes.

10. Perform a quick release and open the pot. Pour in the cooked beans, stir to mix, and select the sauté function. Let the beans warm before serving.

Cornbread in An Instant Pot

Cornbread goes well with many dishes. I love it with ham and bean soup, but it is just as tasty alongside pork chops or a chicken dinner. This recipe is sweetened with a little honey and includes kernels of corn.

I make my cornbread with buttermilk and sour cream to add an air of elegance. My brother calls this my fancy cornbread. You will need an 8-inch round cake pan for this recipe.

Savoring leftover cornbread with honey for breakfast!

Yield: 1 loaf

Ingredients:

    1½ cups yellow cornmeal

    ⅔ cup flour

    ⅔ cup sugar

2 teaspoons salt

1 tablespoon baking powder

2 tablespoons honey

1 cup buttermilk

2 large eggs

¼ cup sour cream

¼ cup butter, melted

1 cup frozen corn, thawed

1 cup water

Directions:

1. In a large bowl, combine the corn meal, sugar, flour, salt, and baking powder. Mix thoroughly.
2. In another bowl combine the honey, buttermilk, eggs, sour cream, and melted butter. Whisk together until well combined.
3. Pour a little of the wet ingredients into the dry ingredients and stir to combine.
4. Fold some of the thawed corn into the dry ingredients.
5. Alternate adding wet ingredients and corn into the dry ingredients until everything is mixed in.
6. Let the batter set undisturbed and uncovered for a full 15 minutes.
7. Pour the batter into a greased 8-inch round cake pan.
8. Pour one cup of water into the bottom of your Instant Pot and insert the trivet. Fold two pieces of foil into strips for a sling and set them, crisscrossed, between the trivet and the pan, bringing the ends up the sides of the pot. This will make it safe and easy to extract the pan without burning your fingers.
9. Set the pan on top of the trivet, being careful not to get any water inside the pan.
10. Seal the lid of your Instant Pot, select the manual, high pressure function, and set the time to 20 minutes.

11. At the end of the cook time, perform a quick release and lift the pan out, using the strips of foil. Let it set, undisturbed, for five minutes before cutting and serving.

Crusty Bread in an Instant Pot

This bread is so simple to make you will be astounded. It is made from five common ingredients. The bread comes out of the pot nice and crusty on the outside but soft and delicious on the inside.

I use a metal coffee can to make this bread. You will need something long and tall that is large enough to hold four cups of bread dough. It also must be heatproof and sized to fit inside your Instant Pot. My mother used to make this bread in her old pressure cooker (the one that set the house on fire); it was our favorite because of the crunchy crust.

Yield: 1 loaf

Ingredients:

1 teaspoon olive oil

2 cups all-purpose flour

½ teaspoon baking soda

1¼ cups plain yogurt made from whole milk

Water

Directions:

1. Pour the olive oil into the container and swirl it around to coat the bottom and the sides.
2. Set the trivet in the bottom of your Instant Pot. The coffee can will set on top.
3. Measure out the flour and baking soda into a large bowl and mix together. Add the yogurt and mix with a fork until you can use your hands and shape the dough into a ball.
4. Knead the dough lightly for a few minutes. The dough will be chunky and a little sticky. Place the elongated ball into the bottom of the coffee can and splash a little more olive oil on the surface of the bread.

5. Take a piece of foil and place it over the opening. Pleat it a little to mound the top and make some room for the bread to expand. Tie the foil to the edge of the coffee can with some kitchen string.
6. Set the can on the trivet and pour water outside the can, bringing water up to about half its height.
7. Lock the lid, select the manual, high pressure function, and set the cook time for 25 minutes.
8. At the end of the cook time, perform a quick release and check the bread for doneness, using a toothpick inserted into the center of the loaf. If it comes out clean, the bread is done. If not, put it back under pressure for 10 more minutes.
9. Carefully remove the can from your Instant Pot and let it cool for 10 minutes before removing from the container and slicing.

Healthy and Delicious Quinoa Chicken Dish

Quinoa bowls are a popular way to eat an entire meal in a container. This recipe includes a range of vegetables and spices along with the chicken. You'll find it very flavorful and quite filling.

Prepared quinoa often has small rings around the seeds.

Yield: 2 servings

Ingredients:

- 2 deboned, skinless chicken breasts, cut into strips
- 1 teaspoon sea salt, divided
- ¼ teaspoon pepper
- 1 tablespoon dried basil
- 1 tablespoon olive oil
- 1 small onion, diced
- 1 clove garlic, minced
- 1 cup uncooked quinoa
- 1 cup water
- 1 red bell pepper, diced
- 1 yellow bell pepper, diced
- 2 cups baby spinach, chopped
- 1 tablespoon Dijon mustard
- 2 tablespoons olive oil
- 2 tablespoons lemon juice
- 1 cup fresh basil leaves

Directions:

1. Set the chicken strips on a plate and season with a half teaspoon of salt, the pepper and the dry basil. Set aside.
2. Select the sauté function on your Instant Pot and let it heat up.
3. Pour in the olive oil, add the onion, and sauté for three minutes. Add the garlic and sauté for another minute.
4. Pour in the uncooked quinoa and let it toast slightly.
5. Add the water and stir.
6. Place the chicken strips on top and seal the lid. Select the manual, high pressure function and set the cook time for five minutes.

7. At the end of the cook time, let the pressure release naturally for 15 minutes.
8. prepare the chopped peppers and baby spinach while you're waiting.
9. Prepare the dressing by mixing in a bowl the remaining sea salt, Dijon mustard, olive oil and lemon juice.
10. Arrange baby lettuce and basil leaves in the bottom of two bowls. Top with the peppers. Add the quinoa mixture on top of that, then the chicken. Drizzle with dressing, and serve.

Irish Soda Bread

Irish soda bread has always been a treat on St. Patrick's Day, but it is so easy to make in our Instant Pot, that we now enjoy it much more often.

The original soda bread did not include raisins; it was just a plain quick bread, rather like baking soda biscuits. The raisins in this recipe add a sweeter flavor and a delightful texture. You can also use dates, dried cranberries, currants, or strawberries instead of raisins.

Soda bread is flaky and moist inside with a hard crust on the outside. You will need a 6-quart ovenproof bowl to help form the hard outer crust. The bread is placed in the bowl, which is then set inside your Instant Pot.

Irish soda bread is crusty on the outside and soft and fluffy on the inside.

Yield: 1 loaf

Ingredients:

    3½ cups all-purpose flour

    1 teaspoon salt

    1 teaspoon baking soda

    ½ teaspoon baking powder

    2 tablespoons sugar

    ⅓ cup olive oil

    1 egg, beaten

1½ cups buttermilk

1 cup raisins

2 cups water

Butter for greasing the pan

Directions:

1. In a bowl, whisk together the flour, salt, baking soda, baking powder, and sugar.
2. Add the olive oil, stirring it in with a fork to moisten the mix as much as possible.
3. Make a well in the center of the dry ingredients. Break the egg in the well and add the buttermilk.
4. Incorporate the dry mix into the liquids by pulling it in from the sides until the flour mixture is all absorbed into the dough.
5. Add the raisins. Dust your hands with flour and knead the sticky dough for a few minutes until a rough ball is formed.
6. Coat the oven-safe bowl with butter and place the dough in the bowl.
7. Set the trivet in the bottom of your Instant Pot and pour in two cups water.
8. Cover the top of the oven-safe bowl with foil and seal the edges around the rim to prevent any water from dripping into the bread.
9. Before placing the bowl on the trivet, make a foil sling, placing two reinforced strips of foil in an "x" shape beneath the bowl. The bread is heavy, so you'll need a little extra support to extract it from the pot.
10. Seal the lid of your Instant Pot and select the manual, high pressure function, setting the cook time for 30 minutes. Let the pressure release naturally.
11. Remove the dish from the pot and remove the foil. Let the bread cool before removing from the bowl and cutting.

Monkey Bread

If you've never had monkey bread, you're in for a treat! These awesome little balls of buttery sweet deliciousness are addictively delectable. The bread dough is rolled into miniature balls that are then clumped together in a ring-shaped dish and baked. Afterwards, you simply peel a roll off from the rest, pop it in your mouth, and enjoy. For this recipe you'll need a Bundt pan that fits inside your Instant Pot.

For a true taste treat, pop one of these into your mouth!

Ingredients:

1 cup granulated sugar

3 teaspoons cinnamon

2 cans of southern style large buttered biscuits

1 stick butter

1 cup light brown sugar

1 teaspoon vanilla

1 cup water

Directions:

1. Combine the sugar and cinnamon in a large closeable plastic bag.
2. Pull the biscuits apart and cut each biscuit into four pieces. Place the pieces in the bag with the cinnamon and sugar and shake to coat each biscuit well.
3. Place the biscuit pieces into a lightly oiled non-stick Bundt pan that fits into your Instant Pot. Just pile them all around the bottom and on top of each other.
4. In a saucepan on the stove or a microwave-safe bowl in the microwave, combine the butter, brown sugar, and vanilla. Stir over the heat until the sugar is dissolved. This is your caramel sauce. Pour this sauce over the biscuits in the Bundt pan.
5. Set the trivet in the bottom of your Instant Pot and make a sling out of two folded pieces of foil that loop beneath the Bundt pan and up the sides of your Instant Pot. This will make it easier to extract the Bundt pan from the pot later. Secure the lid and select the manual, high pressure function for a cook time of 23 minutes.
6. Let the pressure release naturally for five minutes before performing a quick release. Lift out the Bundt pan and let the monkey bread cool for 10 minutes.
7. Lay a plate upside down over the opening and flip them together to extract the bread from the pan onto the plate.

Pinto Beans with Chorizo

In this recipe, the beans are added dry and they cook quickly under pressure. This dish will wake up your taste buds and the chorizo will make them very happy.

I usually serve this with either tortilla chips, like nachos, or wrapped up in a flour tortilla. It can also be served over cooked rice.

Spanish chorizo is spicy enough you might need rice to tame its flavor.

Yield: 6 servings

Ingredients:

- 1 tablespoon olive oil
- 4 ounces dry Spanish chorizo, diced
- 1 onion, diced
- 3 cloves garlic, minced
- 2 cups dry pinto beans
- 2 bay leaves
- ½ teaspoon pepper
- 3 cups chicken broth
- 1 15-ounce can diced tomatoes with juice

Directions:

1. Select the sauté function on your Instant Pot and let it heat up.
2. Add the oil, then the chorizo and stir while sautéing until the meat gets crispy on the edges
3. Add the onion and sauté for three minutes.
4. Add the garlic and sauté for another minute.
5. Pour the beans into the pot along with the bay leaves and pepper.
6. Pour in the broth.
7. Secure the lid on your Instant Pot and select the manual, high pressure function, setting the cook time to 35 minutes.
8. At the end of the cook time, let the pressure release naturally. When it's safe, open the pot and check the beans. If they are not fully done, reset the high pressure cooker for 10 more minutes, again letting the pressure release naturally.
9. Remove the bay leaves.
10. Stir in the can of diced tomatoes. Turn on your Instant Pot to sauté; stir until the pot comes to a low simmer before serving. The mixture should thicken up somewhat.

Pork Chops and Rice

Rice is a highly versatile food because it takes on the flavor of anything it is placed with. This particular recipe combines pork chops and rice, along with some frozen vegetables and broth. I prefer long-grain basmati rice for this recipe because I like the texture. It plumps up in liquid and turns fluffy and light. However, you can use any type of long-grain rice.

Yield: 4 servings

Ingredients:

1 tablespoon olive oil

1 cup onions, chopped

1 cup long grain rice, rinsed

1 teaspoon salt

1 teaspoon pepper

4 thin-cut pork chops

¾ cup chicken broth

½ cup frozen mixed vegetables

1 large carrot, julienned

Directions:

1. Layer the ingredients into your Instant Pot in the order given.
2. Seal the lid, select the manual, high pressure function, and set the cook time for five minutes.
3. Allow pressure to release naturally for 10 minutes, then perform a quick release.
4. Remove the pork chops, stir the pot, and serve.

Savory Chicken and Rice

Here's another rice dish, this time using chicken. The recipe calls for jasmine rice, an aromatic, long-grained white rice. However, if necessary, you can substitute basmati rice. You'll want to rinse the rice to prevent scorching before you place it in your Instant Pot.

Yield: 6 servings

Ingredients:

1 teaspoon salt

½ teaspoon pepper

1 pound boneless, skinless chicken thighs

1 tablespoon olive oil

1¾ cups chicken stock, divided

3 green onions, sliced

3 carrots, diced

1 cup mushrooms, sliced

2 cloves garlic, minced

1½ cups uncooked jasmine rice, rinsed

2 tablespoons fresh thyme leaves, chopped and divided

Directions:

1. Select the sauté setting on your Instant Pot and let it warm up
2. Salt and pepper the chicken thighs liberally.
3. Pour the olive oil in the pot and use tongs to sear the chicken pieces for five minutes on each side. Remove chicken and set aside on a plate.
4. Pour in a third cup of the chicken stock to deglaze the pan and set aside the rest. Scrape up all the brown bits from the bottom, using a wooden spoon.
5. Add the green onion, carrots, and mushrooms; sauté these for about four minutes.
6. Add the garlic and sauté for another minute.
7. Pour in the remaining chicken stock, rice, and thyme leaves, stirring to combine.
8. Set the chicken thighs on top of everything else.
9. See that the rice is covered with liquid before sealing the lid.
10. Select the manual, high pressure function and set the timer for 10 minutes.
11. When the cook time is ended, let the pressure release naturally before opening the lid. Remove the chicken and use two forks to shred the meat.
12. Return the chicken to the pot, stir, and serve.

Southern Black-Eyed Peas and Ham

This is an old southern recipe made new by the Instant Pot. My grandmother used her trusty pressure cooker to make this and served it up with cornbread or hoecakes (a.k.a., baking powder biscuits). When the cupboard is getting bare, this recipe can keep you from going hungry and it costs very little to make.

Black-eyed peas are not peas at all, but a type of bean.

Yield: 10 servings

Ingredients:

    1 pound dry black-eyed peas, rinsed (do not soak)

    1 onion, sliced

    2 cloves garlic, minced

    5 ounces cooked ham, diced

    6½ cups chicken, ham, or vegetable stock

    1 teaspoon dried parsley

    1 teaspoon dried thyme

    Salt and pepper to taste

Directions:

1. Place the black-eyed peas in the bottom of your Instant Pot.
2. Layer in the onion, garlic, and cooked ham.
3. Pour in the stock; sprinkle on the parsley and thyme.
4. Secure the lid and select the manual, high pressure function, setting the time for 30 minutes.
5. At the end of the cook time, let the pressure release naturally and open the pot only when it's safe.
6. Season with salt and pepper to taste, then serve.

Spicy Cajun Chicken And Rice

Here's a flavorful dish from the bayou. And I'll give you my homemade Cajun seasoning, just to make the dish even more special.

Combine in a storage container:

- 1 tablespoon paprika
- 1 tablespoon cracked black pepper
- 2 teaspoons dried thyme leaves
- 2 teaspoons dried oregano leaves
- 2 teaspoons garlic powder
- 2 teaspoons onion powder

Use one tablespoon of this mixture for the recipe and store the rest in a glass jar or bottle in a dark area. I store mine in the refrigerator because it tends to keep a little better there.

The chicken breasts need to be sliced in half to make them thinner, otherwise they won't cook in the allotted time

Yield: 4 servings

Ingredients:

2 large deboned, skinless chicken breasts, sliced in half

1 tablespoon Cajun seasoning, divided

1 tablespoon olive oil

1 onion, diced

2 cloves garlic, minced

1 tablespoon tomato paste

1½ cups jasmine rice, rinsed

1 bell pepper, cut into chunks

2 cups chicken broth

Directions:

1. Select the sauté function on your Instant Pot and let it heat up.
2. Take two teaspoons of the Cajun seasoning and sprinkle both sides of each piece of meat.
3. Pour the oil into the bottom of your Instant Pot and brown the chicken pieces on both sides. Remove to a plate and set aside.
4. Add the onion and sauté for two minutes, then add the garlic and sauté for another minute.
5. Stir in the tomato paste and turn off the sauté function.
6. Add the rinsed rice, the rest of the Cajun seasoning, and the bell pepper; pour in the chicken broth.
7. Stir, but see that all the rice is covered by the liquid.
8. Place the chicken pieces on top and seal the lid. Select the manual, high pressure function and set the cook time for 10 minutes.
9. Let the pressure release naturally at the end of the cook time.
10. Remove the chicken, shred the meat with two forks, and stir back into the pot before serving.

Tasty Garlic Beef and Rice Bowl
Here is another tasty rice bowl, this time combining beef and garlic. I have a friend who takes these to work for lunch and the whole office buzzes when she puts it in the microwave, it smells so good! This recipe is good to have on hand for dinner, too.

The best rices for pressure cooking are basmati and jasmine.

Ingredients:

- 1 tablespoon olive oil
- 1 tablespoon unsalted butter
- 1 onion, sliced
- 4 cloves garlic, minced
- 1 teaspoon sea salt
- ½ teaspoon pepper
- 1¼ pounds chuck roast steak (about 1½ inches thick), cut into strips
- ¾ cup unsalted chicken stock, divided
- 1 teaspoon Worcestershire sauce
- 1 tablespoon light soy sauce
- 1 cup jasmine rice, rinsed
- 1 cup cold tap water

1 12-ounce bag frozen mixed vegetables

2 tablespoons cornstarch

2 tablespoons cold water

Directions:

1. Select the sauté function on your Instant Pot and let it heat up.
2. Add the olive oil and the unsalted butter to melt.
3. Add the onion and sauté for three minutes.
4. Add the garlic and sauté for one more minute.
5. Season the chuck roast strips with salt and pepper and brown them in your Instant Pot for three to four minutes. Then cook and stir for another three to four minutes. Remove to a plate and set aside.
6. Combine in a large glass measuring cup ¾ cup of chicken stock, the Worcestershire sauce, and the soy sauce.
7. Once the meat is removed, deglaze the pot using this mixture.
8. Pour in the rest of the chicken stock.
9. Put the meat and its juices back into the pot.
10. Fill a stainless steel bowl that fits inside your Instant Pot with the rinsed rice and set this on top of the steamer rack above the meat mixture. Cover the rice in that bowl with one cup of cold water.
11. Seal the lid and select the manual, high pressure function for 30 minutes. Let the pot release its pressure naturally for 10 minutes before performing a quick release.
12. While the pot is cooking, prepare the frozen mixed vegetables per the package instructions, then set aside.
13. Mix the cornstarch with the two tablespoons of cold water.
14. Remove the rice bowl and the steamer rack. Pour the cornstarch mixture into your Instant Pot. Stir as it thickens.
15. Add the cooked mixed vegetables, stir to mix, and serve in bowls.

Zingy Southwestern Chicken and Rice

This spicy southwestern recipe can be served over rice or it can be placed in a central dish for dipping and served with taco chips. Any way you serve it, there won't be any leftovers.

Yield: 4 servings

Ingredients:

- 1½ cups brown rice, rinsed
- ¾ cup salsa
- 1 15-ounce can kidney beans, drained and rinsed
- ½ cup frozen corn
- 1½ cups chicken stock
- 2 frozen chicken breasts
- ½ teaspoon onion powder
- ½ teaspoon garlic powder
- 1 teaspoon chili powder
- ¼ teaspoon cumin
- ½ teaspoon salt
- ½ cup shredded cheddar cheese
- Additional cheese for garnish
- Taco chips (optional)

Directions:

1. Put the brown rice, salsa, kidney beans, corn, and chicken stock in your Instant Pot and stir.
2. Place the frozen chicken breasts on top and press them down into the liquid.
3. Mix the onion powder, garlic powder, chili powder, cumin, and salt in a small bowl and sprinkle over the chicken.
4. Dip a spoon into the liquid beneath the chicken and extract a few spoonsful to baste over the frozen chicken, wetting the spices slightly.

5. Seal the lid and select the manual, high pressure function, setting the cook time to 24 minutes.
6. Let pressure release naturally for 10 minutes before performing a quick release. Open the lid and remove the chicken breasts.
7. Shred the chicken with two forks and return it to the Instant Pot, stirring it in and fluffing the rice.
8. Add the cheese and stir to combine.
9. Set on separate plates or on a single plate for dipping and sprinkle more cheese on top.

Zucchini Bread

Instant Pot zucchini bread is so moist and delicious you may even be tempted to make it every day during zucchini-growing season! You will need a 7-inch metal springform pan for this dish.

Harvest your zucchinis for this recipe when they are small and tender.

Yield: 1 loaf

Ingredients:

1 cup water

1½ cups all-purpose flour

½ teaspoon salt

½ teaspoon baking soda

½ teaspoon baking powder

1½ teaspoons ground cinnamon

1 egg plus 1 egg white

½ cup vegetable oil

1 cup granulated sugar

2 teaspoons vanilla

1½ cups grated zucchini

½ cup chopped walnuts (optional)

Directions:

1. Grease and flour the inside of a 7" springform pan.
2. Pour the water into the bottom of your Instant Pot and set in the trivet.
3. In a bowl, whisk together the flour, salt, baking soda, baking powder, and cinnamon.
4. With a mixer, beat the eggs and egg white, vegetable oil, sugar, and vanilla.
5. Gradually add the dry ingredients to the wet ingredients beating well after each addition.
6. Fold in by hand the zucchini and nuts, if desired, and pour the batter into the prepared pan.
7. Put a paper towel over the pan and cover, then seal the pan with aluminum foil.
8. Create an X-shaped foil sling and lay it on top of the trivet, so that the tails come up the sides of the pot.
9. Set the pan on the foil sling, then close and seal the lid.
10. Select the manual, high pressure function and set the cook time for 60 minutes.
11. At the end of the cook time, allow the pressure to release naturally for 15 minutes and then perform a quick release.
12. Carefully remove the pan by lifting up the sling. Remove the foil and paper towel and allow the bread to cool for 10 minutes before removing it from the pan to slice.

In addition to one-pot meals and entrees, your Instant Pot is capable of preparing some pretty memorable side dishes. That's the subject of our next chapter.

Chapter 11: Fun and Delicious Side Dishes

I admit that I don't often make side dishes in my Instant Pot because it is usually occupied with the main dish. However, I have been known to borrow a friend's Instant Pot if I am putting on a dinner party or when serving sides as a main dish.

My family loves twice baked potatoes, so I prepare the baked potatoes in my Instant Pot to speed up the cooking time. We also like macaroni and cheese, so I do make that in my Instant Pot. I've even prepared both a mashed potato bar and a macaroni and cheese bar, letting guests add their favorite toppings before chowing down. I use a separate pot for side dishes often enough that I may soon purchase a 3-quart Instant Pot for this purpose.

Applesauce In An Instant Pot
There is nothing better than warm applesauce served with pork chops or a pork roast. I like mine a little chunky, but this recipe can also make super-smooth applesauce. If you don't like cinnamon in your applesauce, just don't add any, but I *would* suggest keeping the nutmeg, just to spice things up a little. Fresh applesauce will keep for about a week in the refrigerator, if it isn't devoured immediately.

Macintosh apples make an applesauce that is naturally tart and sweet.

Yield: 8 servings

Ingredients:

3 pounds firm red apples, peeled, cored, and quartered. (I prefer Gala, McIntosh, Pink Lady, or Empire)

1 cinnamon stick

¼ teaspoon nutmeg

¾ cup granulated sugar (I often make this without any sugar added)

¼ cup water

¼ teaspoon salt

Directions:

1. Place the apples, cinnamon stick, nutmeg, sugar, salt, and water in your Instant Pot.
2. Seal the lid and select the manual, high pressure function, with the timer set to five minutes.

3. Let the pressure release naturally before opening and carefully removing the cinnamon stick.
4. Use an immersion blender or a potato masher to break up the cooked apple into the preferred consistency. You can also spoon the apple mixture into a regular blender for this step.
5. Taste and add salt if required, then chill before serving.

Bacon and Brussels Sprouts

Brussels sprouts cook up nicely in an Instant Pot. This recipe is has some heat to it, along with wonderful natural bacon flavoring.

Yield: 4 servings

Ingredients:

4 to five strips thick bacon, chopped

1 tablespoon almonds, chopped

¼ cup soy sauce

2 tablespoons sriracha sauce

1 tablespoon rice vinegar

2 tablespoons sesame oil

½ teaspoon red pepper flakes, crushed

2 teaspoons garlic powder

1 teaspoon onion powder

1 teaspoon paprika

½ teaspoon cayenne pepper (optional)

Salt and pepper to taste

2 pounds fresh Brussels sprouts, cut into half

Directions:

1. Select the sauté function on your Instant Pot and let it heat up.

2. Brown the bacon and when cooked, remove to a plate with a paper towel on it to soak up the grease. When cooled enough to touch, crumble and set aside.
3. Add the almonds to the bacon grease and sauté until they start to brown. Turn off the sauté function. Remove the almonds to the same plate as the bacon.
4. Add to the pot the soy sauce, sriracha sauce, rice vinegar, sesame oil, red pepper flakes, garlic powder, onion powder, paprika, cayenne pepper, salt, and pepper, stirring to combine.
5. Add the Brussels sprouts, the bacon, and the almonds.
6. Seal the lid and select the manual, high pressure function for three minutes. Perform a quick release at the end of the cook time.
7. Serve hot.

Baked Potatoes – And Twice Baked – In An Instant Pot

This recipe makes four to eight baked potatoes that come out perfectly every time in just half the time it would take to bake them conventionally. See how to make twice baked potatoes at the end of this recipe.

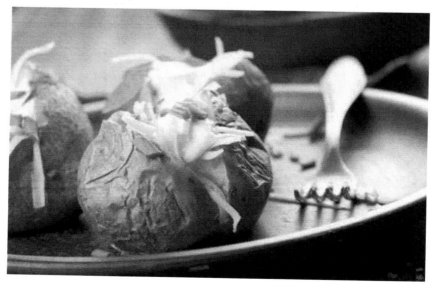

I recommend loading these with cheese, sour cream, mushrooms, and green onions.

Ingredients:
- 1 cup cold water
- 4 to 8 medium russet potatoes
- 2 tablespoons butter
- Sea salt to taste
- Black pepper to taste

Directions:
1. Prepare potatoes by washing them and poking them all over with a fork.
2. Pour the water into your Instant Pot and set the trivet in the bottom.
3. Place the potatoes on top and seal the lid.
4. Select the manual, high pressure function and set the cook time for 10 minutes if using small potatoes, 20 minutes for medium-sized potatoes.
5. Let the pressure release naturally for 10 minutes before performing a quick release.
6. Open the lid and remove the potatoes. Let them cool for five minutes, slice them open, and add butter, salt, and pepper.

Note: To make twice-baked potatoes, set your oven to 400 degrees, Fahrenheit, and prepare a baking sheet with nonstick spray. Remove the pulp of the potatoes to a mixing bowl and set the empty skins on the baking sheet. Add the butter, salt and pepper to the potato pulp and slowly start the mixer. Add enough sour cream to make a smooth mixture (about one cup) and about a half cup of shredded cheddar cheese. Gently fold in the sautéed green onions, crumbled cooked bacon and mushrooms; stuff this mixture back into the skins. Sprinkle with additional shredded cheddar cheese and place in the oven for about 10 minutes.

Basmati Rice

I love basmati rice. It is a long-grain rice that holds up well to boiling without turning mushy. I now use my Instant Pot for rice, because it always comes out absolutely perfect.

When you cook basmati rice with other things, it is best to rinse it first, so it doesn't scorch with the heat of the sauté function on your Instant Pot, but this recipe does not require soaking, because the sauté function is not used. Use broth instead of water for more flavorful results.

Yield: 5 cups of cooked rice

Ingredients:
- 1 cup basmati rice
- 1 cup water

Directions:
1. Place the basmati rice in the bottom of your Instant Pot
2. Pour in the water.
3. Seal the lid and select the manual, high pressure and set the timer for six minutes. If the rice comes out too soft for you, change that to five minutes next time.
4. Let the pressure release naturally for 10 minutes and if there is more pressure, perform a quick release.
5. Open the pot and serve.

Creamy Mac and Cheese

The kids in my family love macaroni and cheese and most of the adults do, too. I use this recipe at least every other week. Sometimes I set up a mac and cheese bar with possible additions in individual bowls. I include chopped green onions, mushrooms, crisp bacon bits, shredded cheese, sunflower seeds and anything I can think that would add flavor. I do this with mashed potatoes on occasion too, and the family just loves it.

Eat your mac and cheese plain or add bacon, mushrooms, onion...the list is endless.

Yield: 4-6 servings

Ingredients:

- 1 pound elbow macaroni
- 4 cups cold water
- 4 tablespoons unsalted butter
- 2 large eggs, beaten
- 1 teaspoon hot sauce
- 1 teaspoon prepared mustard (I use honey mustard or brown mustard)
- 1 12-ounce can evaporated milk
- 14 ounces shredded sharp cheddar cheese
- 6 ounces shredded mild cheddar cheese
- Salt and pepper to taste

Directions:

1. Place the macaroni in the bottom of your Instant Pot with the water and seal the lid.
2. Select the manual, high pressure function and set the timer for four minutes.
3. At the end of the cook time, perform a quick release. Open the lid and if there is quite a bit of liquid left in the pot, drain it off.
4. Add the butter and let it melt. Turn on the warming function.
5. Beat the eggs in a large bowl. Add the hot sauce and mustard and mix well.
6. Whisk in the milk.
7. Pour this liquid into the pot, add the shredded cheeses, and stir with a wooden spoon until the cheese melts.
8. If the dish appears runny, turn on the sauté function and stir constantly while cooking out the extra water. Be careful, because the sauté function can get very hot very fast, and may easily burn the cheese.
9. Season with salt and pepper and serve.

Creamy Mashed Potatoes

If you like creamy, smooth mashed potatoes, this is the recipe for you. The potatoes always come out exactly right. If you set up a mashed potato bar with assorted toppings, your guests will love it.

Mashed potatoes always come out perfect when made in an Instant Pot.

Yield: 4-6 servings

Ingredients:

    4 pounds russet potatoes, quartered

    1 cup cold water

    ¾ cup unsalted butter, at room temperature

    ½ cup milk

    Salt and pepper to taste

Directions:

1. Peel and quarter the potatoes and place them in the steamer basket.
2. Pour the cold water into the pot and set in the steamer basket of potatoes.

3. Seal the lid and select the manual, high pressure function, setting the cook time for eight minutes.
4. As soon as the time has elapsed, perform a quick release and open the pot.
5. While the potatoes are cooking, pour milk in a saucepan and bring it to a simmer. Turn off the heat.
6. Cut the room temperature butter into chunks and add to the milk.
7. Transfer the potatoes to a large bowl and pour out and discard any water. Remove the steamer rack, rinsing and drying the pot with a towel. Return the inner liner to your Instant Pot.
8. Mash the potatoes in the bowl, using a potato masher. Return the mashed potatoes to your Instant Pot and turn on the warming mode.
9. Add the milk and butter, stirring with a silicone spatula until completely smooth and creamy. Add salt and pepper to taste.
10. Keep in your warm Instant Pot until ready to serve.

Deviled Eggs a la Instant Pot

Do you ever have trouble peeling your boiled eggs? Do hard-boiled yolks sometimes appear green on the outside? This won't happen when you prepare your eggs in an Instant Pot.

Yield: 12-16 servings

Ingredients:

1 cup cold water

6 to 8 large raw eggs

1 tablespoon olive oil

2 tablespoons mayonnaise (regular, not low-fat)

1 teaspoon Dijon mustard

1 teaspoon white vinegar

¼ teaspoon sriracha sauce

Salt and pepper to taste

Paprika for garnish

Directions:

1. Pour the cold water into your Instant Pot.
2. Place the eggs in the steamer basket and set it into the pot, sealing the lid.
3. Select the manual, high pressure function and set the timer for 12 minutes.
4. When the cook time is completed, perform a quick release and open the lid.
5. Have a bowl of cold water ready and carefully lift the steamer basket out, setting the eggs in the cold water for five minutes.
6. Peel the eggs under cold running water.
7. Cut the eggs in half and remove the yolks, placing them in a bowl. Set the egg whites on a serving plate.
8. In a small bowl, mix the olive oil, mayonnaise, Dijon mustard, white vinegar, and sriracha sauce.
9. Break up the yolks with a fork, smashing them well. Combine thoroughly with the olive oil mixture and add salt and pepper to taste.
10. Scoop the yolk filling into the whites on the plate and sprinkle with paprika before serving.

Garnished Refried Beans

These refried beans will proudly accompany tacos, quesadillas or enchiladas. The recipe calls for three tablespoons of bacon grease, but you can use all olive oil if you prefer; just keep in mind you will be sacrificing some of the flavor. I use a mixture of bacon grease and olive oil in mine. It gives me the smoky flavor without all the grease.

You won't need to soak the beans in this recipe, but you do need to rinse them well to remove dirt and any debris, then you'll want to cull out any rocks or bad beans.

Refried beans should be slightly chunky for the perfect texture.

Yield: 8-10 servings

Ingredients:

    4 strips of bacon

    7 cups water

    1 pound dried pinto beans

    1 cup onions, chopped

    3 cloves garlic, minced

    1 teaspoon sea salt

1 teaspoon ground cumin

½ teaspoon ground black pepper

½ teaspoon dried oregano

3 tablespoons bacon drippings

Chopped green onions

Chopped fresh cilantro

Chopped fresh tomato

Sour cream

Directions:
1. Fry the bacon on the stove. Set the cooked bacon on a plate and set aside, reserving the bacon fat.
2. Pour the water into your Instant Pot and add the beans.
3. Add the onion, garlic, salt, cumin, pepper, oregano, and reserved bacon drippings to the pot. Seal the lid.
4. Select the manual, high pressure function and set the timer for 45 minutes.
5. At the end of the cook time, let the pressure release naturally for 25 minutes before performing a quick release.
6. Place a colander over a large bowl and drain the beans. Set the liquid in the bowl aside and blend the beans, in batches if necessary. Add some of the reserved liquid to form a creamy consistency.
7. Taste and adjust the flavor with salt and pepper, as needed.
8. Crush the bacon and use it as a garnish, along with the green onions, cilantro, tomatoes and sour cream.

Potato Salad In An Instant Pot

In this recipe, the potatoes and eggs are cooked together in your Instant Pot. This saves time and minimizes dirty dishes. The potatoes and eggs will be cooked perfectly, too.

Yield: 10 servings

Ingredients:
- 2 teaspoons salt
- 3 tablespoons apple cider vinegar, divided
- 4 cups cold water
- 3⅓ pounds potatoes, cut into 1-inch cubes
- 3 large eggs
- 1 small red onion, diced
- 3 stalks celery, finely chopped
- 1 large dill pickle, diced
- 8 stems fresh dill, finely chopped
- 1 cup mayonnaise
- 1 tablespoon whole-grain prepared mustard
- ½ teaspoon garlic powder
- Kosher salt and pepper to taste

Directions:
1. Place the salt, one tablespoon of the apple cider vinegar, and four of cups cold water into your Instant Pot.
2. Add in the potato cubes and make sure they are all under water.
3. Layer the eggs on top and seal the lid.
4. Set your Instant Pot to the manual, low pressure function for 0 minutes. It will take about 24 minutes for the pressure to build up and in that time, the potatoes and eggs will cook.
5. As soon as the pot reaches cooking pressure, perform an instant release and carefully open the pot and remove the eggs to a bowl of cold water.
6. Check the potatoes to see if they are done. If they're still a little hard, turn on the sauté function and let them cook a little longer.

7. In a bowl, combine the red onion, celery, pickle, dill, mayonnaise, mustard, and garlic powder.
8. When the potatoes are done, drain them well and stir them into the bowl.
9. Peel the eggs and chop them, adding them to the potato mixture and stirring to combine. Taste and adjust the flavor with salt and pepper as needed.
10. Cover and refrigerate for no less than three hours before serving.

Quick Corn on the Cob

This is the quickest way to make corn on the cob I know of. I can fit about six ears into my Instant Pot. If more than six ears are needed, it only takes a handful of minutes to make another batch.

Serve your corn on the cob buttered and sprinkled with salt, black pepper, garlic powder, a spritz of lemon juice, and grated parmesan cheese.

Yield: 6 servings

Ingredients:

6 ears of corn, shucked

1 cup water

Directions:
1. Pour the water into the bottom of your Instant Pot.
2. Cut the shucked corn to fit your steamer basket. If I cut off the pointy end, that usually is enough to fit the cobs into the pot.
3. Place the corn in the steamer basket in a crisscross manner and set the steamer in your Instant Pot.
4. Lock the lid and select the manual, high pressure function with a timer set for three minutes.
5. As soon as the cook time has ended, perform a quick release, carefully open the pot, and serve.

Roasted Red Potatoes

I love roasted red potatoes, and this is one of the easiest recipes you'll ever find. The ingredients are few and simple. It only takes 15 to 20 minutes to prepare the dish, so you can even prepare multiple batches if necessary.

Yield: 3-4 servings.

Ingredients:

2 tablespoons fat (butter, olive oil, etc.

½ small onion, sliced

1 clove garlic, minced

2 pounds red potatoes, washed and cut into wedges

1 cup chicken or vegetable broth

Salt and pepper to taste

Directions:
1. Select the sauté function on your Instant Pot and let it heat up.
2. Add the fat and let it heat up.
3. Add the onion and sauté for about three minutes or until translucent
4. Add the garlic and sauté for another minute.

5. Add the potatoes and sauté for five minutes, stirring frequently
6. Turn the sauté function off and add the broth.
7. Seal the lid and select the manual, high pressure function, setting the timer for eight minutes.
8. At the end of the cook time, perform a quick release and carefully open the lid.
9. Taste and add the salt and pepper.

Southern Green Beans

I had a friend in college whose grandmother had been born and raised in southern Virginia. She made the best green beans I have ever tasted, bar none. She used a pressure cooker with fatback (similar to bacon), and onions. The beans were always a little mushier than I prefer, but the flavor was incredible.

This recipe is my attempt to match that flavor. It employs bacon instead of fatback and avoids the mushiness, but otherwise tastes about the same. Sometimes I make it just to remember Charlotte's grandma.

Buttered green beans are versatile; they go well with almost any meal.

Yield: 6-8 servings

Ingredients:

- 3 slices of bacon, diced
- 1 small onion, chopped
- 1 to 2 cloves garlic, minced
- 2 pounds fresh green beans, ends removed and snapped into 3-inch pieces
- 1 cup chicken broth

Directions:

1. Select the sauté function on your Instant Pot and let the pot heat up.
2. Place the bacon in the pot and let it cook completely.
3. Add the onion and sauté for about two minutes, then drop in the garlic and sauté for another minute.
4. Take a small amount of the chicken broth and deglaze the pot, scraping up any brown bits.
5. Add the green beans along with the rest of the broth and seal the lid.
6. Select the manual, high pressure function and set the cook time for 20 minutes.
7. As soon as the cook time is finished, perform a quick release, carefully open the lid, and serve.

Superfast Spanish Rice

Spanish rice is an easy dish to make and it is highly cost effective. You can serve it on the side of almost any meat dish.

Yield: 10 servings

Ingredients:

- 2 tablespoons olive oil
- ½ onion, diced
- 3 cloves garlic, minced
- 2 cups long grain white rice, rinsed (I use jasmine rice)

¾ cup canned crushed tomatoes

2½ cups chicken broth

½ teaspoon garlic powder

½ teaspoon cumin

½ teaspoon paprika

1 teaspoon salt

¼ cup fresh cilantro, chopped

Directions:
1. Select the sauté function and let your Instant Pot heat up.
2. Add the olive oil.
3. Put in the onion and sauté until translucent, then add the garlic and sauté for one more minute.
4. Pour in the rice and stir to coat it.
5. Pour in the crushed tomatoes along with the chicken broth and stir.
6. Add the garlic powder, cumin, paprika, and salt, mixing in thoroughly.
7. Close the lid and lock it in place.
8. Select the manual, high pressure function and time it for eight minutes.
9. As soon as the cook time is finished, let the pot release pressure naturally for five minutes, then perform a quick release.
10. Open the pot, stir in the cilantro, and serve.

Sweet and Spicy Glazed Carrots
This carrot dish is simply to die for. The carrots are sweet and spicy and very different from the typical plain cooked carrots.

You can peel and julienne full-sized carrots or use baby carrots as is.

Yield: 8 servings

Ingredients:

- 1 tablespoon butter
- 1 tablespoon maple syrup
- 1 tablespoon prepared brown mustard
- ¼ teaspoon baking soda
- 1 teaspoon dried thyme
- 2 tablespoons chicken stock
- 3 pounds carrots, julienned

Directions:

1. Turn on your Instant Pot to the sauté function and let it heat up.
2. Put in the butter and let it melt.
3. Add the syrup, mustard, baking soda, and thyme; stir to mix.

4. Pour in the chicken stock and blend it in.
5. Add in the prepared carrots and toss to coat.
6. Turn off the pot and secure the lid.
7. Select the manual, high pressure function and set the timer for four minutes.
8. At the end of the cook time, let the pressure reduce naturally for 15 minutes.
9. Open, stir, and serve.

Tasty Scalloped Potatoes

Everyone seems to like scalloped potatoes and this Instant Pot version is no exception. I recommend serving it alongside ham, chops, or roast.

Let your broiler slightly brown the cheese on top.

Yield: 6-8 servings

Ingredients:

8 small potatoes (about two pounds), cut into quarter-inch thick slices

1 cup vegetable broth

3 tablespoons heavy cream

½ teaspoon salt

¼ teaspoon pepper

½ teaspoon garlic powder

½ teaspoon dried thyme

8 ounces shredded white cheddar cheese (regular cheddar is acceptable)

Directions:

1. Place the potatoes in the bottom of your Instant Pot, along with the vegetable broth.
2. Select the manual, high pressure function and cook for one minute.
3. Let the pressure release naturally, performing an instant release before carefully opening the pot.
4. Remove the potatoes from the pot into a greased casserole dish, but leave the liquid in your Instant Pot. There won't be much.
5. Set your oven to broil.
6. Add the heavy cream, salt, pepper, garlic powder, thyme, and all but two ounces of the cheese to your Instant Pot and turn on the sauté function. Stir until creamy and smooth.
7. Pour the sauce over the potatoes and place it under the broiler for four to six minutes or until the top is bubbly and brown.
8. Sprinkle the rest of the cheese on top and let it melt before serving.

Two Minute Broccoli

Steaming broccoli in your Instant Pot only takes two minutes. How's that for fast?

Steamed broccoli will look much like the raw vegetable, but it's easier to stab with a fork.

Yield: 4 servings

Ingredients:

1 cup water

1 medium sized fresh stalk of broccoli

Salt and pepper to taste

Directions:

1. Pour the water in the bottom of your Instant Pot.
2. Chop the broccoli into florets and set them in the steamer rack.
3. Set the steamer rack in the pot and seal the lid.

4. Select the manual, high pressure function and set the timer for two minutes.
5. When finished cooking, let the pressure release naturally for two minutes before performing a quick release.
6. Open the pot, season with salt and pepper, and serve.

Enough with the healthy veggies! It's time for dessert. You can make all sorts of treats and meal-enders in your Instant Pot. The next chapter will give you plenty to play with.

Chapter 12: Delectable Dessert Recipes

Yes, you can make desserts in an Instant Pot. Many of them will require a six- to seven-inch metal cake pan, a springform pan, or a Bundt pan that will fit inside your Instant Pot. Once you bake a cake in an Instant Pot, it will be hard to go back to making it in the oven, especially if you like moist cakes. You can also make fruit cobblers, pie, pudding, and much more. Your Instant Pot will save you so much time that you can make dessert a regular part of your day.

Apple Cobbler with Rolled Oats
I love old-fashioned cobblers! This recipe actually approaches in the flavor and texture my grandmother's very best. You can use other fruit besides apples, too. Peaches, berries, or cherries all taste great. Simply substitute five cups of other fruit in place of the apples. I have even used three cups of pie filling to make this and it tasted fine.

Serve apple cobbler with whipped cream or ice cream.

Yield: 6-8 servings

Ingredients:

    5 medium apples sliced evenly

    2 teaspoons cinnamon

    ½ teaspoon nutmeg

    1 tablespoon maple syrup

    ½ cup water

    4 tablespoons butter melted

    ¾ cup old-fashioned rolled oats (do not use quick oats)

    ¼ cup flour

    ¼ cup brown sugar

½ teaspoon salt

Directions:

1. Place the sliced apples in the bottom of your Instant Pot and sprinkle with the cinnamon and nutmeg.
2. Add the water and maple syrup.
3. In a bowl, combine the melted butter, oats, flour, brown sugar, and salt; stir well to combine.
4. Drop by the tablespoonful into your Instant Pot on top of the apples.
5. Lock the lid and select the manual, high pressure function, setting the cook time for eight minutes.
6. Let the pot release naturally for five minutes and then perform a quick release.
7. Open and serve with ice cream or whipped cream.

Banana Chocolate Chip Bundt Cake

This recipe is very rich, but because it uses honey and bananas instead of sugar, it is a little healthier than many other desserts. The cake comes out very moist and the chocolate chips...well, chocolate can make everything better. I use a foil sling to extract the pan from my Instant Pot without risking my fingers. The cake must be pulled out of the pot right after pressure is released or it will keep on cooking.

Yield: 6-8 servings

Ingredients:

½ cup plus 1 tablespoon milk

1 tablespoon vinegar

2 bananas, cut into 3 or 4 pieces

¼ cup honey

1 teaspoon vanilla

2 eggs

3 tablespoons coconut oil

1½ cups all-purpose flour

1 teaspoon baking soda

⅛ teaspoon nutmeg

½ teaspoon cinnamon

⅛ teaspoon salt

⅓ cup semi-sweet chocolate chips

⅔ cup water

Directions:

1. Spray a three-cup Bundt pan with baking spray that includes flour, then set it aside.
2. In a small bowl, mix the milk and vinegar. Let it start to curdle, then whisk for a bit to create pseudo-buttermilk.
3. In a mixer, blend the honey, vanilla, eggs, oil, milk, and vinegar until smooth and creamy.
4. In another bowl, stir together the flour, baking soda, nutmeg, cinnamon, and salt. Add gradually to the creamed mixture.
5. Fold in the chocolate chips by hand.
6. Pour the batter into the prepared Bundt pan and slam it on the counter to expel any air bubbles.
7. Set the trivet in the bottom of your Instant Pot, add the water and then insert the foil sling. Set the Bundt pan on top of the foil sling.
8. Secure the lid and select the manual, high pressure setting for 25 minutes.
9. At the end of the cook time, perform a quick release and remove the Bundt pan. There may be some condensation on top of the cake, but that is normal. It will evaporate quickly as the cake cools.
10. Cool for 10 minutes and remove from the Bundt pan. You can dust with powdered sugar if you desire.

Chocolate Lava Cake

You will need four 6-ounce ramekins for this recipe because you are making four individual cakes. These are super-sweet and incredibly rich. When you cut into one, the molten chocolate oozes out like lava.

Top with fresh fruit of the season and whipped cream, if you wish.

Yield: 4 servings

Ingredients:

    1 cup semi-sweet chocolate chips

    1 stick butter

    1 cup powdered sugar

    3 eggs

    1 egg yolk

    1 tablespoon vanilla

    6 tablespoons all-purpose flour

    1 cup water

Directions:

1. Place the chocolate chips and butter in a microwave-safe bowl and heat in the microwave for two minutes. Stir. The mixture should be smooth and creamy.
2. Add the powdered sugar and whisk until smooth.
3. Add three eggs and the egg yolk and whisk until well combined.
4. Add the vanilla and flour and stir well.
5. Oil each container and fill to the top with batter.
6. Set the trivet in your Instant Pot and pour one cup of water in the bottom of the pot.
7. Set the batter-filled ramekins on top of the trivet. You may need to set three in the bottom and balance the fourth on top between their rims.
8. Secure the lid and select the manual, high pressure function. Set the timer for nine minutes.
9. At the end of the cook time, perform a quick release and carefully remove the dishes from your Instant Pot. Turn each one upside down on a plate and shake to remove. Serve while still hot, with a little caramel sauce on top.

Creamy Rice Pudding

Rice pudding is a creamy delicious treat. I remember my grandmother making rice pudding on Christmas Eve; we always left a little bowl out for the mischievous elves that hid household items and clothing. It seemed to help, but perhaps that was just my imagination.

You can add raisins, dried cranberries, chocolate drizzle, or cinnamon...or just eat it plain.

Simple rice pudding is the ultimate in comfort food.

Yield: 6 servings

Ingredients:

- 1 cup basmati rice
- 1¼ cups water
- 2 cups milk
- ¼ cup maple syrup
- ⅛ teaspoon sea salt
- 1 teaspoon vanilla extract
- ¾ cup heavy cream

Directions:

1. Rinse the rice several times with water inside a fine mesh colander. After two or three rinses, place rice in the bottom of your Instant Pot.
2. Add the water, milk, maple syrup, and sea salt, then seal the lid.
3. Select the manual, high pressure setting and set the cook time for 20 minutes.
4. Allow the pressure to release naturally for 10 minutes and then perform a quick release.

5. Open the lid and add the vanilla and the heavy cream, mixing well.
6. Serve hot.

Double Chocolate Cheesecake
This is the cheesecake for all you chocoholic cheesecake lovers. It is so chocolatey and creamy that a little goes a very long way. With this recipe, you prepare the cheesecake in your Instant Pot, inside a six-inch springform pan. To prevent the pan from leaking, (mine always does), wrap the bottom and up the sides with foil before setting it in the pot.

You'll want to prepare a foil sling to place under the pan; this will help you extract the cheesecake without burning your fingers. You can decorate the cheesecake with melted chocolate, piping made from frosting, or drizzled caramel. You'll want to cut thin slices because it's so rich.

While perfect by itself, you can add to cheesecake's decadence with whipped cream.

Yield: 6-8 servings

Ingredients:

    1½ cups chocolate wafer cookie crumbs

    3½ tablespoons cocoa powder, divided

    4 tablespoons melted butter

    1 pound cream cheese, at room temperature

    ⅔ cup packed brown sugar

    ¼ teaspoon sea salt

    1 teaspoon vanilla extract

2 large eggs, room temp

1½ teaspoons instant coffee grounds

1 to 1½ teaspoons water

2 ounces sour cream, at room temperature

6 ounces bittersweet chocolate, melted

1 ounce dark chocolate

1 ounce milk chocolate

1 ounce white chocolate

Directions:

1. Prepare the springform pan by covering the bottom and sides with foil placing a circle of parchment paper in the bottom, and by using baking spray on the inside.
2. Make cookie crumbs out of wafer cookies by placing them in a recloseable bag and using a rolling pin to crush them.
3. Put the cookie crumbs in a small bowl along with 1½ tablespoons of cocoa powder. Pour the melted butter on top and mix with a fork. Press into the bottom of the pan and up about a half an inch on the sides.
4. Set the pan in a preheated 350-degree Fahrenheit oven for 10 minutes, remove. Let the pan cool before proceeding.
5. In a mixing bowl, cream the cream cheese on low power until smooth. Add sugar, salt, and vanilla, combining well.
6. Add one egg at a time, beating thoroughly.
7. In a cup, combine the coffee with the water until dissolved; pour it into the mixing bowl and stir in.
8. In another bowl, combine the sour cream with the rest of the cocoa powder and whisk to combine. Fold gently into the cream cheese mixture.
9. Fold in the bittersweet chocolate until well combined.
10. Pour this batter into the springform pan on top of the crust.
11. Place the trivet inside your Instant Pot and pour two cups of water into the bottom of the pot.

12. Set the foil sling on top of the trivet and up the sides of the pot.
13. Place the springform pan in on top of the sling.
14. Secure the lid and select the manual, high pressure function and set the cook time to 20 minutes.
15. At the end of the cook time, let the pressure release naturally for 10 minutes before performing a quick release.
16. Open the pot and use the sling to lift out the cheesecake, placing it on a cooling rack.
17. Let the cake cool to room temperature before removing the sides and decorating.
18. Melt each of the remaining chocolates in individual bowls or pans. Spread on, dab on, flick on, or do whatever you want to get the chocolate on the top of the cake.
19. Let this set for three hours before serving or refrigerating. Store any leftovers in the refrigerator.

Elegant Crème Brule

Crème Brule is one of my favorite dessert dishes. It is a creamy custard-like substance with a vanilla flavor and a hard sugar shell on top that crunches when you spoon into it. This recipe truly simplifies the process.

The top layer of burnt sugar cracks to reveal the creamy center.

Yield: 6 servings

Ingredients:

    8 egg yolks

    ⅓ cup granulated sugar

    ⅛ teaspoon salt

    2 cups heavy cream

    1½ teaspoons vanilla extract

    6 tablespoons superfine sugar

Directions:

1. Combine the egg yolks in a large mixing bowl with granulated sugar and the salt. Mix with a wire whisk until well blended.
2. Add the cream and vanilla and whisk together.
3. Use a fine wire mesh strainer to strain the liquid into a large glass measuring cup.
4. Pour into six custard cups or ramekins. Cover each with foil.
5. Set the trivet in the bottom of your Instant Pot and pour in 1½ cups of water.
6. Set the six custard cups on the trivet. You will probably need to stack them in layers, balancing them across the edges of the lower cups.
7. Secure the lid and select the manual, high pressure function, setting the cook time for 10 minutes.
8. At the end of the cook time, perform a quick release and remove the lid.
9. Carefully extract the custard cups to a wire rack to cool. When cool, cover and refrigerate for at least two hours and possibly up to two days.
10. When ready to serve, set the custard cups on a wire rack and sprinkle each with a tablespoon of superfine sugar.
11. Light a kitchen torch and move the flame in a circular motion across the custards, staying about two inches above the surface. This will melt and brown the sugar, forming a crispy caramelized top.
12. Serve immediately.

Gourmet Bread Pudding

Bread pudding is an old recipe passed down through my family. It was inexpensive because all you really needed was old bread (the staler the better), some milk, eggs, and sugar. This recipe is a little more complicated, but it is also much tastier than the old recipe because it includes maple syrup or honey and plenty of eggs.

Yield: 10-12 servings

Ingredients:

1 loaf bread (Use any kind you like.)

2 cups whole milk (do not use lowfat milk, but you *can* use high fat coconut milk)

4 whole eggs

2 egg yolks

½ cup maple syrup or honey

1 tablespoon real vanilla extract

¼ teaspoon sea salt

½ cup butter, melted (coconut oil is acceptable, but I prefer the flavor of butter)

Directions:

1. Cut the bread into 1-inch cubes.
2. You will need a stainless-steel bowl that fits inside your Instant Pot. Line it with parchment paper, pressing it flat so there are no folds.
3. Put the bread cubes in the bowl.
4. In a blender or food processor, combine the milk, whole eggs, yolks, syrup or honey, salt, and vanilla.
5. Add the melted butter.
6. Pour two cups of water into your Instant Pot and place the trivet inside.
7. Insert a foil sling to simplify extracting the bowl later, then insert the bowl.
8. Carefully pour the custard into the bowl and press down on the bread cubes to make sure they get all wet.
9. Place a small square of parchment paper over the top of the bowl, folding down any corners that stick out.
10. Secure the pot's lid and select the high pressure function, setting a timer for 15 minutes.
11. At the end of the cook time, let the pressure naturally release for 20 minutes before performing a quick release.

12. Carefully extract the bowl using the sling and set on a rack to cool. Let the bowl cool for five to 10 minutes, uncovered, then place a serving plate upside down and flip everything over. Remove the bowl, take off the parchment liner, slice, and serve with whipped cream.

Low-Carb Chocolate Mousse

This recipe calls for Swerve, a natural sweetener that measures cup for cup like granulated sugar. This recipe is low-carb and dairy-free. You do part of the preparation in a saucepan on the stove.

Top your mousse with a small dollop of whipped cream and a sprig of mint.

Yield: 5 servings

Ingredients:

4 egg yolks

½ cup Swerve

¼ cup water

¼ cup cacao

½ cup almond milk

1 cup whipping cream

¼ teaspoon sea salt

½ teaspoon vanilla

1½ cups water

Directions:

1. Place the egg yolks in a bowl and whisk until they are well beaten, then set aside.
2. In a medium saucepan, combine the Swerve, water and cacao and stirring until everything melts and is combined.
3. Add the almond milk and whipping cream and mix well. Heat up the mixture, but do not let it boil. Once bubbles start forming around the edge of the pan, turn off the heat and remove the saucepan.
4. Add the salt and vanilla and stir.
5. Pour one tablespoon of the chocolate mixture in the bowl with the eggs and swiftly whisk to combine. If you don't do it fast enough the eggs will cook and form chunks. Add another tablespoon and whisk it in, then pour all the chocolate mixture into the eggs and whisk thoroughly.
6. Spray five ramekins with baking spray and apportion the mousse, dividing it equally among all five.
7. Place 1½ cups of water in the bottom of your Instant Pot and insert the trivet. Stack the ramekins on the trivet.
8. Seal the lid and select the manual, high pressure function timing it for six minutes
9. At the end of the end of the cook time, perform a quick release and remove the ramekins as quickly as possible. Let them cool, then place them in the refrigerator for at least four hours, if not overnight, before serving.

Maple Flavored Flan

Flan is a deliciously creamy, sticky desert that comes from Mexico. This custard holds up on its own, covered in rich syrup. It is cut like a pie or cake and served cool. I make it with a 7-inch soufflé dish inside my Instant Pot, but you can also prepare this using a 7-inch cake pan, as long as it is a little taller than a regular round cake pan. You will use the steam function to prepare flan, not the pressure cooker.

Flan is a rich, creamy dessert from Mexico.

Yield: 6-8 servings

Ingredients:

3½ cups water

½ cup maple syrup

¼ cup maple syrup

3 large eggs

4 large egg yolks

1½ cups whole milk

1½ cups heavy cream (whipping cream)

1 tablespoon vanilla

½ teaspoon sea salt

Directions:

1. Pour the water into the bottom of your Instant Pot, insert the trivet, and turn it on sauté to heat it up.
2. In a saucepan, bring the half cup of maple syrup to a simmer. Cook over medium heat for eight to 10 minutes. It might start to smell slightly burnt, but that is fine.
3. Pour it into the soufflé dish and make sure it covers the entire bottom.
4. In a medium bowl, whisk the eggs together with the egg yolks until well beaten, then add the quarter cup of maple syrup.
5. In a medium saucepan, whisk together the milk, cream, sea salt, and vanilla. Heat until it starts to steam.
6. Carefully pour the heated mixture into the egg mixture, whisking quickly to prevent the eggs from cooking.
7. Set the soufflé dish in your Instant Pot on top of a foil sling that will help you remove it later.
8. Strain the liquid through a sieve into the prepared soufflé dish on top of the syrup in the bottom.
9. Cover with the lid but allow it to vent. Select the steam setting, on low heat. I've also found the slow cooker option works very well. Let it steam for 75 minutes. The flan is done when the middle jiggles slightly when shaken or the internal temperature is 180 degrees, Fahrenheit.
10. Turn off your Instant Pot and pull out the soufflé dish using the foil sling, placing it on a cooling rack for an hour.
11. Set the flan in the refrigerator until it is cold. A couple hours at least, although overnight is fine, too.
12. To serve, run a warm knife around the edge of the dish, invert it onto a plate and shake to release. Lift off the soufflé dish and it's ready to serve.

New York Cheesecake in an Instant Pot

Yes, you can make cheesecake in an Instant Pot and boy, does it ever come out nice! There are rarely any cracks and it rises evenly. Make this once and you will never make cheesecake any other way again

I like my cheesecake to have a little zing, so I include orange and lemon zest, but these are purely optional.

You will need a 7-inch springform pan that is prepared with parchment paper and can fit inside your Instant Pot.

You will notice that many of the ingredients need to be at room temperature. I have tried it without setting them out and the results, well, they weren't very good. For some reason, it helps when you follow the directions on this one.

Yield: 6-8 servings

Ingredients:

Crust:

 9 graham crackers

 1 tablespoon granulated sugar

 3 tablespoons butter, melted

Cake:

 ½ cup plus two tablespoons granulated sugar

 2 8-ounce packages of cream cheese, at room temperature

 ½ teaspoon lemon zest (optional)

 ½ teaspoon orange zest (optional)

 2 teaspoons vanilla extract

 ¼ cup sour cream, at room temperature

 ⅓ cup heavy cream, at room temperature

 2 teaspoons cornstarch

 3 eggs, at room temperature

Sour Cream Topping:

¾ cup sour cream

4 teaspoons granulated sugar

⅛ teaspoon vanilla extract

Directions:

1. Cut a circle of parchment paper to fit inside the springform pan, set it in the bottom, and spray with baking spray.
2. Design a foil sling in a crisscross shape. You will use this to lower the pan into the pot and raise it out at the end of cooking.
3. Pour 1½ cups of cold water into your Instant Pot and set the trivet inside.
4. Put the graham crackers and sugar in a food processor and pulse to make them into crumbs. Pour in the melted butter and pulse to mix.
5. Pour the crumbs into the pan and press them against the bottom and slightly up the sides.
6. Set the pan in the freezer to firm up the crust, while you prepare the filling.
7. Cream the cream cheese and sugar until smooth and creamy.
8. Add the lemon and orange zest, vanilla, sour cream, heavy cream, and cornstarch, mixing until combined and creamy.
9. Add each of the room temperature eggs and mix in gently. If you beat the eggs, the cheesecake will have air pockets instead of being dense and creamy.
10. Remove the crust from the freezer and pour the cake ingredients into the pan.
11. Cover the pan with a white paper towel, then a piece of foil, crimping around the edges so it stays on. It does not have to be tight.
12. Place the sling under the pan and up the sides; lower it into your Instant Pot, keeping the ends over the cheesecake so it can be pulled out easily.
13. Lock the lid, select the manual, high pressure function, and set the cook time for 39 minutes.

14. At the end of the cook time, let the pressure release for 20 minutes before performing a quick release.
15. Open the pot, pull out the pan from your Instant Pot, and place it on a cooling rack. Leave it alone for 15 minutes, then carefully remove the foil and the paper towel.
16. The cheesecake will be a little jiggly in the center when it's done. If it is too liquid, cover it back up and return it to your Instant Pot for five more minutes at high pressure, then let the pressure release naturally for 15 minutes.
17. Let the cake cool for one hour.
18. Combine the topping of sour cream, granulated sugar, and vanilla in a bowl, mixing to dissolve the sugar.
19. Spread this topping over the warm cheesecake.
20. Refrigerate for at least four hours. I prefer to leave it in overnight.
21. Remove the cake from the springform pan and slide it onto a serving dish.
22. Serve as is, drizzle with chocolate or caramel sauce, or top with berries.

Perfect Strawberry Fruit Pie

Pies with graham cracker or cookie crusts work better than pastry crusts in the Instant Pot. You will also find that pulpy fruit and crushed berries work best.

This pie is created in a springform pan, using either butter cookies or shortbread cookies for the crust. I make it with strawberries in this case, but you could just as easily use raspberries, blueberries or even passion fruit.

Yield: 6 servings

Ingredients:

Crust:

    1 cup crushed butter cookies or shortbread cookies

    4 tablespoons butter, melted

    Filling:

½ cup frozen strawberries (no sugar added), thawed

4 large egg yolks

1 14-ounce can condensed milk

Topping:

¾ cup frozen strawberries, thawed

½ cup sugar

Directions:

1. Spray a 7-inch springform pan with baking spray.
2. Grind the cookies into crumbs and pour into a bowl.
3. Add the melted butter and mix with a fork until well combined.
4. Press into the bottom of the prepared springform pan and slightly up the sides.
5. Set in the freezer while preparing the rest of the pie.
6. Put the strawberries, egg yolks, and condensed milk in a blender and blend on high until creamy.
7. Remove the crust from the freezer and pour in the filling.
8. Cover the top of the springform pan with foil, crimping it around the edge to keep it in place.
9. Pour one cup of water into the bottom of your Instant Pot and insert the trivet.
10. Make a foil sling and place it under the springform pan and up two sides. Lower the pan into your Instant Pot with the sling. Leave the ends up the sides of your Instant Pot.
11. Close and seal the pot's lid. Select the manual, high pressure function and set the time for 15 minutes.
12. At the end of the cook time, let the pressure release naturally for 10 minutes before performing a quick release.
13. Open the lid, use the sling to remove the pan, and set it on a cooling rack.
14. Remove the aluminum foil cover immediately. The center should be a bit jiggly. Let it cool to room temperature, then refrigerate it for at least three hours.

15. In a saucepan combine the strawberries and sugar. Turn the heat on to medium-low and stir frequently until the liquid reduces and thickens.
16. Pour into a container, and let it cool to room temperature. Pour this sauce over the pie and return it to the refrigerator.
17. When ready to serve, release the sides and cut into wedges.

Pressure-Cooked Pineapple Upside Down Cake

This recipe requires a 7-inch springform pan. If you use a 20-ounce can of sliced pineapple you'll have a few leftover slices. I usually freeze them and use them on top of brown sugar ham.

You can set glazed cherries in the pineapple ring centers.

Yield: 6-8 servings

Ingredients:

2 cups all-purpose flour

1 tablespoon baking powder

½ teaspoon salt

½ cup butter, melted

1½ cups granulated sugar

2 eggs, beaten

1 teaspoon vanilla

½ cup butter, cut into small chunks

½ cup brown sugar

4 slices of pineapple (more if you can fit them in)

Directions:

1. In a bowl, combine the flour, baking powder, and salt. Sift this through a sieve to mix it thoroughly.
2. Cream the melted butter, granulated sugar, beaten eggs, and vanilla, mixing well.
3. Add the flour mixture gradually to the wet ingredients until well incorporated.
4. Spray the springform pan well with butter flavor non-stick spray.
5. Sprinkle chunks of butter on the bottom of the pan and sprinkle the brown sugar on top.
6. Place one pineapple ring in the middle of the pan and the others around it, cutting the sides as needed to fit into the pan.
7. Pour the batter into the springform pan on top of the pineapple rings. Tap on the counter to break up any air pockets
8. Set the trivet in the bottom of your Instant Pot and pour in enough water to come up to the trivet, but not cover it.
9. Make a sling with a piece of foil and place it under the springform pan and up the sides.
10. Carefully lower the springform pan into the pot, using the sling; leave it in place to facilitate removal later.
11. Seal the lid and select the manual, high pressure function for 18 minutes.
12. At the end of the cook time, let the pressure release naturally.

13. Pull the pan out using the sling and set it on a cooling rack.
14. When cool, release the sides, put a serving dish face-down on top of the pineapple upside down cake and flip it over.
15. Remove the bottom of the pan, slice, and serve.

Quick Tapioca Pudding

My mother made tapioca as a regular treat and I still enjoy it to this day. You'll enjoy this recipe if you're a tapioca lover.

Now you can enjoy the simple grace of tapioca pudding.

Yield: 4-6 servings

Ingredients:

⅓ cup tapioca pearls

1¼ cups whole milk (you can use almond milk, but *not* two percent milk)

½ cup water

Zest of ½ lemon

½ cup granulated sugar

¼ teaspoon vanilla extract

Directions:

1. Put one cup of water in the bottom of your Instant Pot and insert the steamer basket.
2. Rinse the tapioca pearls in water, using a fine mesh strainer.
3. Use a 4-cup capacity, heat-proof bowl that fits inside your Instant Pot. Place the rinsed tapioca, milk, water, lemon zest, sugar, and vanilla in the bowl and mix well until the sugar has dissolved.
4. Make a foil sling and place it under the bowl and up the sides. Use it to lower the bowl into the steamer basket inside your Instant Pot.
5. Secure the lid and select the manual, high pressure function, setting the cook time for eight minutes.
6. At the end of the cook time, let the pot release pressure naturally.
7. At the end of the natural pressure release, let the tapioca set closed in your Instant Pot for five more minutes, then open the lid.
8. Use the sling to remove the tapioca from the pot and place it on a cooling rack.
9. Stir vigorously with a fork to distribute the ingredients evenly.
10. Once it's cooled to temperature, cover the dish and refrigerate it for at least three hours, if not overnight. Serve, chilled, in small dishes.

Simple and Sweet Peach Crisp

I love peach flavored anything, so this is one of my favorite desserts. The recipe's simple enough that you can eat it whenever you want. You can top it with whipped cream or ice cream if you want, but I love it just plain.

Peach crisp and homemade ice cream are an unbeatable combination.

Yield: 6 servings

Ingredients:

Topping:

    ½ cup chopped pecans

    1½ cups old-fashioned oatmeal (do not use quick oats)

    ½ cup all-purpose flour

    ¾ cup brown sugar

    ½ teaspoon salt

    1 stick butter

Filling:

    8 cups sliced peach wedges (about six or seven peaches)

    ¼ cup brown sugar

    ¼ cup granulated sugar

    ½ teaspoon cinnamon

1 teaspoon vanilla

1 teaspoon lemon juice

2 tablespoons cornstarch

2 tablespoons water

Directions:

1. In a medium bowl, mix the pecans, oatmeal, flour, brown sugar, and salt. Mix well and set aside.
2. In a medium frying pan, melt the butter.
3. Once melted, pour the pecan mixture into the frying pan and mix vigorously until all combined. Cook, stirring frequently until golden brown, about six minutes.
4. Pour out the mixture onto parchment paper or a silicone mat and let it cool.
5. To make the filling, place the peeled peach wedges in a large bowl. Add the brown sugar, granulated sugar, cinnamon, vanilla, and lemon juice; mix well.
6. Pour the peach contents into your Instant Pot.
7. Seal the pot and select the manual, high pressure function, setting the cook time for four minutes.
8. At the end of the cook time, let the pressure release naturally for 15 minutes before performing a quick release and opening the lid.
9. Stir water into the cornstarch until dissolved and goopy. Gently stir this mixture into the peach sauce in your Instant Pot.
10. Select the sauté function and stir constantly for one to two minutes, until the filling starts to thicken. It will thicken more as it cools.
11. Press cancel and serve warm in bowls, with the topping sprinkled generously over it all.

Sweet Crescent Roll Apple Dumplings

Apple dumplings are somewhat of a tradition in my family. My grandmother made them whenever we came to visit but she never had it *this* easy. Instead of using pie dough and wrapping an entire apple, this recipe wraps individual apple wedges in crescent roll dough, the kind you buy in a can. The results are quite delicious, but are not as massive and calorie-ridden as a whole-apple dumpling.

Crescent rolls in a can are higly versatile.

Yield: 8 servings

Ingredients:

1 8-ounce can of crescent rolls

1 large Granny Smith apple, cored, peeled, and cut into eight wedges

4 tablespoons butter

½ cup brown sugar

1 teaspoon cinnamon

⅛ teaspoon ground nutmeg

½ teaspoon vanilla

¾ cup apple cider (apple juice works in a pinch, but isn't as tasty)

Directions:

1. Select the sauté function on your Instant Pot and let it heat up.

2. Open the can of crescent rolls and roll them out flat on a cutting board.
3. Place an apple wedge on each perforation of the crescent roll and roll them up tight.
4. Put butter in the bottom of your Instant Pot and cancel the sauté function.
5. Add the vanilla and stir, while the butter melts into the vanilla
6. Sprinkle in the sugar, cinnamon, and nutmeg, and stir to mix.
7. Place the wrapped apple wedges in the pot side by side. You may need to stack them.
8. Drizzle the apple cider around the edges of the pot; don't pour it directly on the dumplings.
9. Secure the lid, select the manual, high pressure function, and set the cook time for 10 minutes.
10. At the end of the cook time, let the pressure release naturally, then let it set for five more minutes.
11. Open and serve each wedge on a plate, drizzling some of the remaining syrup over each one.

Want to make your own salsa or ketchup? Perhaps you'd like to make a special treat for Fido or try your hand at making soap or even a highly effective cough syrup. Read on, and you'll discover all sorts of practical – and sometimes weird – things you can make using your Instant Pot.

Chapter 13: Favorite Bonus Recipes

Your Instant Pot is a versatile piece of kitchen equipment that comes in handy in many ways. You can make broth, caramelize mass quantities of onions, create herbal remedies, and create staples such as ketchup. My favorite is melting chocolate; it comes in handy when I make Christmas candies. I just put it on sauté and keep on dipping.

Now you can make your own soap, cough lozenges, and vanilla extract at home, all in your handy Instant Pot. Some of these recipes are weird and wonderful, while others are practical and money-saving. I have a spare insert bowl for my Instant Pot, in addition to the one I use to make food. This is what I use for items that won't be eaten. After all, if you use the same insert for everything, you run the risk of your beef stew tasting like lavender soap, *not* a good idea! It's well worth the price to purchase a second insert.

Bone Broth
Bone broth has recently broken onto the scene as a healthy addition to our diets, and for good reason. It contains useful proteins as well as high concentrations of gelatin, which is especially good for promoting skin health, reducing inflammation, and boosting the immune system. Baking the bones before making the broth only adds to its rich flavor.

The bones are typically simmered for a very long time to extract all the valuable nutrients. At the end of cooking, the bones will be soft. Roasting them beforehand releases collagen and other nutrients in the bones, making for an even more nutritious and flavorful broth.

Your Instant Pot reduces this day-long process to a few hours! I now use bone broth in most of my soups and stews. While beef bone broth is most common, the rest of the world makes broth using chicken and even fish bones. The only drawback to these is that they require so many bones that they are not very practical to make; consequently, I stick to beef for my bone broth.

Roasted beef bones contain rich flavor that enhances bone broth.

Yield: 3 quarts of broth

Ingredients:

- 2 pounds beef bones (use oxtail, short ribs, or marrow bones)
- 2 tablespoons apple cider vinegar
- 3 quarts water (preferably filtered)
- 1 large onion, quartered
- 1 large carrot, chopped into large hunks
- Salt and pepper to taste

Directions:

1. Preheat the oven to 400 degrees, Fahrenheit. Rinse off the bones with water to remove any hairs or dirt, then pat dry with paper towels...
2. Set a rack on a baking sheet with deep sides; cover the interior with non-stick spray.
3. Set the bones on top of the rack and roast for about 30 minutes, until golden brown.
4. Remove the bones from the oven and immediately transfer them to your Instant Pot, using tongs.

5. Add the vinegar and water and turn on the sauté function. Bring the liquid to a boil and skim off any white or gray foam that rises to the top.
6. Seal the lid and select the manual, high pressure function, setting the cook time for 120 minutes.
7. Let the pressure release naturally for 90 minutes.
8. Open the pot, add the onion and carrot pieces, and seal the lid again. Select the manual, high pressure function and cook for another 120 minutes.
9. Let it naturally depressurize for 90 minutes and then open the pot.
10. Remove the bones and strain the broth into a large metal bowl. Discard the bones and the vegetables.
11. Fill a sink with cold water and set the bowl into the sink to cool quickly. Avoid getting any water in the bowl. This should cool the broth to about 50 degrees, Fahrenheit, in 15 minutes.
12. Add salt and pepper to taste and refrigerate for up to a week or freeze in cubes, tightly sealed, for up to six months.

Caramelized Onions

Caramelizing onions typically takes a very long time. You have to cook them low and slow in order to get the right flavor and texture. It takes much less time to do this in an Instant Pot because the heat is more intense and the onions caramelize faster. I use a combination of yellow onions with a few sweet onions thrown in. The onions must be sliced a uniform thickness, about an eighth inch thick.

Caramelized onions go well on a hamburger, with baked chicken or on a steak with mushrooms.

Yield: 2 cups caramelized onions.

Ingredients:

    6 tablespoons unsalted butter (salted butter makes them too salty)

    3 pounds onions, sliced (about four to five large onions)

    ½ teaspoon baking soda

    Sea salt and ground pepper to taste

Directions:

1. Select the sauté function on your Instant Pot and let it heat up.
2. Place the butter in the pot and let it melt, stirring so it doesn't burn.
3. Add the onions and baking soda and stir to combine.
4. Season with salt and pepper and continue to cook, stirring until the onions soften, about three minutes.
5. Seal the lid and select the manual, high pressure, setting the cook time for 20 minutes. Let pressure release naturally for 10 minutes, then perform a quick release.

6. Remove the lid and turn on the sauté function once more. There will be liquid in the bottom of your Instant Pot and you want to reduce that liquid for about five minutes.
7. Your onions are available for immediate use. They also keep, refrigerated, for up to four days will store in the freezer for up to 2 months.

Lip Balm

Homemade lip balm is not as difficult to make as you might think, especially in an Instant Pot. The toughest part is locating 20 containers to hold the balm!

This recipe uses essential oils to scent and flavor the lip balm, so choose something that tastes good. I prefer lemon or strawberry, but if you're dealing with chapped lips, I recommend eucalyptus. It's not very tasty, but it sure soothes those chapped lips. If you don't like the flavor of cocoa butter, you can use mango butter, which adds to the fruity flavor.

Yield: 20 lip balms

Ingredients:

2 cups water

3 tablespoons beeswax

2 tablespoons cocoa butter

2 tablespoons coconut oil

3 capsules Vitamin E oil (poke a hole in the capsule and squeeze out the Vitamin E oil)

10 drops essential oil (strawberry, lemon, or flavor of your choice)

Directions:

1. Add two cups of water to your Instant Pot
2. Use a glass bowl that fits inside and cover the outside, all the way to the top of the pot, with foil. This creates a barrier between the bowl and your Instant Pot, creating a sort of double boiler.

3. Place the beeswax, butter, oil, and Vitamin E in the bowl and mix, using a wooden spoon that is dedicated solely to nonfood items.
4. Select the steam function, close the lid, and steam for 15 minutes.
5. Mix in the essential oil and stir well.
6. Fill the balm containers while still hot. Cover a small baking sheet with wax paper and arrange the containers on top.
7. Let the balm cool, keeping the cap off until hardened.

Chicken Stock

I use a great deal of chicken stock. I freeze some for later use, but I tend to use most of it immediately. I've recently discovered it's very easy to prepare using my Instant Pot. Whenever I buy a rotisserie chicken, I use its bones to make chicken stock. Sometimes I'll even freeze the chicken carcass until I'm ready to make stock. I don't even need to thaw the carcass before I start. I also save vegetable scraps in the freezer until I amass three cups, then I incorporate them into the process, for the added flavor.

A good chicken stock should be clear and bright yellow.

Yield: 12 cups chicken stock

Ingredients:

Bones from a whole roasted chicken

2 to 3 cups vegetable scraps including onion peels, carrot peels, ends of celery, garlic, etc.

1 sprig thyme or one teaspoon dried thyme

1 tablespoon sea salt

1 teaspoon whole peppercorns

2 bay leaves

10 cups cold water

Directions:

1. Put everything in your Instant Pot and seal the lid.
2. Select the manual, high pressure function and set the time for 45 minutes. It will take some time to heat up and actually start cooking if you use frozen chicken and vegetables.
3. At the end of the cook time, let the pressure release naturally for 30 minutes before performing a quick release.
4. Strain through a fine sieve into a bowl and let it cool. Throw away the solids.
5. Use immediately or freeze for up to three months.

Cough Syrup

This cough syrup really works! It tastes okay too, but I wouldn't want to take it all the time. It is easy to make, and I just store it in a canning jar.
I also freeze it in ice cube trays and then pop them out into a resealable container for use as needed. The frozen cubes help to soothe a sore throat.

Yield: 1½ cups of syrup

Ingredients:

2 cups water

¼ cup fresh ginger root, finely chopped

8 sprigs of fresh thyme

1 cup honey

1 lemon, juiced

¼ teaspoon cayenne pepper

Directions:

1. Place the water, ginger and thyme in your Instant Pot and press the sauté button.
2. Let them come nearly to a boil, then simmer until the mixture is reduced by half.
3. Turn off your pot and let the mixture cool to a warm state. This will steep the herbs. I let it go for about 20 minutes.
4. Strain the herbs from the liquid and discard the solids.
5. Place the liquid back into your Instant Pot and whisk in the honey, lemon juice, and cayenne pepper. It should be warm enough to melt the honey.
6. Place in an airtight jar or freeze in cubes. After thawing, keep refrigerated.

Dog Food

Now you can occasionally give your dog a homemade dinner. This recipe offers your pet protein, vitamins and fiber. Just to be clear, this does *not* provide all the nutrients a dog needs to be strong and healthy, so do not feed it to your pet exclusively. Nevertheless, your dog is guaranteed to love it.

Watch Out! Your cat may feel left out and want some homemade food, too.

Ingredients:

    1 cup brown rice, uncooked

    2 chicken breasts

    ½ cup fresh or frozen green beans, chopped

    ½ cup peas, frozen

    2 carrots, cut into small pieces

    1 medium sweet potato, chopped

    1 cup fresh blueberries

    2 cups water

Directions:

1. Rinse and drain the rice. Place it in the bottom of your Instant Pot.
2. Set the chicken breasts on top of the rice
3. Add the beans, peas, carrots, sweet potato and blueberries on top of the chicken.
4. Pour in the water.
5. Seal the lid and select the manual, high pressure function and set the time to 25 minutes.

6. At the end of the cook time, let the pressure release naturally for 10 minutes if all fresh ingredients are used, 20 minutes if some of the ingredients were frozen.
7. Perform a quick release and open the lid.
8. Remove the chicken and shred the meat, returning it to the other ingredients and stirring to combine well.
9. Store any leftovers in the refrigerator or freeze them for later.

Eggs

Eggs are cooked in several different ways and most of them are easily made in an Instant Pot. The only egg preparations I have been unable to recreate are fried eggs and eggs over easy, but I'm still trying. Here you will find how to make hard and soft-boiled eggs, scrambled eggs and poached eggs.

Hard, Medium, or Soft-Boiled Eggs

Always set your eggs out about one hour prior to cooking, so they come to room temperature before proceeding. Use the steam basket to make these and lay them out in a single layer. Do not stack them or they won't cook properly.

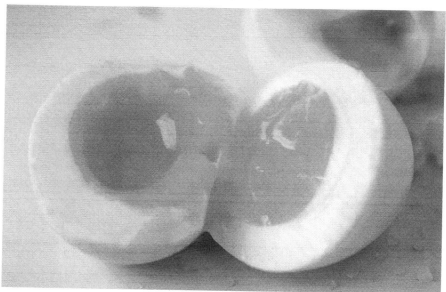

Soft boiled eggs come out perfect every time in an Instant Pot.

Ingredients:

    1 cup water

    Eggs

    Ice water

Directions:

1. Pour the one cup of water into your Instant Pot.
2. Set the eggs in a single layer in the steam basket and insert into your Instant Pot.
3. Lock the lid and select the manual, high pressure function.
4. Set the timer for two minutes for soft boiled eggs, four minutes for medium eggs with a slightly runny yolk and six minutes for hard cooked eggs.
5. While cooking, prepare a bowl full of ice water will immerse the eggs.
6. As soon as the cook time has finished, perform a quick release and open the lid.
7. Use tongs to remove each egg and carefully set it in the ice water. This will arrest the cooking process. Leave the eggs in the water for five minutes for hard boiled eggs. Soft boiled eggs will go in the water to stop the cooking, but are pulled out almost immediately in order to serve them hot.

Scrambled Eggs

This recipe feels like cheating, because all you do is use the sauté function and scramble the eggs, but if you are traveling and taking your Instant Pot with you, you might need to know how to make them.

Ingredients:

    4 eggs

    ¼ cup milk

    1 tablespoon butter

    Salt and pepper to taste

Directions:

1. Crack the eggs into a mixing bowl and add the milk. Whisk until frothy.
2. Select the sauté function on your Instant Pot and let it heat up.
3. Drop the butter into the bottom of the pot and let it melt. Stir it around.
4. Add the eggs and stir with a wooden spoon or a silicone spatula.
5. Turn off the sauté function when they are done to your liking and serve them on a plate, seasoning with salt and pepper to taste.

Poached Eggs

I have a problem making poached eggs on the stove. They never seem to come out right. In the Instant Pot, however, they come out fine. I use single-serving silicone cups and it works great.

Poached eggs come out great in an instant pot without all the fuss.

Ingredients:

1 cup water

4 large eggs

Salt and pepper to taste

Directions:

1. Set the trivet in the bottom of the pot and pour in the water.
2. Spray each silicone cup with non-stick spray
3. Crack each egg and put one in each of the four silicone cups.
4. Salt and pepper to your liking.
5. Carefully place the filled silicone cups on top of the trivet in your Instant Pot.
6. Secure the lid on your Instant Pot and select the steam function.
7. Set the time for three to five minutes. If you like your poached egg really runny, steam for three minutes, but if you like it a little more solid, go for five minutes.
8. Release the pressure immediately to prevent hardening of the yolk.
9. Use tongs to remove the silicone cups from the pot and run a spoon around the sides, then pop them out.

Herbal Balms/Salves

I make herbal salves in my Instant Pot to treat my chapped skin in the winter. They are easy to make and work like a charm. I purchased a second inner pot that I use only when I make non-food items, so my beef stroganoff won't taste like eucalyptus or calendula.

You make an infusion of the herbs in the pot using the slow cooker option. I store these in small one-pint jars that have lids. I keep the finished product in the refrigerator, just to keep it fresh longer.

Ingredients:

Infusion:

1 ounce, herb of choice

1¼ cups olive oil

Salve:

¼ cup infusion

¼ cup beeswax, grated (or beeswax pellets)

6 to 8 drops of essential oil

Directions:

1. Place the fresh herb in a canning jar that fits into your Instant Pot. I use one pint jars or smaller jars designed to hold small amounts of jelly.
2. Cover the herbs with the olive oil so it comes about one inch above the herb on the jar. Make sure to use at least 1 ¼ cups of oil, because you'll need one cup of finished oil to make the salve.
3. Set the jars, uncovered, into your Instant Pot. I can get 3-quart jars in my 6-quart Instant Pot.
4. Secure the lid of your Instant Pot.
5. Select the yogurt setting and set the timer for 24 to 72 hours. The longer you let it simmer, the more fragrant and potent the oil will be.
6. When done, remove the jars with tongs and use a fine strainer or cheesecloth to strain the herbs out of the oil into a bowl or another jar. Press the herbs into the sieve or cheesecloth to get out as much as you can.
7. Fill your Instant Pot with about two inches of water and select the slow-cooker option.
8. Pour the infused oil into a 4-cup oven-safe measuring cup and place it in the pot.
9. Set the timer for 30 minutes.
10. Place one cup of the infusion into a canning jar.
11. Add the beeswax and stir with a wooden skewer or Popsicle stick. Set the canning jar in your Instant Pot with at least one cup of water in bottom. Make sure not to get any water inside the jar.

12. Keep stirring until the beeswax melts, about 20 to 30 minutes. Note: your Instant Pot is not on at this time.
13. Check the consistency by letting a few drops fall onto a piece of wax paper. Let it cool and see if it hardens. If it is too hard, add a little more oil, but if it comes out too soft, add more beeswax.
14. Remove the jar from your Instant Pot
15. Add drops of essential oil and pour into smaller individual jars. Leave open to cool.
16. Screw on the lids and they are ready to use or give away.

Note: I use lavender and keep it in the kitchen. If I get a burn, I rub it with the salve and the burn does not blister. I use chamomile or calendula flowers for a skin soothing salve and yarrow flowers to heal chapped and irritated skin. You can also use eucalyptus for a powerful, healing salve.

Herbal Infusions – Water-Based

Herbal Infusions are great to use for home remedies. Now you can make them in your Instant Pot. Just stuff fresh herb into a quart or pint canning jar and fill with water. Using the slow cooker option, put two to three cups of water in the bottom and place the jars in your Instant Pot for about 24 hours. Do not put the lids on the jars, but do put the lid on your Instant Pot.

Use herbal infusions to add to soaps, or drink them as tea.

Ingredients:

Enough fresh herbs to almost fill a canning jar

Filtered water to fill the canning jar

2 to 3 cups of water

Directions:

1. Pack the canning jar with fresh herbs.
2. Pour in the filtered water to a half inch from the lip of the jar.
3. Pour tap water into your Instant Pot.
4. Place the jars in your Instant Pot, without their lids.
5. Select the slow cooker option and close the lid.
6. Let this cook for 12 to 24 hours, making sure there is plenty of water in the bottom of your Instant Pot at all times. You may need to add more, part way through.

7. Lift out the jars from your Instant Pot using tongs. Set the jars on a counter to cool
8. Once cool, strain out the solids and discard them.
9. Pour the strained liquid into clean jars and screw down the lids.
10. These will keep in a dark cupboard for about three weeks or in the refrigerator for several months.

Suggestions:
1. You can make lavender infusions and apply this to your face and neck to keep your skin looking young.
2. Make calendula flower infusions and freeze them in ice cube trays. Melt directly on the skin, to relieve sunburn.
3. Use mint leaves to make an astringent for your face.

Herbal Soap

I love making herbal soap, but caution must be taken. Do not allow animals or kids around when you are making it; the lye used in the recipe is very caustic. You don't want anyone to breathe or even touch it. Soap-making is not dangerous if you are careful and know what you are doing.

Only use a glass bowl or measuring cup that fits inside your Instant Pot. The soap reacts when it comes in contact with metal. The inner pot is made out of a non-reactive substance, but I do not suggest you use it directly with your soap. Few people can afford two Instant Pots; if you want to use your pot for food again without getting a nasty aftertaste, use a glass bowl inside the inner pot. Lye should never come in contact with any metal.

You'll want to work in a well-ventilated area to minimize the buildup of caustic fumes. Read up on how to make soap before you start, so that you understand the process and the dangers of working with lye.

You will use the slow cooker function on your Instant Pot, so the issue of caustic fumes will be less, but it is still important to protect yourself from them. It is also important for your measurements to be precise, so I highly recommend using a scale to portion out these ingredients.

Ingredients:
- 16 ounces coconut oil
- 16 ounces olive oil
- 4.8 ounces lye
- 12 to 16 ounces herbal infusion
- 1 ounce essential oils (one, a mixture, or to match the herbal infusion)

Directions:

1. Measure the coconut oil and olive oil into the glass bowl that fits into your Instant Pot. Set the bowl inside the inner pot. Activate the high heat function.
2. Measure the lye and the herbal infusion in disposable plastic cups. Use two cups – one for the lye and another one for the liquid.
3. Carry outside a large canning jar and the cups with the lye and the herbal infusion. This will minimize the fumes when you mix the lye.
4. Pour the infusion into the canning jar.
5. Put on eye and hand protection (heavy rubber gloves) and pour the lye into the infusion – DO *NOT* POUR THE INFUSION INTO THE LYE as it will cause a major reaction and will release even more caustic fumes.
6. Carefully stir, using a stainless-steel spoon devoted to soap making alone. Do not splash the liquid or get it on your skin. A cloudy white mixture will form, and it will get very hot. Let the jar set in a safe place outside for 10 minutes or until the jar cools.
7. While cooling, check the oils in the pot and make sure they are at 120 to 130 degrees, Fahrenheit. Once they reach the correct temperature, pour in the lye infusion and stir.
8. Rinse the canning jar with water and pour it down the drain. Pour white vinegar into the jar, swirl it around and rinse it down the drain.

9. Mix the liquid in the bowl with your spoon and then use an infusion blender for four to five minutes or until it starts to thicken and become opaque. Rinse the stick blender immediately and pour vinegar over it and rinse.
10. Pull the lid down on your Instant Pot and change to low heat. Set the timer for 15 minutes and check. It should be bubbling on the sides. After 45 minutes or so, the mixture will thicken and the entire surface should start to bubble with the sides collapsing in.
11. Turn the heat off and remove the bowl. I use a foil sling under the bowl to get it out without burning my fingers.
12. Add the essential oils and stir in.
13. Spoon into soap molds. I use silicone or plastic molds, but you can use an empty box lined with parchment paper if you don't have molds. Cover the molds with parchment paper and put in a cool, dry place to harden.
14. Harden for 24 hours and pop the soap out of the molds, or cut into bars. Let the soap sit on parchment for two days so it dries well.

Instant Pot Ice Tea

You might think it silly to make ice tea in an Instant Pot, but I am here to testify if you do it once, you will always make it this way. When you cook under pressure, food cooks without boiling and it works the same with tea. The tea gets hot, but it doesn't boil, creating a smoother flavor that is never bitter. You can use regular tea, green tea, or herbal tea. You can sweeten your tea using sugar, honey or Splenda or you can drink it plain. I am a big tea drinker; When I am at home, I make my ice tea this way and none other.

Keep ice tea in the refrigerator and add lemon and/or mint leaves.

Ingredients:

    4 regular sized tea bags, five if you like your tea strong

    6 cups water

    Sugar, Splenda or honey to taste (I use a half cup of sugar or a quarter cup of honey or Splenda when I do sweeten it.)

    1 pinch baking soda (makes the tea mellow by cutting the tannins)

Directions:

1. Cut the strings off the teabags and toss them into the bottom of your Instant Pot.
2. Pour in the water and add the sweetener, if desired.
3. Add the pinch of baking soda and stir.

4. Seal the top, select the manual, high pressure function, and set the cook time for four minutes.
5. Allow the pressure to release naturally 15 minutes and perform a quick release, if necessary.
6. Let the tea cool 15 to 20 minutes and serve over ice.

Suggestions:

- Use a combination of tea. EXAMPLE: two regular tea bags and two orange flavored ones or two regular and two Chai tea. Get creative.
- I make two batches and pour into a big pitcher to keep in the refrigerator. The tea is very strong so be sure to serve it over a lot of ice cubes, so it dilutes it a bit.

Hot Sauce

Hot sauce is a staple in my home. I would go broke if I didn't make it. This recipe is very flavorful and easy to prepare in an Instant Pot. It makes about four – 5-ounce bottles of sauce that will keep for a long time in the refrigerator or can be frozen if you don't think you will use them up in three to six months. Always wear rubber gloves when working with pepper. I have a hard time because I seem to be allergic to the hot stuff in peppers when I touch it, so I use heavy rubber gloves and wear long sleeves with safety glasses. If you do get it on you, rinse your skin with milk to stop the burning and then use some of that lavender salve you made to get rid of any irritation.

Yield: 20 ounces

Ingredients:

1 pound Cayenne pepper or Fresno peppers (or a pepper of your choice)

¼ cup carrots, shredded

5 gloves garlic, minced

1 roasted red pepper, chopped

¼ cup apple cider vinegar

½ cup white vinegar

½ cup water

¾ tablespoon paprika

½ tablespoon sea salt

Directions:

1. Cut the tops and bottoms off the peppers and slit them down one side. Open them up and remove the seeds. (this is where you really need gloves)
2. Chop them in thirds and place in your Instant Pot.
3. Add the carrot, garlic, red pepper, vinegars, water, paprika and salt and stir.
4. Secure the lid and select the manual, high pressure and time for two minutes.
5. Let the pressure release naturally as it will fill the house with pepper fumes that will make your eyes water.
6. Open the pot and let the ingredients cool. Either put in a blender or use an immersion blender (don your gloves and other protective gear) and blend until smooth.
7. Strain through a fine strainer and fill bottles. Do not use for three to five days because it mellows with age.

Jam in an Instant Pot

I love a little jam on my toast in the morning and strawberry is my favorite. I get fresh local strawberries, process them, and then freeze the jam for use in the off-season This jam is so good you will never want to buy it premade again. I use a canning jar and make several batches when I can get local strawberries. The orange sweetens the jam without using too much sugar and adds depth to the flavor.

Serve jam on toast or biscuits or as a topping over ice cream.

Ingredients:

    1 pound strawberries, rinsed, tops removed, and sliced in half

    ⅛ cup granulated sugar

    1 fresh orange

Directions:

1. Put the sliced strawberries in your Instant Pot.
2. Sprinkle with sugar and let sit with nothing on for 10 minutes. This gets the juices flowing and put moisture into the mixture.
3. Cut the orange in half and use a reamer or juicer to juice it into a 4-cup measuring cup.
4. Measure out one ounce of the juice and pour it over the sugared strawberries.
5. Secure the lid and select the manual, high pressure and time for one minute.
6. Let the steam release naturally for 15 minutes.
7. Open the lid and transfer to a blender or use an immersion blender. I do not blend until completely smooth because I like some chunks of strawberry in mine. Store in a covered

canning jar in the refrigerator or put in freezer bag and freeze.

Ketchup

Once you taste this ketchup, you'll never want to buy it at the store again; the stuff is simply delicious. I store about a cup in a bottle in the refrigerator and freeze the rest. When I need more I thaw some out, blend it a little, and put it in the bottle.

Always use plum tomatoes to make your ketchup. They hold up well under pressure and have the right texture to make excellent ketchup. Some of the ingredients might surprise you, but they all blend together to make a ketchup you will love.

Homemade ketchup is jam-packed with flavor.

Yield: 3 cups

Ingredients:

2 pounds plum tomatoes, rinsed and quartered

1 tablespoon paprika

¾ teaspoon sea salt

⅛ teaspoon garlic powder

⅛ teaspoon ground cloves

⅛ teaspoon ground cinnamon

¼ teaspoon celery seed

1 tablespoon honey

1 tablespoon onion, chopped fine

⅓ cup raisins

6 tablespoons apple cider vinegar

1 tablespoon cornstarch

1 tablespoon water

Directions:

1. Place the tomatoes, paprika, salt, garlic powder, cloves, cinnamon, celery seed, honey, onion, raisins and vinegar into your Instant Pot and use a potato masher to smash everything as well as possible.
2. Close and secure the lid. Select the manual, high pressure function and set the cook time for five minutes.
3. Perform a quick release and set your Instant Pot to sauté.
4. Simmer for 10 minutes and the liquid should be reduced by half.
5. If you want to thicken it, mix the cornstarch with the water to make a slurry and pour into the tomato mixture. Blend until smooth.
6. Pour into a bottle and let it cool before using or refrigerating. Your ketchup should be good for about six months.

Kettle Corn

Popcorn in your Instant Pot? Why not! It works quite well, actually. You can also cook regular popcorn without the sugar, using this recipe, but if you want sweet kettle corn, you'll want to include the sugar. You can even enhance it with a half tablespoon of cinnamon mixed into the sugar before you add it. This makes plenty to share.

Throw some nuts in when you add the sugar, for added flavor.

Ingredients:

- 2 tablespoons oil
- ¼ cup popcorn kernels
- 1½ tablespoons sugar
- Dash of salt

Directions:

1. Turn your Instant Pot to sauté and let it heat up
2. Add the oil and wait one minute

3. Put three popcorn kernels in your Instant Pot and close the glass lid. Wait one to two minutes and if they don't pop by then put in three more.
4. Once the three kernels have popped, pour in the rest of the kernels and sprinkle with sugar.
5. Cover with the glass lid
6. Using pot holders, grab the cover and your Instant Pot's inner liner. Lift it up and swirl to coat the kernels with sugar and oil. Do this every two minutes or so.
7. When the kernels stop popping or slow down, remove the inner pot and set it on a heat-safe surface.
8. Wait until the kernels completely stop popping before removing the lid, salting to taste, and enjoying.

Lotion Bars

Normally you need a double boiler to make lotion bars, but if you have an Instant Pot, all you need is its "keep warm" button. This recipe makes several lotion bars in a short amount of time. You will need molds for the soap and you'll want to use pot liner that is dedicated for making nonfood items; otherwise, your food will taste – interesting.

Ingredients:

1 cup cocoa butter, grated

1 cup beeswax pellets or grated beeswax

½ cup extra virgin olive oil

1 teaspoon Vitamin E oil

20 drops essential oil of your choice (optional)

Directions:

1. Grate your cocoa butter and beeswax and place it in the cold Instant Pot.
2. Add the olive oil and press the Keep Warm button.
3. Stir with a wooden spoon occasionally and it should all be melted in 12 to 15 minutes.

4. Pour the liquid in the pot into a 4-cup glass measuring cup and whisk in the Vitamin E oil.
5. Quickly whisk in the essential oil.
6. Pour into molds. I sometimes use a greased muffin tin for this purpose
7. Set aside to harden. You can place them in the refrigerator to speed up the hardening process.
8. Pop the hardened soaps out of their molds and wrap in parchment paper.
9. Store in airtight containers if you are not using them immediately.

Dipping Chocolate

This really isn't a recipe but rather a method of preparing melted chocolate for dipping. I make tons of chocolate-dipped pretzels, cookies, apricots, dates, cherries and other goodies for the holidays. I'm tired of having to re-melt my chocolate in the microwave every few minutes.

With the Instant Pot, my frustrations are a thing of the past. Now I set the trivet in my Instant Pot, pour hot water in the bottom, turn on the warming function, and then I place a glass bowl with the chocolate pieces on top of the trivet. The chocolate stays melted for about two hours, giving me more than enough time to dip everything my little heart desires.

Your Instant Pot is perfect for keeping warm your dipping chocolate.

Ingredients:

    3 cups water

    Chocolate pieces

    Anything you want to dip

Directions:

1. Pour the water into your Instant Pot and set the trivet inside.
2. Put glass bowl on top of the trivet with about a cup of chocolate pieces inside.
3. Turn on the sauté function until the water begins to boil, then switch to the warm setting.
4. Go ahead and start dipping.
5. Add more chocolate as necessary.

Ricotta Cheese

I have a problem with store-bought ricotta cheese. I often find it rubbery and I spend a lot of time stirring and fussing with it, trying to get the soft and fluffy consistency I prefer.

Now, when I make it in my Instant Pot, it comes out perfect every time. This recipe makes two cups, which is usually enough for a pan of lasagna.

Ricotta cheese should be creamy and smooth

Yield: 2 cups

Ingredients:

8 cups whole milk (do *not* use two percent)

⅓ cup fresh squeezed lemon juice or ¾ cup citric acid

¼ teaspoon salt (taste first, you might not need it)

Directions:

1. Pour the milk into your Instant Pot and cover with lid used to make yogurt.
2. Select the yogurt function and set it to boil. This will set the time.
3. When cooking time is up, remove the lid and don't let any condensation drip back into your Instant Pot.

4. Place a hot pad on the counter and carefully use another hot pad to remove the inner pot. Place it on the hot pad on the counter.
5. Add the lemon juice or citric acid and stir gently. You want the milk to start to coagulate and separate making chunks of curd. This should happen in 30 seconds and you will want to keep stirring for another 30 seconds.
6. Stop stirring and let set for five minutes.
7. Line a colander with cheesecloth and set it over a large bowl.
8. Pour in the milk mixture and let it drain for five minutes. If you want a firmer consistency let it drain longer. The cheese can drain for up to four hours at room temperature without any negative consequences.
9. Taste and stir in salt as needed when you're finished draining the cheese. The cheese remains in the cheesecloth while the bowl will contain the whey. Set the whey aside for other uses.
10. Transfer the cheese into an airtight container and refrigerate for up to five days or freeze it for up to three months.
11. Stir before using.

Roasted Garlic

I used to roast garlic in my oven. Not anymore. I now do this in my Instant Pot and it takes half the time. I love to squeeze out the softened garlic onto crackers and eat it plain. The recipe calls for eight heads of garlic; note that this does not mean eight *cloves* of garlic. The heads contain the cloves.

Squeeze the softened garlic paste out of each clove for a mild tasty treat.

Yield: 8 heads of roasted garlic

Ingredients:

⅔ cup water

8 heads of garlic

2 tablespoons virgin olive oil

1 teaspoon sea salt or kosher salt

Directions:

1. Pour the water into the bottom of your Instant Pot and set the trivet inside.
2. Cut the tops of the garlic cloves about a quarter inch down and leave the papery outside substance intact. You should

be able to see the cloves peeking out through cut you made.
3. Place the garlic heads cut-side-up on the trivet.
4. Drizzle the olive oil over the heads of garlic and sprinkle with salt.
5. Close the lid and secure it.
6. Select the manual, high pressure function and set the cook time for 15 minutes.
7. Let the pot release naturally for about 10 minutes and perform a quick release.
8. Remove the garlic with tongs, peel off the papery substance, and serve the softened cloves.

Salsa

This recipe produces a thick and tasty salsa and you will never buy it in a jar again. It takes just a little time to prepare, so you can have it around all the time. Store it in a canning jar in the refrigerator and just see if it lasts more than a week. It probably won't.

I often add a little frozen corn to my salsa before cooking, when I make it as a dip.

Ingredients:

3 large yellow onions, diced

2 medium green peppers, seeded and diced

12 cups seeded tomatoes, diced

1 cup jalapeno peppers, seeded and chopped (wear gloves)

3 6-ounce cans tomato paste

½ cup apple cider vinegar

3 tablespoons granulated sugar

2 tablespoons garlic powder

2 tablespoons cayenne pepper (I use one because I don't like it very spicy)

1 teaspoon sea salt

4 tablespoons fresh cilantro, chopped

Directions:

1. Place the onions, green peppers, tomatoes, jalapenos, tomato paste, vinegar, sugar, garlic powder, cayenne and sea salt into your Instant Pot and stir.
2. Secure the top on the pot, select the manual, high pressure function and set the cook time for 30 minutes.
3. Let the pressure release naturally and open the lid
4. Allow it to cool before adding the cilantro and mixing it in.
5. Store in jars or freeze.

Vanilla Extract

You may not know you can make your own vanilla extract. The stuff you buy in the store is expensive and making your own probably doesn't save you money because you need to use vanilla beans. However, the flavor is going to be superior to what you find in the grocery store. You might want to try it.

Vanilla beans come in grades. I usually use grade B beans. I also would use vodka that is at least 80 proof. This recipe makes six cups of extract and your homemade brew will last for a few months, as long as you store it in dark containers in a dark place. I use three 16-ounce jars with lids when I make mine.

Vanilla beans

Yield: 6 cups

Ingredients:

- 6 vanilla beans
- 6 cups vodka
- 1 cup water

Directions:

1. Cut the vanilla beans, splitting them in half from top to bottom.
2. Scrape out the black specks of vanilla and divide the beans equally among the jars. I use two beans per jar.
3. Divide the vodka equally among the jars.
4. Seal the jars.
5. Pour the water in the bottom of your Instant Pot and place the trivet inside.
6. Set the jars on the trivet, giving them a little space between the jars.
7. Seal the lid of your Instant Pot, select the manual, high pressure function, and set the cook time for 60 minutes.

8. Let the pressure release naturally. Don't open the pot for one hour.
9. Remove the jars with tongs and let completely cool on a rack or folded kitchen towel on the counter.
10. Use after 24 hours.

Conclusion

I hope you have enjoyed all the incredible recipes in this book. Now that you know how to use your Instant Pot, what are you going to explore first? Desserts? Sandwiches? Or are you more interested in making yogurt? Or pasta? Wherever you start, you're going to have a great time getting to know this appliance that will quickly become one of the favorite parts of your life. There's no need to hesitate. Don't let all those buttons scare you. Go ahead and choose your favorite recipe and get started.

Now you can cook faster, healthier, and tastier than ever before! With your Instant Pot and these recipes, you're well on your way.

Thanks for reading.

If this book has helped you or someone you know then I invite you to leave a nice review right now; it would be greatly appreciated.

My Other Books

For more great knowledge of the world, be sure to check out my other books and author page at:

USA: https://www.amazon.com/author/susanhollister

UK: http://amzn.to/2qiEzA9

Or simply type my name into the search bar: Susan Hollister

Thank You

Made in the USA
Lexington, KY
05 July 2018